he challenge of work and life integration is real for all types of employ-, but this challenge is especially intense for women in corporate roles t offer little flexibility to support personal demands. But creating this egration requires a partnership of men, women and employers. Dr. unt's research and years of real-world experience provide prospective l practical solutions through an industry-focused lens. Extremely use-for anyone juggling work and family!"

—Karen Horting, Executive Director & CEO, Society of Women Engineers (SWE)

e addresses a very important and seldom approached aspect of our dern society: the hurdles, barriers and socio-psychological difficulties ed by dual-career couples. There is a constant battle in one's life, pri-rily in the life of a parent, to juggle with work commitments, career spects and family life. Eve's book addresses these uncomfortable issues a highly pragmatic and well-researched manner, providing potential utions for both couples and employers on how to address such issues."

—Ella Minty, Founding Chartered Public Relations Practitioner, The Chartered Institute of Public Relations, United Kingdom

runt has lived the cultural revolution that has led to an ever-increasing nber of dual-career couples facing the challenges of finding a work-balance. With clear, concise language backed by data, Ms. Sprunt ws on a wealth of experience to provide compelling arguments and nd advice. Dual-career couples just entering professional life, as well vell-seasoned managers, will gain valuable insight from this book."

—John H. Bradford, President, Society of Exploration Geophysicists and Professor, Boise State University

e Sprunt offers valuable, original insights in this must-read book, ch provides abundant information, practical findings, and impor-t recommendations on how to successfully cope with the challenges ng dual-career couples."

—Giovanni Paccaloni, President, Paccaloni Consulting International, Italy

Advance Praise for
A Guide for Dual-Career Co

"The revolution wrought by working women has . .
couples make choices and share their future. Yet res
this complex terrain have been few. Eve Sprunt's
organized book provides dual-career couples with an
showing organizations how to benefit from a trend t

—**Sally Helgesen, Author,**
The Female Advantage, T

"As a female trailblazer in the petroleum industry a
expert in analyzing data, Dr. Sprunt knew just the r
and brilliantly analyzed thousands of responses she
career couples. This very accessible book is a 'mu
career women and their spouses, but also for emplo
uinely concerned about gender equity."

—**Rosalind S. Simson, Associate Profe**
Women's and Gender Studie

"Finally . . . a book targeting the key career manager
and millennials. No, it's not child care, it's pursuir
careers. Executives should pay attention to manage
boom talent."

—**Janeen Jud**
Society of Pe

"The definitive handbook for both men and wor
sue a dual-career lifestyle. Just like its author, this
innovative with a strong dose of realism. Every co
personal success in today's 24/7 workplace will fin
to help juggle their roles as professionals, partners,

—**Janet Bandows Koster, Executive**
Association for

"This work has great value for working couples who are engaged in dual careers. The data analysis and experiential knowledge provide useful guidance in setting objectives and making choices."

—William L. Abriel, Owner, Orinda Geophysical

"Simple to read and full of smart and practical advice that empowers dual-career couples to surmount challenges and have rewarding and successful careers."

—Maria A. Capello, Senior Advisor in Kuwait Oil Company, Kuwait

"This ground-breaking book addresses an important problem that is increasingly affecting men and women around the world who have globetrotting careers. The author touches on issues both from a personal and a professional standpoint with great attention, sensibility and an outstanding understanding of both business and human needs."

—Loris Tealdi, Society of Petroleum Engineers, Italy

"A must read . . . as a dual-career working woman I found the list of questions for couples inspiring."

—Dr. Tammy Wong, CEO, Fostering Executive Leadership, Inc.; Author of *The Hour Glass Effect, Leveraging Female Talent for Your Competitive Advantage*

"Give this book to your daughter . . . it's a roadmap for how to have both a career and a life."

—Harbo Jensen, loving father, Chevron Vice President, and MIT Trustee

"A must read for anyone looking to navigate the career and life lattice. Provides great insight on how to make dual careers work both at the office and at home."

—Katie Mehnert, CEO and Founder, Pink Petro

A Guide for Dual-Career Couples

A Guide for Dual-Career Couples

Rewriting the Rules

EVE SPRUNT, PhD

PRAEGER™

An Imprint of ABC-CLIO, LLC

Santa Barbara, California • Denver, Colorado

Library of Congress Cataloging-in-Publication Data

Names: Sprunt, Eve, author.
Title: A guide for dual-career couples : rewriting the rules / Eve Sprunt, PhD.
Description: Santa Barbara, Calif. : Praeger, [2016] | Includes
    bibliographical references and index.
Identifiers: LCCN 2015051216 | ISBN 9781440850097 (alk. paper) |
    ISBN 9781440850103 (ebook)
Subjects: LCSH: Dual-career families. | Work and family. | Marriage. | Career
    development.
Classification: LCC HD4904.25 .S676 2016 | DDC 650.1085—dc23
LC record available at http://lccn.loc.gov/2015051216

ISBN: 978-1-4408-5009-7
EISBN: 978-1-4408-5010-3

20 19 18 17 16   1 2 3 4 5

This book is also available as an eBook.
Visit www.abc-clio.com for details.

Praeger
An Imprint of ABC-CLIO, LLC

ABC-CLIO, LLC
130 Cremona Drive, P.O. Box 1911
Santa Barbara, California 93116-1911
www.abc-clio.com

This book is printed on acid-free paper ∞

Manufactured in the United States of America

To my grandchildren,
Viola Sprunt, Rosalyn Sprunt,
Scarlet Broeker, and Quinn Broeker

Contents

Preface

When I was completing my PhD in geophysics at Stanford University in 1976, I thought my biggest challenge was coordination of two careers. My husband needed two years to complete Stanford's combined JD and MBA program. To solve my short-term challenge, I arranged to continue at Stanford as a research associate. I wasn't concerned about the implications of the fact that I was the first woman to receive a PhD in geophysics from Stanford (January 1977). Naively, I thought that gender discrimination was no longer a problem.

The postdoctoral period gave me time to conduct a systematic job search and to have my first child. My son was born nine months after I defended my PhD thesis. When he was 13 days old, I returned to work. My son joined me in the office at Stanford that I shared with a male graduate student and a male postdoc.

My son went everywhere with me in a baby pack. It was like being pregnant on the outside. When he was two months old, my son accompanied me when I gave a poster presentation at a large technical conference. Fortunately, he slept through my session.

Later, when he was almost six months old, I was asked on short notice to cover a class. I couldn't line up a babysitter, so I wore him in a backpack. I don't know what it was like for the class, but it was very distracting for me and I don't recommend it.

When my son was about six months old, he was awake enough of the time to interfere with my productivity. I arranged for one of the graduate student wives to babysit for him. When I stopped bringing him with me every day, all of my colleagues and the staff (including to my surprise the librarians) told me that they missed him.

One of my deliberate decisions was to bring my son to a job interview when he was about two months old. For years the interviewers had asked me illegal questions about my child-bearing plans. I picked an interview time when I was reasonably certain that my son would be asleep. I walked into the interview with my son asleep in the Snugli pack. I introduced my son to the interviewer by saying, "Here's the question you are not supposed to ask." The interviewer, Dr. Ed Witterholt of Cities Service (an oil company that long ago vanished in a merger), responded perfectly. He invited the entire family to an interview in Tulsa, Oklahoma, providing expenses for everyone and arranging a babysitter during our stay in Tulsa. The on-site interview was followed by a job offer.

With the pattern set by Cities Service, I asked all of the companies to provide babysitting services when they invited me to interview at their facilities, because I had no one to watch my son. My husband was in class all day and studying in the evening. We had no relatives in the area who could babysit. We never contemplated my husband taking care of our son overnight.

The strategy my husband and I had for coordinating two careers was that I would find a job first, because as a research scientist, I was more geographically limited than he was with business and law degrees. After I selected a job, he would limit his search to that location. We naively assumed that geographic mobility would not be a major consideration in my career. I started looking for a job about a year before we planned to leave Stanford.

I was approached by MIT, where I had received my bachelor's and master's degrees in science in earth and planetary sciences, about a faculty position. However, I was worried about the seven-year tenure clock. My son limited my ability to work evenings and weekends and I wanted to have another child. In those days before in vitro fertilization and genetic testing, the combination of declining fertility and increasing birth defects with maternal age made it unwise to postpone maternity. First-time mothers over the age of 30 were considered old and having a baby after the age of 35 was considered to be high risk. I declined to apply for the position at MIT, because I thought that there would be fewer barriers for a working mother in industry. That turned out to be an incorrect assumption.

In the late 1970s the oil industry was booming. My job search yielded job offers from six different oil industry research laboratories in four cities in three states. I was impressed by the personal attention paid to me during the recruiting process by the head of the Mobil

Research Laboratory in Dallas and decided to accept that offer. Mobil had a couple of business units in Dallas, so I thought that I could remain in Dallas without limiting my career.

When I formally accepted the job offer, I noticed the first warning signal that my plan might not be as obstacle-free as I hoped. The hiring manager blurted out, "We're so glad to have you and we're so glad you are a woman." Once I started work, the honeymoon rapidly ended. The research project I was asked to lead suffered from serious technical flaws and I couldn't convince any of the much older men that a different approach was needed. For the first time in my life, I felt trapped. With two careers to coordinate and a toddler, I couldn't just quit and move to take another position.

I persevered, but was told by my boss's boss, "You can't have a younger woman supervising an older man." Fortunately, he didn't have a problem with a young woman supervising research projects and male technicians. Within a couple of years, I was managing multiple projects and doing what I considered to be "publishable quality" work. However, the company avoided giving me a managerial title and just had me manage the research to avoid the issue of a younger woman supervising older men. I was an "activity leader" instead of a manager.

Having my second child was not as easy as the first. I delayed attempting to have another child until I had worked for Mobil for a year. Then, I was devastated to have several pregnancies that ended in miscarriage. I kept the pregnancies and the miscarriages secret and told no one.

Then when I was a little more than three months pregnant, I had a business trip to the Nevada Test Site, which is the location north of Las Vegas where nuclear weapons were tested. My visit concerned hydraulic fracturing, not nuclear testing. I was going to see the results of a Department of Energy research project on hydraulic fracturing that was conducted in a tunnel in one of the mines that was also used to test nuclear weapons.

The visit was going just fine, when our hosts decided to use some extra time to give us a grand tour of the Nevada Test Site. First we were taken to see the "Sedan crater."[1] On the rim of this giant crater, which was formed as part of an appraisal of using nuclear explosions for excavation, there was a giant sign explaining how much radiation a person standing at that location received from the residual radioactivity. Since I was pregnant and had suffered at least two and probably three miscarriages, all I wanted to do was get away from the radioactive material, but the tour went on and on. We visited the locations where studies were conducted to evaluate the effects of a nuclear bomb blast on different types of buildings. By the time I returned to Las Vegas, I envisioned myself as being coated in radioactive dust. I was devastated by the idea that I had jeopardized my unborn baby. A few days later, I became alarmed that I was miscarrying again. Fortunately, I didn't miscarry. Six months later, I gave birth to a healthy baby girl.

Many people tried to make me feel guilty about being a working mother. When my daughter was born, I took the six weeks of sick leave allowed for a routine birth. Then she started in full-time daycare. For many years afterward, my husband would delight in sharing that the daycare center where our daughter spent her early months subsequently became a dog kennel.

When my children were young, one of the arguments for women staying home with their infants and toddlers was that their children would get more attention and instruction and be better able to compete when they went to school. I realized that this was a myth for the middle class. The children of the affluent had been cared for by nannies and nursemaids for millennia. Despite having limited contact with their exalted parents, those children of the upper crust would go on to be the leaders of the next generation. Being raised by servants did not impair their intellectual development.

At the age of three, our daughter was accepted for one of the 22 positions in the preschool at the Hockaday School, which was and is the most exclusive school for girls in Dallas. For me, her admission to Hockaday was proof that her daycare experience had not been detrimental. I refused to feel guilty about sending her to daycare when she was only six weeks old.

Hockaday was where the well-do-do in Dallas sent their daughters. The Bush twins, Jenna and Barbara, attended for several years before moving to Austin when their father, George W. Bush, later the 43rd president, became governor of Texas. The twins were a grade behind my daughter, but Jenna ran track with my daughter. Since the twins were the grandchildren of the sitting president (George H. W. Bush), there was much gossiping about the Secret Service agents protecting the twins at school.

The preschool program at Hockaday was only half a day. Arranging transportation to and from a daycare center to Hockaday became an ordeal. There was a daycare center a mile from Hockaday, but it insisted that a minimum of five children was required to provide drop-off and pick-up service. Swallowing my pride, I called every one of the other 21 girls' mothers. It was a humiliating experience and

I couldn't find a single other girl who needed daycare. In desperation I went back to the daycare center and asked what I would have to pay for the center to provide the pick-up service for just my daughter. It turned out to be only paying the cost of full-day care. If I had known that, I never would have wasted my time and embarrassed myself calling all of the other moms.

My daughter ended up being a "lifer" at Hockaday, continuing on through high school graduation. When my daughter was graduating from high school, much to my amazement, the mother of another lifer admitted that she envied me, because I never did car pool. At the annual school fund-raising auction, first place in line for car pool always sold for an outrageous sum.

Until my daughter was old enough to drive herself to her various activities, I was dependent on the generosity of other mothers. I was embarrassed to ask for favors, but I developed a thick hide and did so. My daughter was able to participate in Brownies, because another mother transported her to and from the meetings.

Besides frequently swallowing my pride and asking favors from the other parents at the prestigious schools my children attended, I had to be tough to survive at work. Despite rules to the contrary, women were expected to ignore repeated slights. My complaints to human resources were summarily dismissed.

One boss, "Barney," liked to creep up behind me and put a hand on my shoulder. When I expressed an objection to working with a colleague, "Robert," who failed to properly credit me for my accomplishments, Barney insisted that the real reason was that my love affair with Robert had gone sour. In my defense, I truthfully told Barney that I was a virgin when I married and had never had relations with anyone but my husband. Undaunted, Barney maintained that was nonsense and explained that he and his wife had an open marriage. The head of human resources dismissed my complaints saying, "You know Barney is crazy!"

Another man with whom I had a technical disagreement responded to my protests by saying, "Why aren't you home with your kids?" The response by human resources to my grievance was, "You know he is nasty to everyone."

With oil prices in a death spiral, staff reductions became a regular occurrence. Initially, I believed that my record of technical accomplishments with major economic impact would protect me. Then I got my first female boss, who had previously been very nice offering advice. Once she shared that she had never had children, because her husband was sickly. When she became my boss, she suddenly saw me as competition and did everything she could to destroy my career. One day she walked into my office, looked at the pictures of my children and said, "You've had everything." It was as if she felt that because I had children, I shouldn't have a career as well. From that point on, I was under continual attack. She sought to retroactively discredit all of my accomplishments and did everything that she could to run me off. I thought to myself, "I can't quit now, I've worked the entire time my kids were preschoolers and now they are both in school."

Short of quitting, I tried to escape, but she poisoned every contact I made. Now, I know that she was a bully. At the time, I didn't have a word to describe the devastating experience. In hindsight, recognizing the behavior as bullying makes the dynamic of that horrible period easier to understand.

Oil prices were very low, so jobs were scarce, but I secured an external job interview. Unfortunately, as is usually the case when someone is being bullied, my self-confidence was very low. I blew the interview by mishandling the question about why I was interested in changing jobs.

After a couple of years of misery, I had the opportunity to discuss the bullying with the instructor of a company course. A few weeks later, the instructor came to see me. His message was, "Sit tight. It may take six months, but things will improve." Within six weeks, the bully-boss announced her retirement and promptly vanished.

That was my first experience with prolonged bullying. It is a devastating experience that destroys your self-confidence. In hindsight, I realized that the problem was that I felt trapped. The job market in my industry was terrible. My husband was pleased with his job and the schools our children attended and did not want to relocate. I felt that my only options were to allow myself to be bullied or to give up my career.

My next boss was a nice man, but he initially kept me on a very short leash. When he retired a few years later, he called me into his office and said that he was shredding all of the material that the bully had placed in my file.

My salvation during that terrible period was my involvement with the Society of Petroleum Engineers. As someone trained in geophysics, I did not immediately think of that group as my preferred professional society. However, one of the most senior scientists in my company, Aziz Odeh, without my knowledge nominated me for a position on the "Geology and Geophysics" Subcommittee of the Annual Meeting Program Committee. The chairman of the subcommittee moved to the Middle East, failed to fulfill any of his responsibilities, and then asked me to represent the subcommittee at the Annual Program Committee Meeting. I went into that meeting with no preparation, but attending that meeting changed my life.

During the Annual Meeting Program Committee meeting, I patched together the geology and geophysics session. Shortly afterward, I was asked to chair the Geology and Geophysics Subcommittee. A year later, I was asked to head the entire Annual Meeting Program Committee. Thrilled and surprised by that opportunity, I went to see Aziz Odeh to thank him for nominating me a couple of years earlier for the subcommittee and to ask his advice on how to get company permission to take on the first of what turned out to be the cliché series of positions of increasing responsibility (albeit in a volunteer organization). His advice was, "Tell them you will do as much as possible on your own time, and do so. It will get easier with time." For a mother with elementary school children, it was not easy to handle the work associated with these volunteer positions during nights and weekends. But I followed Aziz's advice and he was right.

In those days, we didn't talk about mentors and sponsors. In hindsight, I realize that Aziz was my sponsor for positions in the Society of Petroleum Engineers. I always wondered why Aziz didn't try to sponsor me within Mobil, only externally. The male contemporary of mine, whom Aziz sponsored within the company, rose to become head of the research laboratory. When Aziz died, two people were asked to give eulogy addresses, myself and the man who was the head of the laboratory. Until that time, I had no idea that anyone knew that Aziz had played such an important role in my life.

Several years earlier a white male colleague had said to me, "You better hope that you never work for a Middle Eastern man." He could not have been more wrong. Aziz Odeh was born in Palestine. My best friend at Mobil was a man born in Syria. Over the years, many of my good friends and colleagues have been men of Middle Eastern origin. I've learned that you never know who is going to turn out to be a loyal and true friend and to not prejudge people.

During the long downturn in the petroleum industry, I continued to be active in the Society of Petroleum Engineers. After chairing the Annual Meeting Program Committee, I was tapped to serve as the editor of one of the technical journals. Next, I was surprised one Sunday morning to receive a call inviting me to be the first woman to serve on the society's board of directors. As my term on the board was drawing to a close, I guessed that the volunteer position managing all of the organization's publications, "senior technical editor," would be vacated soon and I asked if I could be considered. The reaction was, "Are you sure you want that? It is a lot of work!" I said, "Yes" and got the position.

The "carrot" for me was that the senior technical editor wrote a monthly editorial in the flagship journal that was mailed to all of the society's members. I thought that I would never get an opportunity to be president of the society, so the next best thing was to have the editorial column. The position was a lot of work, but I loved having the column.

My goal in writing my editorial columns was to be as truthful and provocative as I could without getting fired. I visualized what I was doing as walking along the edge of a cliff. With two children and a husband who had lost his job as a result of a merger, I could not afford to get fired. However, I wanted people to read what I wrote and to realize that my abilities extended far beyond experimental rock physics.

Twice I was called in by my boss to defend one of my editorial columns. The first time was because I had written about a sensitive subject, quoting news stories with the offending company's name redacted. A high-ranking executive in Mobil was convinced I was writing about Mobil and called my boss to complain. Fortunately, I was able to prove that the quotes were not about Mobil. The second time was because I was trying to be nice. I was praising a colleague, but another colleague who had been the greatest obstacle to success had complained that I did not credit her! My boss was a good guy and there were no lasting repercussions.

By the time I began looking for a job in response to the Exxon-Mobil merger, I had been writing the editorial column for six years. A friend had given me a great suggestion, "You can contact anyone you want in the industry, and ask to interview them." I had taken his advice, and contacted many industry leaders. Now, it was time to start working my contacts.

The industry was still caught in a protracted downturn, but the status quo was no longer an option. My husband was not employed and I needed to work. My daughter was a senior in high school and my son was in college. It was time for me to test my wings. When the chief technology officer at Chevron, Don Paul, talked to me about opportunities and career development, I was hooked. He said that I had "the ability to recreate myself" and was giving me the chance to do it again.

When the ExxonMobil merger was consummated, I didn't even wait to find out what the merged company planned to do with me. After 21 years with Mobil at the age of 48½ and only 18 months away from qualifying for the full Mobil annuitant health care benefit, the siren song of opportunity held me in its thrall. I triggered the severance package eligibility by getting the appropriate person to go on the record that I would not be able to get a position in Dallas.

At Chevron, I had the opportunity to reinvent myself several times. My first position was managing the corporation's global climate change policy. After the merger of Chevron and Texaco, I was part of the management team for several of Chevron Technology Ventures' venture capital funds. Subsequently, I managed alternative energy research.

In the early 1990s I was convinced I would never have the opportunity to serve as the president of the Society of Petroleum Engineers, but I was selected as the 2006 president of the society. Chevron supported me while I served in that capacity. After meeting with people around the world as the 2006 president of SPE, I realized that people in dual-career couples everywhere were struggling with many of the same problems.

After my service as president of the Society of Petroleum Engineers, I managed Chevron's worldwide university philanthropy and recruiting. That was followed by serving as business development manager for Chevron Energy Technology Company, and finally coming full circle at the end of my career back to research and earth sciences with a final role as adviser, Geological Research and Development. I retired from Chevron late in 2013.

In 2013, I received the Society of Women Engineers' highest award for "game-changing contributions to the petroleum industry, to the science and practice of geosciences and petroleum engineering, and to the advancement of women engineers."

In 2015, the Association for Women Geoscientists honored me with its ENHANCE award for my "life-long commitment to advancing the status of women in the geosciences, participation in nominating fellow female scientists for deserving recognition, and recent push for transparency to shareholders in terms of gender figures and salary differences at ExxonMobil and other major companies."

My big question for myself in retirement was, "What can I do now, that I couldn't do earlier in my career?" While I don't want to entirely give up science and technology, my main focus is on helping women advance. As a retiree, I don't have to adhere to company rhetoric. I can speak my own mind.

My focus is on helping dual-career couples, because for women to advance, we need to enlist men as allies. Properly recognizing many factors that historically were considered women's issues as dual-career couple issues better aligns men's and women's interests. One-on-one mentoring is great, but written words can reach far more ears. My goal in writing this book is to help women and men better navigate the obstacles confronting dual-career couples and in that way to create a more level-playing field for both genders at work and at home.

Acknowledgments

No one succeeds alone. We are influenced by many people and aided and supported by many more. When I wanted to gather data on dual-career couples, I was fortunate to have Susan Howes as my collaborator. The surveys that Susan and I led would not have been possible without the support of Tom Whipple of the Society of Petroleum Engineers. When I became actively engaged with the Women's Network Committee of the Society of Exploration Geophysicists, Maria Angela Capello and Nancy House were valuable allies.

My husband of over 40 years, Hugh Sprunt, deserves special thanks. We have been through a lot together, marrying young and journeying through life together. He has been willing to follow and support me, even when I have embarked on risky adventures. We were a dual-career couple long before anyone thought about anything from that perspective. When we met and married, the talk was of women's liberation and bra burning, not the partnership between women and men. With no role models, we forged our own path and did well. From the beginning, Hugh eliminated one common source of marital discord, by asking that we keep our finances separate. I was not thrilled, but the test of time has shown it to be a fantastic way to balance power in the household.

I am grateful to my literary agent, Gail Fortune, for her advice and support and to Hilary Claggett of Praeger for guiding me through the publication process.

Introduction

Countless books have been written on how people can achieve greater success in their careers. In addition to the unisex advice books aimed at both women and men, many other volumes provide women with recommendations on everything: what to wear, how to speak, where to sit, and even whom to marry. Women have been networking, leaning in, and speaking up for years, but nevertheless are covered with bumps and bruises from banging into "glass" barriers.

Women's woes are compounded by hostility from men who resent programs and policies that they believe create reverse discrimination. For women to reach equality in the workplace, the interests of men and women must be better aligned. This book guides the way to better alignment of the interests of men and women.

Practical advice for dual-career couples has been distilled from research and life experience. The emphasis is on the work side of the work–life balance with guidance focused on three key factors—opportunity, flexibility, and documentation of accomplishments. Emphasizing the three key factors makes it easier to develop strategies and tactics for having a rewarding career that works for you. There is no unique solution, because everyone has different priorities and constraints.

NEED FOR A DIFFERENT APPROACH

Women have been acquiring the education they need to succeed for many years. The U.S. National Science Foundation reported that, since the late 1990s, 57 percent of all bachelor's degrees have been awarded to women. The Association of American Medical Colleges found that in 2014 women received 47 percent of medical degrees. Catalyst observed that in every year since 2002 women have earned between 34 percent and 37 percent of MBA degrees. According to the University of California, San Diego, Center for Research on Gender in the Professions, women have earned 40 percent or more of all law degrees since 1986 and 45 percent or more since 1998.[1] With so many well-qualified women, why are there so few women in leadership roles?

Let's take the case of female attorneys. According to Catalyst, in 2013 women comprised almost 45 percent of associates in law firms, which is about what you would expect given that is approximately the percentage of female law school graduates.[2] But despite surviving law school, which is notoriously difficult, between the entry level in law firms, of "associate," and the next level, of "counsel," the percentage of women drops from 45 percent to 38 percent. Even greater attrition occurs in the big step up to partner. Only about 20 percent of law firm partners are women.

Where are these female attorneys if they aren't in the law firms? They are not judges; only 24 percent of federal judges and 27.5 percent of state judges are women. They haven't risen to the top of academia; only about 21 percent of law school deans are women. Why despite having the endurance and stamina to suffer through law school are women so underrepresented in senior legal positions?

The salaries of female attorneys were only 83 percent of men's, and in 96 percent of law firms the highest paid partner is male. Nevertheless, female attorneys earn a higher percentage of their male counterparts' wages than the national average for working women.

Data collected by the U.S. Census Bureau indicate that in 2013 women who worked full time, year-round earned only 78 percent of the pay of their male counterparts and that progress toward eliminating the gender pay gap has stalled since 2007. Even after adjustments for factors including hours worked, educational differences, and job type, the Census Bureau notes that 10 to 40 percent of the gender pay gap remains unexplained.

In occupation after occupation, we see the same pattern that was documented for female attorneys. Women are well represented at entry level, but there are fewer and fewer women at progressively higher levels of management. Are we seeing discrimination as each promotion becomes increasingly competitive and the selection process is more subjective?

Discrimination is still a major problem for women. Multiple studies using identical resumes except for changing the gender of the name have shown that both women and men judge women more harshly.[3] Also, the surveys that I led show that while there is discrimination against both men and women who are part of a dual-career couple, the repercussions are more severe for women. Prejudice decreases opportunities for women at midcareer.

The scarcity of women in the upper ranks of organizations is often attributed to women dropping out of the workforce because they were unable to attain an acceptable work–life balance. The key is the word *balance*. We seldom stop to think that, when we complain about balance, we must look at the factors on both sides of the balance. The focus tends to be on the life side, but in a balance both sides are equally important. If you only investigate the life side, you will never understand or solve the problem.

Life is about pain–gain and risk–reward trade-offs. People are reluctant to make sacrifices for a reward that they perceive to be beyond their grasp. Midcareer women, who are discouraged about their career potential, are more likely to drop out of the workforce than women who believe that they are making progress toward their goals and have exciting opportunities in their profession.

Evidence indicates that advancement stalls midcareer for many women. The underrepresentation of women above a certain level suggests that something is effectively creating a "glass ceiling." If a woman thinks her career has reached a dead-end, her work–life balance tilts sharply and she feels as if she is making too many sacrifices in her personal life for a career that is going nowhere. The absence of women in the upper echelons of organizations and high midcareer attrition are linked.

LIFESTYLE DISCRIMINATION

In addition to the altered gender ratio, the presence of a large number of well-qualified women in the workforce has resulted in lifestyle changes that are not obvious. As a result of the increase in ambitious career women, a major fraction of the workforce is composed of people with high aspirations, who are in a long-term, committed relationship with another person, who is equally focused on his or her career. Both men and women in these dual-career couples are underrepresented in the executive ranks of many organizations, so top management often does not appreciate the ramifications of the proliferation of members of dual-career couples in the workforce.

Until the last 20 years or so, the professional and managerial workforce was overwhelmingly composed of men who were the dominant source of income for their family. The lifestyle and priorities of both male and female members of the dual-career workforce are significantly different from those of the old sole breadwinner workforce. This new workforce is ambitious and hardworking, but needs greater flexibility than the old sole breadwinners, who had someone managing their household.

Top management continues to be dominated by people who have a partner in the role of "domestic engineer" (homemaker), or people who are single. When executives speak about the success they have achieved in their careers, they almost always acknowledge the support that they received from their spouses. Corporate wives (and they usually are wives not husbands) handle the household logistics and pack their spouse's suitcases. These wives tend to brag about managing a dozen or more family relocations. With their spouse's support, the executives can focus all of their attention on their work, working late, traveling, or relocating on short notice.

Too many executives cannot imagine someone following in their footsteps unless they have a partner providing similar domestic support or are single with minimal family obligations. These executives are more apt to closely question female employees than male employees about their partner's career, because they are accustomed to thinking of women as being in the domestic support role. Employers are perplexed as to how to manage people who are part of dual-career couples, when the members of the couple think that both careers are important. Employers want the couple to decide which career is most important, but many couples depend on both incomes and/or are both are dedicated to their vocations.

The differences in economic and logistical constraints between sole breadwinners and members of dual-career couples create significantly different lifestyles, which constitute a form of invisible diversity. Like other forms of diversity, these differences can result in prejudice and misunderstanding. Management that is overwhelmingly composed of dominant sole breadwinners tends to be out of touch with the issues impacting the members of dual-career couples in their workforce. This leads to conflict, which in turn increases attrition.

Executives are thrilled if they can find a talented young woman with a partner in the support role. They get the visible gender diversity on which organizations are being scrutinized without the lifestyle differences associated with a majority of women. Unfortunately, women, who have persuaded their domestic partner to assume a support role, are often even harder on other women than male dominant earners. These female sole breadwinner or dominant earners can also be difficult managers for men who are part of a dual-career couple. Once someone has suffered under this type of female boss, they are more likely to avoid working for another woman. Having management that is out of tune with the workforce is not a prescription for success.

REFRAMING WOMEN'S ISSUES AS DUAL-CAREER COUPLE ISSUES

My goal is to help women advance into senior positions by reframing so-called women's issues including child care as dual-career couple issues. This approach makes men and women allies in pushing for change, and shifts the focus from gender to lifestyle diversity.

Members of dual-career couples do not have a partner providing domestic logistical support, so they need greater flexibility than the sole breadwinners. They are not less ambitious, but they are living with different constraints. Furthermore, couples composed of people earning about the same amount of money usually rely on both incomes. These couples rarely can afford to sacrifice one career for the other.

When women were just beginning to penetrate the technical and managerial workforce, child care was considered a female responsibility. While women are the childbearers, both parents can share responsibility for postnatal child-rearing. For women to succeed, child care and household management should be considered a shared responsibility. If women are equal earners, men should be equal caregivers and do their share of the household tasks. However, access to the flexible work arrangements required to manage child care and domestic logistics should be available to everyone (not just parents). Equal access will minimize resentment and penalization of those who use the flexible work arrangements.

Child care is more of a challenge in some countries than in others. In places in which women are still a small fraction of the well-paid workforce, older female relatives are often available for full-time child care. In those countries, low-cost household help also tends to be obtainable. Some other countries subsidize daycare, making it less expensive and more accessible. Variations in child care affordability and availability impact the flexibility dual-career couples have to travel on business and to work long and/or irregular hours.

We also need to consider willingness to relocate as a dual-career couple issue. Managers tend to believe that women are more reluctant to relocate than men although data do not support this. As a result, these managers think that many women are not serious about their careers.

GUIDANCE FOR MEMBERS OF DUAL-CAREER COUPLES

The guidance shared in this volume is based on: (1) surveys that I led on the subject that gathered over 10,000 responses, (2) feedback in response to my publications and presentations on the survey results, (3) discussions with a wide range of people, (4) research on what has been written on similar and related topics, (5) over 35 years' working full time in the male-dominated petroleum industry as a research scientist and manager including an assignment in human resources as the manager of worldwide college recruiting, and (6) as a granddaughter, daughter, mother, and grandmother looking at the issues in a multi-generational context.

In this book, I have tried to concentrate on the major implications of the research, without burying people in the details. For those who want to read the detailed research reports, I have included references to technical publications.

A major part of analyzing data is identifying patterns. Often in hindsight the patterns are intuitively obvious. The survey results reveal the importance of opportunity in people's decisions to take a job, to leave an employer, to drop out of the workforce, or to consider returning to work. However, what constitutes an irresistible opportunity varies from person to person and even for a single person can change radically over the course of his or her career.

When people complain about work–life balance, it means that they think that the opportunities that they have available to them are not worth the sacrifices required. Access to flexible work arrangements that address the person's pain points can make the work–life balance acceptable.

Everyone wants flexibility to handle unforeseen events and personal priorities. Single parents can make a strong argument that they need even more flexibility than people in dual-career couples. Unfortunately, even when flexible work arrangements are available, many people are afraid that making use of them will damage their career. Tips are provided on using work flexibility and minimizing career impact.

To enhance your chances of receiving raises and promotions, it is important to gather credentials and document your performance. Understanding the biases that creep into competency assessment is important in developing strategies to minimize the impact. Multiple studies using identical resumes with the gender switched have shown that both women and men judge women more harshly.[4] Also, using flexible work arrangements may reduce critical "face time," so you should have a plan to maintain visibility and rapport with key people and also to document your accomplishments.

In creating your strategy to succeed as a member of a dual-career couple, you should keep three factors in mind: opportunity, flexibility, and competency. Management doesn't want to "waste" an important career-building opportunity on someone they think is not serious about their career and well qualified.

A woman in a dual-career couple with a young child may be eager to seize the opportunity to be on the fast track and willing to make sacrifices to open the door to future advancement if she has sufficient flexibility. However, she may never be given the opportunity, because a dominant breadwinner manager may think that she is neither qualified nor interested. You must have a strategy to combat this type of subtle and unconscious bias.

Just because your organization doesn't work for you doesn't mean that there aren't other places that would be much better fit. Organizations often cannot change quickly enough for people who are working for them to avoid damaging their career. Don't be afraid to look for other alternatives. You may be surprised by which organizations are flexible and which are not. If you have strong credentials, plan to negotiate for what you need to succeed and to have a thriving personal life.

SURVEYS ON DUAL-CAREER COUPLES

I was inspired to take action in 2010 when I heard about older male managers intimidating young women by asking them, "When are you going to put your career first?" These men believed that being willing to relocate was essential to gaining experience and being promotable. They would not accept that someone could gain equivalent experience and be fully productive without being geographically mobile. In effect, these bosses were looking for someone who emulates their old sole-breadwinner lifestyle rather than focusing on capability and productivity.

To better understand the issues and to create a persuasive argument for change, I needed to move beyond anecdotal evidence to meaningful statistics. Management is data-driven. Thus, I decided to gather data to document the prevalence of dual-career couples in the workforce as well as statistical information on how members of dual-career couples differ from members of the dominant-breadwinner workforce.

My approach was to start with my own industry, the petroleum industry. Having served as the 2006 president of the Society of Petroleum Engineers (SPE), I knew whom to approach in that organization about conducting a survey. It is always beneficial to have a good collaborator. I was fortunate that Susan Howes, who is not only a petroleum engineer but also a certified human resources professional, was interested in the initiative to conduct surveys on dual-career couple issues. The staff liaison for the SPE Talent Council, Tom Whipple, was also supportive in helping us secure approval for the study and in its implementation.

Susan and I developed the survey questions, which had to be approved by the members of the SPE Talent Council, several of whom were human resources professionals. We recognized that a survey by a professional society offered significant advantages over a survey by an employer. In a voluntary, professional society survey, we were able to ask questions that if asked by an employer would be viewed as inappropriate invasion of an employee's privacy. We could also explore broad trends that extended beyond a single organization or geographic area.

We did not collect information to identify unique individuals and participation was completely voluntary. We pledged to never share the raw data beyond a small circle of people. Furthermore, we promised not to release any information that could be linked to a specific person.

In May 2011, SPE e-mailed a link to the survey to over 46,000 members all around the world. A total of 5,570 members responded for a response rate of 12 percent, which was better than the typical "good" response rate of 10 percent to a survey by SPE. People of 98 different nationalities responded with more than 100 responses from 6 countries.[5]

Analyzing the data, I was like a kid in a candy shop. I was constantly thinking of new ways to "interrogate the data" to uncover patterns through different cross-correlations. I played with the spreadsheets until my hands ached from repetitive stress syndrome. Nights and weekends were filled with looking for ways in which people in dual-career couples differed from those in other types of domestic relationships.

With a PhD from Stanford University in geophysics and bachelor's and master's degrees from Massachusetts Institute of Technology, I had ample experience designing research projects. I was accustomed to ignoring technical and disciplinary boundaries. My university degrees were in earth sciences/geophysics, but I had spent my career imper-sonating a petroleum engineer. In their work, scientists ask, "Why?" Engineers seek to solve problems. My forte was solving problems at the junction of multiple disciplines by identifying the most important variables.

There are only a few other surveys on dual-career couples in the public domain. An excellent survey was conducted by Schiebinger, Henderson, and Gilmartin under the auspices of Stanford University's Clayman Institute for Gender Research.[6] Schiebinger et al. gathered information from more than 9,000 full-time faculty at 13 leading U.S. research universities. While only 10 percent of those in the Clayman Institute study were part of a dual hire, 30 percent of the women and 32 percent of the men were partnered with another academic; 72 per-cent of university-level academics have an employed partner. Half of those partners are also in academia. Only 14 percent of university-level academics are single and only 13 percent fit the traditional model with a stay-at-home partner. In the report on that study, I saw many simi-larities between the dual-career couples in academia and those in the petroleum industry.

Schiebinger et al. learned that 10 percent of the faculty contacted in the survey were part of a "dual hire" at their current institutions.

Ten percent is a small, but important, proportion of faculty hir-ing. Universities are in danger of losing some of their most prized candidates if suitable employment cannot be found for qualified partners. In independent internal studies analyzing factors influ-encing failed faculty recruitment, two prominent U.S. research universities found that partner employment ranked high (num-ber one or two) in lists that included salary, housing costs, and some 15 to 16 other factors.[7]

The first SPE survey whetted my appetite, leaving me hungry for more data. Susan and I were able to persuade the SPE Talent Council and the SPE Young Professionals Group to allow us to conduct another survey to better understand how being part of a dual-career couple impacted people under the age of 45.

The second survey was e-mailed in December 2011. The response rate was 5 percent as opposed to 12 percent in the first survey. The lower response rate may have been because of survey fatigue or because the survey was distributed in December, when many people were on vacation. Nevertheless, we still gathered 1,392 responses.[8] The results from the December 2011 SPE survey were consistent with the prior SPE survey, which was conducted in May 2011, and also with the 2008 Stanford Clayman Institute survey of academics. A key observation in both the Stanford Clayman Institute survey and the December 2011 survey was that most members of dual-career couples consider both careers to be equally important.

A 2012 survey of alumni of the Harvard Business School that compared expectations shortly after graduation with those years later found that early in their careers women expected their careers to be as important as their partners, but subsequently were disappointed that life did not turn out that way.[9] The female Harvard graduates also reported that their partners did not share child care and household chores as equally as they anticipated, leaving them to shoulder most of the burden.

When we shared the findings of the second SPE survey with petroleum industry management, those executives who were dominant breadwinners were still reluctant to consider equally important careers to be a realistic concept. As long as they could hire people who mimicked their own lifestyle, they saw no reason to make changes.

The motivation for the third SPE survey was to collect data to convince those traditional executives that continuing to populate the "fast track" to advancement and the executive ranks with people whose lifestyle and value system were significantly different from the bulk of the workforce would lead to problems. These managers tend to think that employees will always grumble and want more accommodations. What makes a difference is when people "vote with their feet." Problems hiring and retaining employees catch their attention. We needed another survey to show the impact on attraction and retention of employees.

The SPE Talent Council authorized a third survey that focused on factors impacting attraction and retention of employees. We worked with the alumni associations of multiple universities that train petroleum industry technical professionals in an attempt to contact people who had dropped out of the workforce. To understand how petroleum engineers compared with other technical professionals, we reached out to other technical professional organizations posting in multiple LinkedIn groups the solicitation to participate. We were not given authorization to distribute the link by e-mail to SPE members, because of complaints from some SPE members about being spammed with too much e-mail, so we posted the solicitations to participate on the SPE website and through SPE discussion groups. We kept the survey open for about six months gathering 1,737 responses.[10] The survey was closed when the SPE staff statistician determined that incremental responses were not significantly changing the metrics that he was monitoring.

As a "data junkie," I was constantly looking for new ways to feed my habit of gathering information on dual-career couples. When I was approached by the president of the Society of Exploration Geophysicists (SEG) about forming a women's network, I accepted, because I saw it as another opportunity to collect data. The SEG Women's Network Committee collectively developed an exhaustive set of questions on women's and dual-career couples' issues. However, the SEG staff balked at the number of questions, so the set of survey questions was reduced to a more manageable size. The link to the SEG survey was e-mailed to members in May 2013. Almost 1,600 people responded, about 5 percent of the 33,000 members.[11]

The results of the 2013 SEG survey were consistent with those of the three SPE surveys, but probed more deeply into several important issues that impact dual-career couples. We found significant differences in willingness to relocate (which is a requirement for being on the fast track at some companies) as a function of both gender and the percentage of household income earned by the person participating in the survey. A person's income has a significant impact on decision making and family dynamics. In this volume we follow the money and see how it is changing the workforce.

CHAPTER 1

What Is a Dual-Career Couple?

People have a wide range of definitions of what it means to be a dual-career couple. The broadest definition is: two people who are in a long-term, committed domestic relationship with each other and who both have high aspirations for their careers. They don't have to be legally married. They don't have to be of opposite sex. They don't have to be well paid or working full time. They just have to be planning on a life together while continuing to pursue their careers.

ESSENTIAL DISCUSSIONS

Career planning for a single ambitious person is daunting. Merging the career goals of two domestic partners with high hopes for their life's work is far more challenging. Open and honest discussions of career priorities and decision-making criteria are essential to forging a satisfying and enduring partnership.

The people in a relationship may have significantly different expectations. One partner may think they are in a long-term, committed relationship and the other person may see the arrangement as more temporary. The partners may have different perspectives on the relative importance of their careers. They may not agree on key criteria for deciding how to proceed when actions in support of one career may adversely impact the other. Whether or not the couple is married or plans to marry, an individual in a dual-career couple should understand the priorities of his or her partner before doing anything that compromises either his or her own career or that of his or her partner.

In a romantic relationship, conversations about finances and career interaction can be awkward. Nevertheless, it is essential to talk about these issues. Don't avoid the chat just because you might not like what you hear. Failure to discuss the issues doesn't make them go away.

One woman shared with me that she broke off an engagement, because her fiancé told her that, in the event of conflict between their careers, the career of the person who was making the most money should always come first. She was wise to identify that incompatibility before rather than after marriage.

You and your partner should confer on these matters not only when considering whether or not you wish to marry or live together, but also periodically throughout your relationship. Life deals us many surprises that can drastically alter our priorities. For example, after a year of battling a rare type of cancer in 2007, I decided that my focus should be more on helping other women rather than on advancing my own career in the petroleum industry.

Many life events can alter our perspectives and goals. If as a couple, you have frequent discussions, you are in a better position to evaluate against your criteria an opportunity that pops up out of the blue and requires a rapid response.

Advance planning pays off when you are trying to determine if you can make a business trip on short notice or uproot the entire family and move to a new location. You can arrange the chats with your partner at a relatively convenient time. Decisions made when the clock for a response is rapidly ticking may not be as well-informed and wise. The discussions will be more productive if they are conducted when you both are under less pressure and are more relaxed.

QUESTIONS FOR COUPLES TO DISCUSS

- What do you agree is the relative priority of your careers?
- If you believe that your careers are equally important, what does that mean to each of you?
- If one career is considered to be more important, what factors make that career more important and what is the relative weighting of those factors?
- What factors do you think are most important in making joint career decisions?

- How will you manage your finances? Will you combine your earnings or keep your earnings separate and share household expenses?
- How will you share household chores?
- Who will be primarily responsible for unanticipated urgent home repairs?
- Do you hope to have children? If so, how many? How do you plan to share and manage child-rearing responsibilities?
- Do you anticipate eating dinner together during the week? How much time do you think you will spend together in a typical week?

KEY DIFFERENCES IN DUAL-CAREER COUPLES

Some major factors that shape dual-career couple relationships include:

- Financial—What percentage of the household income does each partner contribute?
- Marital status—Are the partners married? Do they intend to marry? Are they legally able to marry?
- Gender—Is it a heterosexual or same-sex relationship?
- Children
- Children from prior relationships
- Relative age of the partners—Is one partner older and more established in his or her career than the other?
- Extended family obligations
- Does the couple share an employer? Do they want to share any employer?
- Citizenship or residency status
- Academic tenure

FOLLOW THE MONEY

Whether you like it or not, money is power. When women could not earn a living wage, marrying a good breadwinner and keeping him happy was essential to maintaining a decent quality of life. It was no wonder that marrying well was a key success variable for women. Many stereotypical male and female behavior patterns that now bedevil women in the workplace have their origin in a woman having to hang onto her man to protect her standard of living and to ensure food and shelter for her children. A woman's lifestyle was at risk if she failed to "love, honor and obey" her husband.

The ability of a woman to earn sufficient money to maintain her standard of living is revolutionary. Although on average, women still have not reached complete economic parity, women have made sufficient progress such that, in a heterosexual relationship, a woman's earnings are often a significant fraction of the household income. That has facilitated a huge shift in power in domestic relationships.

Women's ability to be self-supporting could be a key factor in the declining rate of marriage in the United States. According to the Pew Research Center, the percentage of American adults who have never married has been rapidly increasing since about 1980.[1] From 1960 to 1980, there was little change in the percentage of men and women over 25 who were unmarried. However, between 1980 and 2012, the percentage of unmarried women over the age of 25 has risen from about 9 percent to 17 percent, while the percentage of unmarried men has increased from about 11 percent to 23 percent.

The increase in unmarried adults coincided with the increase in women's compensation relative to men's.[2] Data collected by the National Committee on Pay Equity show that between 1960 and 1980, women's pay wobbled between 56 percent and 60 percent of men's pay. Then between 1980 and 2001, women's pay rose from 60 percent to 76 percent of men's. Unfortunately, since the turn of the twenty-first century, there has been relatively little progress such that, as of 2014, women were still earning just 78.6 percent of men's wages. Although progress toward gender pay equity has stalled, it is much easier for a woman to support herself earning almost 79 percent of a man's income than it was when the average woman earned just 60 percent.

Cultural norms and gender behavior expectations have lagged behind the growing importance of women's wages in family well-being. The expectations of society are evolving, but transitions are difficult. As traditional gender patterns become increasingly obsolete, individuals must define their own roles instead of simply following traditional patterns. Behavior and attitudes depend on how much of the household income each partner contributes. A woman who can be self-supporting has no need to be as submissive as a "kept woman."

When one partner depends on the other for his or her financial well-being, the dominant partner can and often does call the shots.

The dependent partner then must manipulate and bargain to get what he or she wants. My grandmothers and my mother had to beg their husbands for money. I never have.

When my husband and I married in the early 1970s, he had much more money than I did. He asked that we keep our finances separate, but we didn't have a formal prenuptial agreement. I wasn't thrilled, but I agreed. For the first couple of decades of our marriage he was better off financially than I was. Then for the last two decades I have gradually built up a bigger and bigger lead over him.

One evening he complained that I didn't bother to manipulate him. By that he meant that I didn't conform to the stereotypical female behavior of coaxing him into thinking that something I wanted to do was really his idea. I was shocked by his request. To me, "manipulating" was a devious and underhanded way of interacting with my spouse. Since I was working full time and extremely busy, I didn't have the time or energy to waste manipulating him so that he could think something was his idea. I was able to take care of myself financially and didn't have to wheedle and cajole him. I thought it was more honest to tell him what I planned to do and in a straightforward way lay out the facts in support of my decision. I could make my own decisions and take credit (or blame) for them.

In dual-career couples, how much each partner currently contributes to the household finances and their relative future earning potential are important factors in family decision making. For example, career opportunities that require relocation can jeopardize the budding career and wages of the other partner. Thus, the relative portion of the household income provided by each partner is likely to be a major factor in decisions as to whether or not one partner's career is to be compromised for the benefit of the other partner's career.

As we move down the path to gender pay equity and full equality for women, many women still anticipate being equal earners or the lesser contributor in a dual-career household. However, life throws us many unanticipated punches. A partner may lose his or her job, be physically or mentally incapacitated, or die. There are many reasons why a woman may unexpectedly find herself the family's dominant earner and/or source of medical benefits.

The burden of being responsible for the family's welfare is a heavy load that until relatively recently was considered to be a man's responsibility. When a woman unexpectedly assumes those responsibilities, she undergoes a major shift in priorities and attitude if she feels she must keep a job she doesn't like. Our careers and our earnings shape our attitudes and our relationships.

EQUAL EARNERS

"Equal earners" are people in couples in which both partners contribute about the same amount to the household income. When a couple depends on both incomes to support their lifestyle, anything that significantly reduces either income is a major concern.

If one partner's job requires a move to a new location, it can be highly disruptive to the other partner's career and to the family. If both members of the couple work for the same organization and are offered transfers to the same location, relocation can be relatively easy. However, if they work for different employers and the other partner must find another position or give up his or her career, the family faces some very difficult decisions. Some people may prefer living separately to compromising one career and/or losing the income from the "trailing spouse."

My surveys found that an overwhelming percentage (more than 80%) of people in equal-earner couples consider both careers to be equally important. Economic equality tends to promote more equal division of household responsibilities. If the couple is managing without full-time hired household help, their delicate daily balance can become difficult to sustain when anything out of the routine occurs, whether it is emergency home or car repairs or a sick child.

Despite the daily strain of maintaining an equal-earner household without a hired housekeeper, these couples may also have children. To better establish their careers before taking on the added burden of parenthood, they may wait until they are in their thirties to become parents. At any age, the addition of children makes it more difficult to work irregular hours, stay late on short notice, or travel. Equal-earner parents highly value flexible work arrangements that when necessary allow them to work from home or modify their schedule.

DOMINANT EARNERS

If one partner in a dual-career couple provides 70 percent or more of the household income, I have classified that person as a "dominant earner." As the fraction of the household income provided by the higher earning partner increases, the dominant earner is increasingly likely to think that his or her career is more important than his or her partner's career. The dominant earner may believe that the less-well-compensated partner should be the one to handle emergencies and should assume a larger share of the housework and child-rearing.

Different types of careers are associated with radically different pay scales and lifestyles. Many people choose careers that do not pay well, because they are passionately interested in the work. As a result, people's pay does not directly correlate with their academic qualifications and level of professionalism. Just because some jobs do not pay well does not mean that there is not a lot of competition for the positions. An influential and highly qualified person can be a star performer in a poorly paid field and still earn far less than his or her partner, who is at a lower level in a better compensated profession. Thus, members of these couples may consider both of their careers to be equally important.

Some professions with a high percentage of women tend to be more poorly paid than professions that are dominated by men. Many people feel that if "the money I earned" is providing most of the financial support for the family, their partner should be responsible for more of the household chores. Studies show that women still spend more time on housework and childcare, even though the time spent by men has been increasing.

SOLE BREADWINNERS

In one survey I conducted on dual-career couple issues, a 56-year-old man commented: "While you may not consider my wife and I to have a dual-career, I do by the fact that without her assistance my daily life would be very difficult. Her role is as important as mine since she is the one that takes care of what I consider the part of our daily life that makes our life possible."[3]

The man and his wife in the example above do not meet the definition of a dual-career couple. In the definition (two people, who are in a long-term, committed domestic relationship with each other and who both have high aspirations for their careers), the emphasis is on more than one career.

Many "traditional" executives and managers still have a wife, whose role is to support her husband. The couple has a common goal to advance the man's career. The wife serves as his domestic personal assistant, packing his bags for business trips and entertaining his guests. Her role is to make him look good to his superiors, colleagues, and customers. In the ideal, this type of wife was the perfect, submissive wife satirized in the 1972 novel, *The Stepford Wives*, by Ira Levin and in the movies of the same name released in 1975 and 2004.

I have attended executive retirement events at which the invaluable role the wife played in her husband's career was acknowledged and celebrated by both the employer and the executive. The executive and his spouse describe the career as "we did." One man explained his wife's valuable role as a hostess saying that over a 21-year span, she welcomed over 6,000 people into their home. He announced that both of them needed a rest. Even though his wife had never been a paid employee, both husband and wife were effusively thanked and presented with retirement gifts. This epitomizes the old "two for the price of one" career. Sad to say, when I asked his successor if his wife was playing the same role, he said that she was.

At another retirement event, a top executive was profuse in his praise of his wife. "She proved especially adept at bringing national and expatriate spouses together for social and school activities—a critically important role in ensuring a harmonious team." This executive also noted that during his 41 years with the company, they had lived in 18 different homes. He bragged that his wife "has always been ready to pack up and go."

Some supervisors consider it to be essential to not just to have a spouse, but a wife in the support role. A female friend of mine was denied a transfer to the Andean region of South America, because her boss did not think her husband or any man could provide sufficient household support.

My friend was well aware of the challenges she would face in that part of South America. Her father worked as a mining engineer in the Andes. She spent more than a decade in the region as a child, closely observing the role played by her mother, who prior to her marriage had been an airline stewardess.

For the purposes of this book, a relationship in which one person's career is to provide support for his or her partner's career is *not* a dual-career couple. It fits the traditional model for executives, people who will go anywhere at any time with the full support and cooperation of their partners. Although such couples are an employer's dream team, they represent the past in which the woman was financially dependent on her spouse, not the future in which the woman has a career of her own and can be financially self-supporting.

PART-TIME CAREERS

Initially I thought that both people working full time should be part of the definition of a dual-career couple. My attitude was adjusted by vehement responses I received through social media to the 2013 Society of Petroleum Engineers (SPE) survey on factors impacting attraction and retention of employees.[4] Within minutes of posting an invitation to participate in the survey on an MIT alumnae website, I received angry e-mails from three women. They were outraged that the survey did not include an option for people who worked part-time.

To better understand the perspective of these irate alumnae, I corresponded with them. Two of the women agreed to allow use of anonymous quotes from their e-mails in publications. These women, who currently work part-time, were emphatic that working part-time did not reflect how serious someone was about their career. They stressed that it took a tremendous effort on their part to build their own businesses, for which they now work part-time.

One woman wrote, "I have left the corporate environment and work as an independent consultant precisely because I want to work half-time. . . . Job-wise, it would've been much easier for me to find a default full-time job than spend time creating my part-time profession, but I want to spend time raising my kids. In this sense, part-time workers are just as committed to their careers as full-time workers."[5]

As a result of the feedback from these women, how many hours per week the individuals work is not included in the definition of a dual-career couple. These women presented convincing reasons why people who are very serious about their vocation may choose to work part-time.

Dame Stephanie Shirley describes in her March 2015 TED Talk how in the 1960s, she founded a software company, Freelance Programmers, in the United Kingdom with women working part-time in their homes. "I recruited professionally qualified women who'd left the industry on marriage, or when their first child was expected and structured them into a home-working organization. We pioneered the concept of women going back into the workforce after a career break. We pioneered all sorts of new, flexible work methods: job shares, profit-sharing, and eventually, co-ownership when I took a quarter of the company into the hands of the staff at no cost to anyone but me."[6]

The women working part-time for Dame Shirley in their homes writing computer code were clearly very self-disciplined. However, Dame Shirley describes herself as a workaholic even though she created a company that relied on part-time workers. It is ironic that her company was for many years staffed solely with women, when tech companies now find it difficult to recruit women. Part-time work and telecommuting can enable people to sustain their careers while caring for young children.

CHAPTER 2

Why Now?

The transition from a workforce that was overwhelmingly composed of dominant male breadwinners to a workforce with a large fraction of dual-career couples has occurred during my lifetime. I have witnessed and benefited from the amazing progress that women have made toward equality in the last half century that enabled the growth of the dual-career couple workforce.

If I had been born a decade earlier, my career might never have gotten started. As a woman I would have had a very difficult time securing satisfactory employment. If I was born a few decades later, my career would not have been as adversely impacted by the barriers to women that have left me battered and bruised.

Thanks to legislative and legal actions in the 1960s and early 1970s, when I was ready to look for work in the late 1970s, I had my pick of job offers. I was part of a generation of women, who, since they were there for the changes, gathered "firsts" as in the first woman to hold certain positions or earn degrees or other forms of recognition for their accomplishments.

My "firsts" are not nearly as impressive as those of Sally Ride, who was the first American woman in space, but we were the only two women in a first-year graduate physics class at Stanford from the fall of 1973 through the spring of 1974. I never got to know her, because I was a geophysicist and she was a physicist. The geophysicists sat together. Our academic discipline was a stronger "tribal" factor than gender. We stuck with our own kind and didn't socialize across the divide.

MAJOR LEGAL CHANGES IN
THE UNITED STATES

The Equal Pay Act of 1963 was signed into law in June of 1963 by President John F. Kennedy shortly before I turned 12 years old. I was in my final month of sixth grade and didn't appreciate the significance of the new law, which subsequently has had a profound impact on my life and the job opportunities and earning ability of all American women including myself. The Equal Pay Act created a labor standard that required employers to pay men and women the same wages when performing jobs that were equal or essentially equal. It was the first national labor standard in the United States that prohibited paying women less than men merely because of their gender.

The following year, the Civil Rights Act of 1964 prohibited discrimination on the basis of sex, race, color, national origin, and religion. Despite the passage of that act, six years later when I was hunting for a summer job after graduating from high school in 1969, the "help wanted" advertisements in the newspapers were still divided into "male" and "female" sections.

The entry-level jobs for women were primarily for receptionists, secretaries, or keypunch operators. There were lots of openings for keypunch operators, who were employed to type computer programming code into a machine that punched holes into the stiff paper cards that were used to input programs and data into computers. That dead-end job category morphed into a "data entry keyer" when computer terminals replaced batch processing, but almost a quarter century after the Civil Rights Act, Carol Kleiman noted in a *Chicago Tribune* article on August 2, 1987, that 92 percent of those employed in that poorly compensated role were female. The main job opportunities for women when I finished high school were in low-paid, dead-end positions.

I missed most of the changes prompted by Title IX of the Education Amendments of 1972, whose goal was to eliminate discrimination by educational institutions that received federal financial assistance. I started at the Massachusetts Institute of Technology (MIT) in the fall of 1969, when women were about 5 percent of the undergraduates. Toilet facilities for women were few and far between, and unlike the men, the freshman women were not required to take physical education. To MIT's credit, the percentage of female undergraduates at MIT has increased almost continuously for almost half a century, rising from just a few percent in 1961 to about 46 percent, a tremendous accomplishment for a university focused on science and engineering.

While I was at MIT, there were scarcely any female faculty and I never took a course from one of them. However, the percentage of female faculty at MIT has risen continuously since the mid-1980s, with about 22 percent of the total faculty positions now held by women. Young women now have much more reason than I did to think that their careers can and should be as important as those of their male contemporaries.

In 1977, I was the first woman to be awarded a PhD in geophysics from Stanford. I arranged to continue at Stanford as a research associate in the Department of Geophysics, because my husband was still working on his graduate degrees. My secret project was to have a child, so I selected from the choice of Stanford health care plans the one that provided the most economical maternity care coverage. My son was born nine months after I defended my PhD thesis.

I didn't feel comfortable asking anyone for guidance. There were no female faculty in my department, so I had no role models. I never learned if at that time Stanford University offered any maternity leave for staff members. I just assumed there was none. Having worked right up until delivery, I decided it was reasonable to take two weeks off. When my son was 13 days old, I put him in a front carrier Snugli pack and brought him into my office, which was close to the machine shop and next door to the laboratory in which I worked. As a research associate, I shared the office with two men, a graduate student and a Japanese research associate. To have privacy while I nursed my son, I strung up a bedsheet between a pair of tall bookcases. My son came into work with me every day until he was about six months old.

In 1978, I started work at Mobil's Field Research Laboratory in Dallas, Texas. At that time, there were almost no female staff members other than clerical workers and librarians. There were still a few male secretaries from the days when Mobil wouldn't even hire women for clerical roles. One of the librarians was just a few years older than myself. She shared with me that each of the three times she got pregnant, she was terminated, and when she was ready to return to work, Mobil rehired her.

The same year that I started working for Mobil, the Pregnancy Discrimination Act of 1978 amended Title VII of the Civil Rights Act of 1964 to prohibit sex discrimination on the basis of pregnancy. The Pregnancy Discrimination Act required that "women affected by pregnancy, childbirth, or related medical conditions shall be treated the same for all employment-related purposes, including receipt of benefits under fringe benefit programs, as other persons not so affected but similar in their ability or inability to work."[1] Employers could no longer force pregnant employees, like my friend the librarian, to quit or be terminated if they were pregnant.

Thanks to that Pregnancy Discrimination Act, when my daughter was born in 1981, I was eligible for pregnancy-related sick leave. For an uncomplicated vaginal birth, the new mother was considered to be medically disabled for only six weeks. I received four weeks' full pay with the remaining two weeks at half pay, because I had not yet earned six weeks of full-pay sick leave in the two and a half years that I had worked for Mobil.

In the late 1970s and early 1980s only about 45 percent of the women with children under the age of 6 were employed.[2] There was not a lot of support for working mothers with infants and preschoolers. When my children got sick, it was a mad scramble and wild juggling act, because there were no provisions for taking time off to care for ailing children or other relatives. I was trying to prove that a woman could do a man's job, so I didn't think that I could ask for any flexibility.

The Family and Medical Leave Act was not enacted until 1993. That act required employers to provide to employees job-protected and unpaid leave for qualified medical and family reasons if the person had been employed for at least 12 months, worked at least 1,250 hours in the past 12 months, and at a location where the company employed 50 or more employees within 75 miles. Qualified medical and family reasons include personal or family illness, family military leave, pregnancy, adoption, or the foster care placement of a child.[3]

The Family and Medical Leave Act meant that men were entitled to take unpaid paternity leave. When my two children were born, there was no question of my husband taking time off to assist me. He drove me to and from the hospital, was present for my labor and delivery, and otherwise minimized his time away from work. However, when my first grandchild was born in 2011, thanks to the legal progress in the interim, my son took off two weeks to help with the new baby. Allowing men take paternity leave is a huge step in encouraging men to be more involved in the care of their children and to more equally share child-rearing responsibilities.

Many professional women of my generation felt that they had to choose between having a career and having a family. According to the Pew Research Center that is no longer true. In 1994, 30 percent of women aged 40 to 44 with a master's degree or higher had no children, but now only 22 percent of equivalent women are childless. The change has been even greater for women with an MD or PhD. In

1994, 35 percent of those women were childless, but now only 20 percent are. Pew found that not only are highly educated women more likely to have children, but also they are having more children.[4]

NARROWING THE PAY GAP

I entered the workforce shortly before the gap between men's and women's earnings began to narrow after decades of no progress. It took almost two full decades after the Equal Pay Act of 1963 for the provisions of that act to have an impact on women's wages. Then for the next two decades, there was steady progress toward narrowing the wage gap. Unfortunately, in this century little progress has been made.

The generation of women who preceded me encountered numerous obstacles to their careers. Not only did women not receive financial compensation that was equivalent to men's, but also women's ideas and accomplishments were often claimed by men or attributed to male colleagues (a pattern that still too frequently occurs).

Rosalind Franklin's experience in the United Kingdom is a classic example of a woman not being recognized for her major contributions. She was the British biophysicist and X-ray crystallographer whose X-ray diffraction images of DNA led to discovery of DNA double helix. Unpublished drafts of her papers show that she was the first to determine the form of the DNA helix. Two men, James Watson and Francis Crick, were awarded the 1962 Nobel Prize in physiology or medicine in recognition of their discovery of the structure of DNA in 1953 using her data, but they didn't acknowledge her work.

Like Rosalind Franklin, my mother was born in 1920. I grew up listening to my mother's stories of the challenges that she encountered during her career as a commercial artist. When she asked for a raise, her bosses would refuse by explaining to her why a man had to be paid more than a woman. The prevailing belief was that if the man was married, he needed the extra money to support his family or if he was single he needed the money to take women out on dates. My mother always resented this attitude. She was supporting herself and contributing to the support of her mother.

The job market for women was grim in 1948 when my mother's sister Audrey received her PhD in English literature from Johns Hopkins University. To her dismay, Audrey found that the department chairmen at most universities would not even interview women for faculty positions. She had supported herself while she was working on her doctorate by working as the secretary for the English department.

When her employment opportunities seemed to be nonexistent, the department chairman at Johns Hopkins University considered allowing her to continue working as a secretary. Finally, a friend offered her a nontenure track position at Mills College, a women's college in Oakland, California. Audrey wrote, "Like the old maids in eighteenth century novels, I was not choosy."[5]

Almost a decade later, Audrey was still was paid less than a milkman. Although she had sacrificed for decades to pursue her career, when she finally found love, there was no question as to whose career took precedence. Audrey had made tremendous sacrifices to get her education, because her father didn't think college education was worthwhile for women. In contrast, Audrey's future husband had spent four years in college at his father's expense, but never settled on a major and left without a degree, when his father cut off his funding. The huge disparity between women's and men's compensation in the 1950s meant that even if a woman was better educated than her husband, the financial imperative was that the man's career came first.

When I entered the petroleum industry in 1978, I had no trouble getting hired. After onsite interviews with eight companies, I received six job offers. Under pressure from the government, companies were hiring women, but they weren't sure what to do with the women once they were employed. However, I almost immediately slammed into the glass ceiling. My boss's boss told me, "You can't have a younger woman supervising older men." In effect, that blocked women from acquiring the management experience that the company deemed to be essential for advancement. Not surprisingly, there were no women in management.

I was the third female PhD hired to work at Mobil's Field Research Laboratory in Dallas. The second female PhD was hired one year before me. The other woman, who was hired in the 1950s, was embittered by her experiences and convinced that she could not have children and maintain her career.

Going into a male-dominated area of science turned out to be a wise career move. A U.S. Department of Commerce, Economics and Statistics Administration, August 2011 report on "Women in STEM [Science, Technology, Engineering and Mathematics]: A Gender Gap to Innovation" observed that the gender wage gap was smaller in STEM careers. A 2013 White House report noted,

By 1980, thanks to advances in women's educational attainment, the number of women in STEM fields began to increase—even though women still comprised 25 percent or less of the total employed in the STEM occupations. Notably, women who hold STEM degrees and work in STEM occupations earn 33 percent more, on average, than women in non-STEM jobs; and, while women in non-STEM occupations typically earn 23 percent less than their male colleagues, the salaries of their counterparts in STEM are only 14 percent less than those of their male co-workers.[6]

When I became the first woman to receive a PhD in geophysics from Stanford in 1977, I was well positioned to benefit from the higher compensation in STEM fields and the narrower gender wage gap. That said, I still encountered prejudice and gender-based career obstacles. Fortunately, in the ensuing decades many of the barriers have vanished or diminished.

Sadly, too few women have discovered how much fun science and engineering are. Women continue to be underrepresented in well-compensated STEM professions. In most disciplines, the gender pay gap is much larger than the 14 percent cited in the White House report for women in STEM careers.

CURRENT GENDER PAY GAP

The U.S. Census Bureau reports that on average women's earnings are about 80 percent of men's earnings, with no substantial improvement in a decade.[7] The Census Bureau's analysis is based on weekly earnings for full-time workers, who are defined as people who usually work at least 35 hours per week. This methodology lumps together as full-time workers people who work different numbers of hours on a weekly basis. Of those the government defined as working full time, 26 percent of the men but only 14 percent of the women indicated that they worked more than 40 hours per week. Thus, in the Census Bureau's weekly pay comparison the results would tend to overestimate the gender pay gap, because men work more hours on a weekly basis than women.

In contrast with Census Bureau evaluation of the gender pay gap, the Pew Research Center bases its assessment on hourly earnings, because 26 percent of women but only 13 percent of men work part-time.[8] Using hourly earnings adjusts for the differences in the number of hours worked. On the basis of hourly data as of 2012, the gender pay gap was smaller, but women's compensation was still only 84 percent of men's.

Digging deeper, a 2013 White House report observed, "Controlling for differences in the types of jobs women and men typically perform, women earn less than men in male-dominated occupations (such as managers, software developers, and CEOs) and in female-dominated occupations (such as teachers, nurses, and receptionists)."[9] The White House report drew this conclusion from a report by the Institute for Women's Policy Research.[10]

Ariane Hegewisch, a study director at the Institute for Women's Policy Research, said in 2012, "These gender wage gaps are not about women choosing to work less than men—the analysis is comparing apples to apples, men and women who all work full time—and we see that across these 40 common occupations, men nearly always earn more than women."[11]

An example of women earning less than men when all known factors were taken into consideration was a study of the starting salaries of physicians immediately following completion of their residency programs in New York State between 1999 and 2008. That study concluded that there was a significant gender gap in starting salaries that could not be explained by medical specialty, work hours, or other characteristics. In 1999 starting salaries of the female physicians were an average of $3,000 less than their comparably trained male peers. By 2008 the gap had widened with the salaries the women physicians received an average of $16,819 less than the salaries of comparably qualified men.[12]

As of February 12, 2015, the current population survey of the U.S. Bureau of Labor and Statistics still shows a large gap between the median weekly wages for men and women (Table 2.1).[13] In not a single one of the top 50 paying professions for men was women's pay at parity. The gap doesn't correlate with the percentage of women in the job classification and cuts across all professions. Women can try to escape the female job classification ghetto, but they can't seem to avoid the pay inequities.

Female purchasing managers were closest to equality receiving 93 percent of men's wages, but that job category is the 29th best paid. In only 3 of the 50 best paid professions for men did women earn 90 percent or more of men's wages. Besides the purchasing managers, civil engineers, and registered nurses were at 90 percent or more of parity. In the top 10 best compensated roles for men, female pharmacists and female computer and information systems managers were most successful relative to their male peers, receiving 87 percent of men's pay.

Table 2.1 Gender Pay Equity for Top Paying Professions

Occupation	Men's Median Weekly Earnings ($)	Percentage of Females	Women's Pay as a Percentage of Men's
Chief executives	2,246	26	70
Pharmacists	2,176	52	87
Physicians and surgeons	2,002	37	62
Lawyers	1,915	34	83
Human resources managers	1,827	76	71
Legal occupations	1,765	55	57
Computer and information systems managers	1,763	27	87
Software developers, applications and systems software	1,736	20	84
Financial managers	1,671	53	67
Management analysts	1,665	42	74
Personal financial advisers	1,637	40	61
Marketing and sales managers	1,624	45	71
Physical scientists, all other	1,547	35	82
Financial analysts	1,493	41	82
Physical therapists	1,478	61	88
Computer systems analysts	1,460	35	86
Operations research analysts	1,457	54	85
Management occupations	1,454	42	78
Medical scientists	1,449	50	79

(*Continued*)

Table 2.1 (Continued)

Occupation	Men's Median Weekly Earnings ($)	Percentage of Females	Women's Pay as a Percentage of Men's
Medical and health services managers	1,448	72	84
Computer programmers	1,447	19	87
Education administrators	1,439	62	81
Computer and mathematical occupations	1,435	25	81
Management, business, and financial operations occupations	1,416	47	75
Architecture and engineering occupations	1,413	15	82
Managers, all other	1,412	38	82
Postsecondary teachers	1,409	47	81
Civil engineers	1,406	17	91
Purchasing managers	1,366	43	93
Securities, commodities, and financial services sales agents	1,356	35	65
General and operations managers	1,350	30	84
Management, professional, and related occupations	1,346	52	73
Business and financial operations occupations	1,310	57	75
Professional and related occupations	1,286	55	74
Training and development specialists	1,280	55	75

Occupation	Men's Median Weekly Earnings ($)	Percentage of Females	Women's Pay as a Percentage of Men's
Market research analysts and marketing specialists	1,269	61	79
Human resources workers	1,257	73	73
Health care practitioners and technical occupations	1,256	74	78
Life, physical, and social science occupations	1,247	41	85
Web developers	1,245	35	79
Compliance officers	1,237	48	88
Accountants and auditors	1,236	63	81
Business operations specialists, all other	1,229	57	77
Registered nurses	1,190	89	90
Credit counsellors and loan officers	1,188	60	77
Diagnostic related technologists and technicians	1,156	73	81
Social and community service managers	1,142	62	86
Education, training, and library occupations	1,141	73	79
Computer occupations, all other	1,122	24	88
Sales representatives, wholesale and manufacturing	1,120	28	78

Data from the United States Bureau of Labor and Statistics, median weekly earnings of full-time wage and salary workers by detailed occupation and sex (February 12, 2015), http://www.bls.gov/cps/cpsaat39.htm.

Consistent with the New York State study that found large gender compensation differences for doctors with equivalent qualifications immediately after the completion of their residencies, the census data determined that female physicians and surgeons earned just 62 percent of what their male peers did. No matter how well educated they are, on average women are paid less than comparable men.

The fifth highest-paying profession for men is human resources managers. What I find most depressing is that although 76 percent of human resources managers are women, those women earn just 71 percent of their male counterparts' wages. Human resources managers are generally responsible for ensuring gender pay equity within their organizations. Despite the role of human resources managers in preventing discrimination, these female human resources managers have not been able to eliminate the gender pay inequities in their own profession. Bias against women in compensation determination is clearly very pervasive and resistant to elimination.

When there are C-level and other high-ranking positions in human resources to be filled, I noticed that well-qualified, internal female candidates tend to be passed over with a man selected either from outside the company or brought in from another career track within the organization. Using executive level, well-compensated human resources positions as developmental assignments for "high flying" men in effect discriminates against female human resources professionals. What hope is there for women in general, if the female watchdogs can't protect themselves?

The Pew Research Center's evaluation of the wage gap for workers between the ages of 25 to 34 offers a ray of hope.[14] In 2012, young women between the ages of 25 and 34 earned 93 percent of their male counterparts' income. The gender pay equity gap for these younger women is much smaller than the 84 percent of men's wages netted by women overall. Furthermore, for the 25- to 34-year-old women, the pay gap appears to be narrowing at a faster rate than the gap for women overall.

We have come a long way from the 1960s, but new initiatives are needed to accelerate elimination of the gender pay gap. Greater transparency is needed. Just as organizations annually release financial data, organizations should be expected to release information on gender pay equity. What is publicly reported gets attention.

In 2015 I submitted a shareholder proposal to ExxonMobil, asking for an annual report on gender pay equity at different percentiles of compensation. Unfortunately, relatively few investors care about gender pay equity. My shareholder proposal received only 5.8 percent of the votes. The managers of mutual funds who own many of the corporate shares did not vote in favor of the pay equity report. Women's pay matters and we need to leverage our savings and investments to make our voices heard on this matter.

EVOLUTION OF FAMILY INCOME

The U.S. Bureau of Labor and Statistics reports on the comparative earnings of husbands and wives in "Women in the Labor Force: A Databook."[15] The earliest year for which data on married couples was provided was 1967. In that year, husbands were the sole earners in 36 percent of married couples and wives were the sole earners in 2 percent of married couples.

By 1970, the first year for which the contribution of wives' earnings to family income was reported, the percentage of families with sole breadwinner husbands had declined to 33 percent. The percentage of sole breadwinner wives remained at 2 percent. The median percentage that wives' earnings provided to the family income was just 26.6. The discriminatory wage practices that handicapped women meant that, in virtually all families, the man's income was the primary source of support.

In 1978, when I started work at Mobil as a young research scientist, I felt under constant pressure to prove that as a woman, wife, and mother of a toddler, I could be as valuable an employee as a man. At that time, 26 percent of husbands and 3 percent of wives were sole earners and the median contribution of wives to the family income had declined to 26.1 percent from 26.6 percent eight years earlier. As part of a dual-career household in which my salary was slightly higher than that of my husband, I was a statistical anomaly. It seemed to me that everything I did was closely scrutinized. I didn't dare ask for greater flexibility to manage child care and household challenges. Women were a novelty in my occupation and not considered to be an important part of the petroleum industry workforce.

It was not until 1987 that the Bureau of Labor and Statistics began collecting data on the percentage of wives who earned more than their husbands if both partners had earnings. The percentage of husbands who were sole earners had declined in nine years from 26 percent to 19 percent, and the percentage of wives who were the sole earners had doubled, increasing to 4 percent. In families in which both husbands and wives worked, 17.8 percent of the wives earned more than their husbands. The fact that in 1987 the Bureau of Labor and Statistics decided to collect information on the percentage of wives earning more than their husbands in "married couple families in which both wife and husband have earnings from work" indicates that by that time the percentage of dual-career couples in the workforce had grown to be large enough to be noticeable.

As of 2011, the percentage of husbands who were the sole earners was still 19 percent, the same percentage as in 1987. However, the percentage of wives who were the sole earners nearly doubled again, increasing from 4 percent to 7 percent. Furthermore, wives earned more than their husbands in 29.2 percent of the families in which both married partners worked—an increase of 11.4 percentage points since reporting began 24 years earlier. Women are now an important part of the workforce and as a result so are members of dual-career couples.

The survey that I conducted in 2011 of petroleum engineers showed that percentage of equal earners peaked at the 30- to 34-year-old age bracket.[16] Those in the younger age groups were still pairing off with the percentage of equal earners increasing with age. For male petroleum engineers over age 34, the probability of being part of a dual-career couple declined with age. The overall pattern suggests that, with the passage of time, equal earners will become a larger and larger segment of the workforce as older workers retire and are replaced by those in dual-career couple relationships.

Data from a 2013 survey of members of the Society of Petroleum Engineers found that a significant fraction of the people who reported that they were in a long-term, committed dual-career relationship (just over 9 percent of the men and 17 percent of the women in their thirties) were not officially married.[17] The survey polled individuals, not both members of a couple, so the reason for this gender difference is open to speculation. However, my guess is that in the absence of a wedding ceremony, more women than men believe that they are in a long-term, committed relationship.

INVISIBLE DIVERSITY

Members of dual-career couples face different challenges on a daily basis than members of dominant earner families. People in dual-career couples in effect have a different "culture" than dominant earners. Their daily lives are shaped by the absence of a helpmate whose role is to manage household logistics, and also by the ongoing trade-offs between their career and their partner's career. The differences between "dual-career couple culture" and "dominant earner culture" constitute a type of hidden diversity and as in all diversity differences can be a source of misunderstanding and friction.

Older managers and executives who rose through the ranks as part of a couple with a single dominant breadwinner consider the concept of equally important careers to be naïve and unrealistic. They refuse to accept that both members of a couple can sustain high-powered careers. Unfortunately, management with an antiquated mind-set still dominates the upper ranks of many organizations.

Desai, Chugh, and Brief surveyed 718 married men and found that "men in more traditional marriages compared to those in modern ones tend to view the presence of women in the workplace unfavorably, perceive that organizations with higher number of female employees operate less smoothly, find organizations with female leaders unattractive, and are more likely to deny qualified female employees opportunities for advancement."[18]

Desai et al. define a "traditional marriage" as one in which the wife is not employed. In their study, a "neo-traditional marriage" is one in which the wife is employed part-time, and a "modern marriage" is one in which the wife is employed full time. They suggest that even though men in traditional marriages resist what they call the "gender revolution in the workplace," they are not "cold-hearted, calculated sexists; rather, it is perhaps more the case that they are unaware of their gender biases." They also find that these men "are more likely to populate the upper echelons of organizations and thus, occupy more powerful positions."

Executives, managers, and coworkers in traditional marriages may intend to be supportive and caring, but their perspective is warped by their drastically different domestic culture. Often they cannot relate to the aspirations of members of dual-career couples and are ignorant of the crises those couples face and surmount on a daily basis. They cannot imagine how couples, who are not willing to sacrifice one career for the other, can successfully climb the corporate ladder.

Furthermore, because of their lifestyle with a dependent wife, many of the dominant earner managers and executives unconsciously perceive the accomplishments of all women as merely logistical support and fail to recognize any female's performance as indicative of strong management ability. One woman in a senior role complained to me that her C-level boss always complimented her performance in terms that were more appropriate for someone whose job was to provide assistance. His typical response, when she did an outstanding job, was to say, "very efficient and well organized," instead of recognizing her intellectual contribution.

Desai et al. suggest a way in which the growing fraction of the population that is part of a dual-career couple with children will in the long run create an environment in which more women can succeed. They believe that children "reared by a working mother would enter the workforce with more egalitarian attitudes (e.g. less benevolent sexist attitudes) than those reared in traditional families."

More children of working mothers are in the pipeline. The U.S. census shows that participation of married women with children in the workforce has increased since 1970. As of 2014, about 68 percent of married mothers with a spouse present were working, including about 58 percent of those with an infant under a year old.[19] An even higher percentage (about 75%) of mothers with "other marital status" are in the workforce. Unfortunately, waiting for the next generation of management does not help those currently in the workplace, who are struggling with archaic executives who don't recognize or appreciate women's contributions.

KNOWLEDGE IS POWER

Members of dual-career couples can't wait for the children of working mothers to grow up and become managers. They need a strategy to deal with the diversity divide. Understanding the invisible diversity differences that plague members of dual-career couples is important. If you understand the consequences of the differences and have strategies to overcome them, you can enhance your chances of success.

Savvy employers will recognize the importance of the dual-career couple workforce and "surf the wave" to leverage the wave's energy rather than trying to "hold back the tide." More flexible work arrangements can benefit both employer and employee. However, as an individual, you should not wait for your employer to change. If you cannot negotiate a satisfactory work–life balance with acceptable advancement and recognition in your current position, you should look for a better fit. That may mean changing employers or finding a more enlightened boss within your own organization.

Eventually when attraction and retention of employees become a problem, those organizations that fail to offer career paths that are compatible with being part of a dual-career couple will feel the pressure to change. When people "vote with their feet," employers take notice. However, as an employee, you need to keep an eye on your "career clock." Don't let the clock run out by waiting for your employer to recognize the problems and make amends.

Better understanding of how being part of a dual-career couple influences your career is important. If you understand how the "other side" of dominant earners thinks, you are in a better position to create a strategy for personal success.

CHAPTER 3

Why Reframe Women's Issues as Dual-Career Couple Issues?

Women need the support of men. At work, women need the backing of men at all levels of the organization to advance. At home, women need a more equitable division of household responsibilities so that they can focus as much on their careers as men can. As couples, we must move beyond outdated gender-based behavior expectations as to who does what kind of tasks both at home and at work. Everyone wants greater flexibility to enable them to better integrate their work and their personal life.

REVERSE DISCRIMINATION

My husband likes to ask, "When do fat, balding, white guys get their turn?" He is certain that 20 years from now, there will be affirmative action for men, because women are now earning more than half of college degrees and benefiting from special programs.

Since we have been married for well over 40 years and he has heard endless descriptions of the challenges that I have faced at work, I still marvel at his rants. However, human nature is such that we often fail to appreciate what we have, and covet what we don't. As a white male, my husband doesn't recognize or appreciate the advantages he has enjoyed. Actions that I perceive as working to level the playing field, he sees as discriminating against men like himself.

Men and women may live together in heterosexual dual-career couples, but they frequently still fail to see eye to eye on many issues. Just because a man is a part of a dual-career couple doesn't mean that he understands the challenges that his female partner encounters at work. We all have complicated, mixed, and sometimes contradictory emotions. A man may be proud of his female partner's accomplishments at the same time that he feels competitive with her and jealous if her career is more successful than his.

Male colleagues have dropped by my office to complain about reverse discrimination. Some of the most forthright and strident conversations have been with men whose wives were fellow professionals. One male member of a dual-career couple complained that he couldn't get a promotion, because all of the promotions were going to women including his wife.

From the women's perspective, the company still had a glass ceiling. Women were reasonably represented up to midlevel, but few managed to break into the executive ranks or even the top tier of technical professionals. A high-level human resources professional privately confessed to me that the question wasn't whether women were fairly compensated relative to male peers in their salary grade, but whether or not the women were in the appropriate salary grade. A strong sponsor was required for a woman to secure an executive position or to be promoted into a top technical role. If a woman was in an executive grade and she lost her sponsor, her progression tended to come to an abrupt halt, after which she would be relegated to dead-end positions.

In a 2015 survey conducted by Interaction Associates of more than 400 people "across the business spectrum," the conclusion was that, "the gender gap in how men and women view gender bias on the job is huge. Less than half of the women surveyed say both genders are treated equally but 2/3 of the men surveyed say they are. And when asked if gender bias exists in their organization, nearly half of the women surveyed say it does but less than a third of the men agree."[1]

Corporate statistics support the female perspective. The Catalyst's "pyramid" illustrates how poorly represented women are in the upper ranks of S&P 500 companies.[2] The broad base of the pyramid represents the women who comprise 45 percent of the labor force in S&P 500 companies. Women become increasingly underrepresented at higher levels of the pyramid. One step up from the bottom are first and midlevel officials and managers of whom only 36.8 percent are female. Moving up another level to executive and senior-level officials and managers, women are only 25.1 percent of the total. Next up are board members of whom only 19.2 percent are female. Finally at the pinnacle, only 4.6 percent of the CEOs are women.

Given that a large percentage of professional degrees have been awarded to women for many years, the Catalyst pyramid supports the conclusion that there are gender-related barriers that hinder the advancement of women. As noted in the introduction, women have earned 40 percent or more of all law degrees since 1986 and 45 percent or more of law degrees since 1998. Also, women have earned between 34 percent and 37 percent of MBA degrees since 2002. The scarcity of women in the upper ranks of S&P 500 companies is prima facie evidence that numerous obstacles still inhibit the advancement of women. A huge impediment to eliminating those barriers is that many men refuse to admit that they exist.

In a 2013 survey, McKinsey found that, "Just 19 percent of male respondents strongly agree that reaching top management is harder for women." Moreover, McKinsey also found that, "Men are notably less likely than women to see value in diversity initiatives, less aware of the challenges women face, and more likely to think that too many measures that support women are unfair to men."[3] Like my husband, these men believe that they are the disadvantaged ones and are suffering from reverse discrimination.

The fifth edition of the *American Heritage Dictionary of the English Language* that was published in 2013 defines *reverse discrimination* as, "Discrimination against members of a dominant or majority group, especially when resulting from policies established to correct discrimination against members of a minority or disadvantaged group."

To avoid antagonizing men, employee policies and programs should be gender-neutral. This not only defuses complaints about reverse discrimination, but also can minimize the stigma attached to making use of the programs.

HOUSEHOLD DUTIES

The role of women has changed dramatically in the last century. One hundred years ago, relatively few women worked outside of their homes. Traditionally, women were responsible for household chores: cooking, cleaning, and child-rearing.

At the same time more and more women began working for monetary compensation outside of their homes in the twentieth century, another big change was under way—the mechanization of the home. Refrigerators and freezers meant that women no longer had to acquire fresh food on a daily basis. Food processors, electric mixers, and microwaves have reduced the time required to prepare home-cooked meals. Packaged and processed foods meant meals could be ready in minutes with minimal cleanup. Nonstick pans and dishwashers expedited the cleanup after meals. Hot water heaters with thermostats, washing machines, and clothes dryers have reduced the time needed to do the laundry and dishes. Women no longer had to devote an entire day of the week to doing the laundry. Electric steam irons have expedited ironing, while no-iron shirts and synthetics have eliminated the need for ironing. Vacuum cleaners and even robotic vacuum cleaners have reduced the time required to clean the house. Women could get their chores done in far less time.

While technology was drastically reducing the time required for daily household chores that traditionally had been women's responsibility, women's compensation was growing relative to men's (as discussed in Chapter 2). When women could earn more money, there was greater incentive for married women including those with children to be employed full time outside their homes.

A large portion of the workforce is now composed of members of dual-career couples, but we still tend to think of child care, cooking, and cleaning as being primarily the female partner's responsibility. It is time for that to change. Men should not feel noble if they assist their wife with these chores. They should consider it to be part of doing their share of what it takes to keep the household going.

When I started working, I was busy trying to prove that I could do it all—be a good wife, mother, and gourmet cook. My husband prided himself on "being liberated as hell." He would drop the kids off at daycare or school and reduce his work hours to take care of the children when I traveled. But on a day-to-day basis, I still spent far more hours than he did on household chores. When my husband hired someone to mow the lawn, I decided it was time to hire someone to clean the house. I wasn't going to be on my knees cleaning a toilet while he watched TV.

Old gender-based behavior expectations die hard. Government statistics show that women who work full time are still shouldering more than their share of the load at home (Table 3.1). The U.S. Bureau of Labor and Statistics determined that on average from 2009 through 2013, married men in households in which both partners worked full time had more time for leisure and sports than their spouses, even though they also spent more hours at work. While the amount of time that women and men devoted to household activities, caring for and helping household members, and purchasing goods and services

Table 3.1   Daily Use of Time by Parents Working Full Time

	Married mother employed full time (hours/day)	Married father employed full time (hours/day)	Ratio of time, woman/man
Own children under age 18			
Personal care*	9.0	8.7	1.0
Household activities	1.9	1.2	**1.6**
Purchasing goods and services	0.5	0.3	**1.7**
Caring for and helping household members	1.3	0.9	**1.4**
Working and work-related activities	5.3	6.1	0.9
Leisure and sports	2.9	3.6	0.8
Travel	1.4	1.4	1.0
Other	1.7	1.8	0.9
Own children, youngest under age 6			
Personal care*	9.0	8.6	1.0
Household activities	1.7	1.1	**1.5**
Purchasing goods and services	0.5	0.4	**1.3**
Caring for and helping household members	2.1	1.3	**1.6**
Working and work-related activities	5.2	6.0	0.9
Leisure and sports	2.7	3.5	0.8
Travel	1.3	1.4	0.9
Other	1.7	1.8	0.9
Own children, ages 6–17, none younger			
Personal care*	9.0	8.7	1.0
Household activities	2.0	1.3	**1.5**
Purchasing goods and services	0.5	0.3	**1.7**

(*Continued*)

Table 3.1   (Continued)

	Married mother employed full time (hours/day)	Married father employed full time (hours/day)	Ratio of time, woman/man
Caring for and helping household members	0.8	0.5	**1.6**
Working and work-related activities	5.4	6.1	0.9
Leisure and sports	3.1	3.8	0.8
Travel	1.4	1.5	0.9
Other	1.8	1.8	1.0

U.S. Bureau of Labor and Statistics, Daily Time Use among Married Mothers, TED: The Economics Daily, May 8, 2015, http://www.bls.gov/opub/ted/2015/daily-time-use-among-married-mothers.htm.

*Personal care includes the time spent sleeping.

depended on the age of the children, the ratio of the time women and men expended on these activities as well as on work, leisure, and sports remained constant independent of their offsprings' ages.[4]

With women now providing much of the financial support in many families, it is time for a more equal distribution of domestic chores. A more evenly balanced division would benefit women both at home and at work. If there was a fairer split of the child care, food preparation, and cleanup, women could like men choose to work longer hours to advance their careers and/or to spend more time on leisure activities.

To fix the work–life balance challenges for women that are associated with child care and housework, we must manage these activities as dual-career couple issues. Members of dual-career couples should unchain themselves from the traditional gender stereotypes as to who does which type of labor at home to more appropriately divide the household overhead. If both careers are considered to be equally important, the daily distribution of time use at work and at home should be better balanced.

When partners spend about the same amount of time on the household tasks, it may be easier to mutually agree on hiring help for some of the tasks. The investment in third- party assistance will seem more worthwhile to each of the partners, if it creates more discretionary time for both of them. The family may be better off in the long run spending more money for domestic help, if that expenditure enables both partners to devote extra time to work and increases the probability of both of them advancing.

GENERATIONAL SHIFTS

In May 2015, EY released the results of a research study of about 9,700 full-time workers in eight countries (United States, Germany, Japan, China, Mexico, Brazil, India, and the United Kingdom).[5] One-third of the full-time workers, who participated in the study, reported that managing work–life has become more difficult in the past five years.

The EY investigation found that, in the United States, 62 percent of full-time employees had a spouse/partner who worked at least full time and that the odds of having a partner who worked full time were significantly higher for millennials and Gen X, than for boomers. Many boomers are beyond the child-rearing stage of life, so it is not surprising that 70 percent of parents versus 57 percent of nonparents have a partner employed full time.[6]

Definitions of the generations vary. In the EY study, boomers (or baby boomers as they are also known) were born between 1946 and 1964 and at the time of the study were between the ages of 50 and 68. Members of Gen X were born between 1965 and 1980 and were between the ages of 34 and 49. Millennials, who are also called Gen Y, were born between 1981 and 1996 and were between the ages of 18 and 33.

Four of the top six conclusions in the press release for the EY study are consistent with reframing women's issues as dual-career couple issues.

- The millennial generation is advancing into management roles and working more hours simultaneously with becoming parents.
- Greater responsibilities at work and at home, combined with stagnant salaries and increasing expenses, are creating work–life balance problems.
- Worldwide, insufficient opportunities for advancement prompt more parents to quit than nonparents.

- In the United States, about 16 percent of millennials report that using a flexible work schedule has adversely impacted them, and over twice as high a percentage of millennials, 38 percent, claim that they would relocate to another country for better parental leave benefits. (However, I doubt that such a large percentage would really walk the talk and move for better benefits. I suspect that the responses were a method of registering dissatisfaction with their existing leave options.)

Monica Marquez, the West Region Diversity Inclusiveness and Flexibility Leader of EY, highlighted an issue of paramount importance: "Generation X and Boomers have this kind of misconception . . . that these people that want flexibility might be less committed to their work, less committed to their career progression . . . For the Millennials, they're saying we want this flexibility, but we aren't any less aggressive about our career."[7] Amen!

ACCESS TO FLEXIBILITY

Some men think that employers are more understanding of women's need to make use of work flexibility programs. Thus, these males believe that their working wife should be the one to go home to take care of a sick child or to handle other child-related issues.

The results of the survey that I conducted for the Society of Petroleum Engineers (SPE) on dual-career couple issues in December 2011 do not support that rationalization.[8] In that survey about 13 percent of both men and women reported that within the prior year they had encountered resistance from their manager when they tried to make use of their company's work–life balance policies. Contrary to some men's convictions, more women than men (20% of the women versus 15% of the men) responded that they had received negative feedback from colleagues for trying to utilize family-friendly programs. Colleagues and supervisors do not have a greater tolerance for women using family-friendly programs than they do for men.

One woman wrote, "Females always end up feeling inadequate and guilty if we have to take time off to be with children during emergencies. We are also usually passed up for promotions, which is unfair considering most females I know work harder and multitask to keep up with their workloads."[9]

Another woman observed, "As long as male colleagues do not take advantage of family benefits, it will be difficult for female workers to manage their family and compete with their male colleagues."[10]

The EY study found that fewer men than women were willing to make use of their parental leave. Only 60 percent of the men as opposed to 71 percent of the women felt empowered to take all of the parental leave to which they were entitled. A total of 78 percent of the women but only 66 percent of the men agreed that "all parents should have an equal amount of paid parental leave time," and 71 percent of the women but only 61 percent of the men agreed that "we need both women and men to take parental leave in order to combat the stigma associated with taking parental leave."[11]

Women are not granted more leeway than men. Not only should women and men have equal access to flexible work arrangements, but also they should feel equally empowered to make use of them.

In busy work environments, no one has a free ride. Women, especially women with children, are closely observed by their peers, who are checking to see if mothers are pulling their own weight. When both partners are contributing to the household income, they should take turns handling household responsibilities including routine and emergency child care and unexpected home repairs.

Work–life integration challenges such as child care should be viewed as a parental, not a maternal, responsibility. Note that I did *not* say work–life problems should be managed as a dual-career couple issue. Anyone may face a domestic emergency. In many ways, single parents are more challenged than dual-career couples. Even dominant earners with a supportive spouse can find themselves in a jam if they have young children and their wife contracts a serious illness. Everyone benefits from flexibility with the emphasis on work performance, not face time.

In her book, *The Balance Myth*, Teresa Taylor described her child care crisis.[12] Despite the nanny's excellent recommendations, Taylor became concerned that her nanny took too long to answer her calls. She also wondered why her son hated sitting in his infant swing. To check out the situation, she made a midmorning stealth visit to check on her nanny, who was the 20-year-old daughter of a colleague. To her horror, Taylor found the nanny chattering on the phone with friends, while her son was strapped in his swing in another room. Her neglected infant was still in his night clothes with an incredibly filthy diaper. She fired the nanny on the spot, but was then stranded without child care.

Taylor, who later became the chief operating officer of Quest, a Fortune 200 company, wrote, "I knew the unwritten code. People can have family emergencies, trips to the hospital, or car accidents, but the actual moment when a woman's career is instantly flushed down the toilet is the moment the words *day care* pass from her lips to the boss's ear."[13]

It shouldn't be that way. People should not have to lie about why they need flexibility. Everyone—male, female, married, separated, divorced, single, old, and young—should feel that they have equal access to the flexible work arrangements offered by their employer without retaliation from their management or pressure from their peers. Use of these flexibility benefits should come without stigma, so that they are not effectively limited to lower-level employees.

A 2013 survey that I led for the SPE asked if people had changed employers for better work–life balance.[14] People were not asked how many times they had switched jobs for this reason. In that survey, 61 percent of women and 42 percent of men were part of a dual-career couple relationship. Members of dual-career couples were more likely than others to have shifted employers for better work–life balance. Overall, 30 percent of all women and 21 percent of all men had switched employers to secure more favorable work–life balance. But of those in dual-career couples, 42 percent of the women and 37 percent of the men had changed jobs for that reason—far more than average for their gender. Men and women in dual-career couples struggle more with work–life balance than those in traditional relationships.

The stigma of reverse discrimination for women is eliminated if flexible work arrangements are available to all employees. The focus should not be on whether or not a person uses certain benefits, but rather on their performance.

SINGLES' CONCERNS

Some single people are concerned that they are expected to work more, because they have fewer domestic responsibilities. These individuals fear that they will end up picking up the slack for coworkers.

A single woman complained about being asked to cover for men. She described being asked by men to finish up their work as they walked out the door saying, "If I don't get home now to my wife and kids, I might not have a wife any longer." She reported feeling that, "If I don't get out of this office, I will never meet a spouse and have kids!"[15] We all need sustainable work–life integration with sufficient personal time, no matter how we use the time.

GEOGRAPHIC MOBILITY

Hearing about instances in which male supervisors harangued young women about their reluctance to relocate prompted me to take action to reframe "reluctance to relocate" as a dual-career couple issue. I brought my concerns to the Women's Network Committee of the Society of Exploration Geophysicists. The women's group persuaded the society to conduct a survey in 2013 that included an extensive investigation of members' willingness to relocate.[16]

The survey was distributed to the society's approximately 33,000 members about half of whom reside outside of the United States and received almost 1,600 responses. The results of that survey were published in two articles in the society's journal, *The Leading Edge*, which is distributed to all members. Some of the conclusions from Table 3.2 were shared in those articles, but the complete table has not been previously published.

The survey included questions about 18 factors that could influence an individual's decision to accept or decline a relocation. The analysis compared the responses of men and women, and further divided the gender groups by how much of their household income they contributed, in particular whether or not they were equal earners providing between 40 percent and 60 percent of the household income or dominant earners who were providing more than 69 percent of the household income.

In Table 3.2, the percentages given are the percentage of that gender group, who responded that they would be willing to relocate for that reason. The rank reflects how many affirmative responses were received from that demographic group for that factor relative to the 17 other factors. The factor that received the most positive responses is ranked "1" and the factor with the fewest positive responses is ranked "18." In Table 3.2, the factors are listed according to the preferences of the equal-earner women from 1 to 18, with 1 being the factor that would stimulate the largest number of them to relocate.

"Valuable experience" and "international experience" are the strongest motivators for men and women in general. After that there are some major differences that can be a source of friction, both between members of a couple and between employee and supervisor.

Table 3.2 Willingness to Relocate

	All women		All men		Equal women		Equal men		Dominant women		Dominant men	
	Per-centage	Rank	Per-centage	Rank	Per-centage	Rank	Per-centage	Rank	Per-centage	Rank	Per-centage	Rank
To gain valuable experience	55	1	45	2	59	1	55	1	55	2	49	1
For international experience	52	2	46	1	54	2	49	2	52	4	49	2
To a location where my partner can find work	36	6	20	9	50	3	37	5	41	7	21	9
To a better location from a personal perspective	47	3	39	4	43	4	48	3	55	3	44	4
For a promotion	34	7	32	5	37	5	33	7	39	8	33	6
To avoid unemployment	37	5	32	6	36	6	37	6	51	5	41	5

For more money	37	4	40	3	35	7	40	4	58	1	47	3
To a location with more work opportunity	33	8	27	7	33	8	29	8	33	10	29	8
If my employer was shutting down my location	31	9	26	8	32	9	24	9	49	6	32	7
If I had no children living at home	21	11	14	13	25	10	16	11	22	12	15	12
To a location closer to my family	26	10	14	11	24	11	11	13	36	9	17	11
To a location where my children could attend a better school	16	12	18	10	17	12	20	10	25	11	18	10

(Continued)

41

Table 3.2 (Continued)

	All women		All men		Equal women		Equal men		Dominant women		Dominant men	
	Per-centage	Rank	Per-centage	Rank	Per-centage	Rank	Per-centage	Rank	Per-centage	Rank	Per-centage	Rank
If my children were too young to attend school	8	14	6	16	11	13	5	17	10	14	5	17
To a location with affordable housing	12	13	9	15	11	14	9	14	16	13	8	15
Not willing to relocate under any circumstances	4	17	9	14	4	15	8	15	4	17	9	14
Anywhere if asked	7	15	14	12	3	16	13	12	4	16	11	13
To a location where I can go to school part-time	3	18	3	18	2	17	2	18	3	18	4	18

| To a location where my partner can go to school | 5 | 16 | 6 | 17 | 2 | 18 | 8 | 16 | 9 | 15 | 7 | 16 |

Note: Data in the table are sourced from a survey conducted by the Society of Exploration Geophysicists in 2013. The table has not been previously published. Selected results from that study were published in Eve Sprunt, Nancy House, and Maria Angela Capello, "SEG Survey on Dual-Career-Couples and Women: The Hidden Diversity of Dual-Career Couples," *The Leading Edge* 33, no. 7 (2014): 812–816, http://dx.doi.org/10.1190/tle33070812.1; and Eve Sprunt, Nancy House, and Maria Angela Capello, "SEG Survey on Dual-Career-Couples and Women: Implications for the Future of Our Society," *The Leading Edge* 33, no. 4 (2014): 460–462, http://dx.doi.org/10.1190/tle33040460.1.

Management is accustomed to money being a very powerful motivator. For dominant earner women, more money is the strongest incentive to relocate with 58 percent of them saying they would relocate for that reason. However, only 47 percent of dominant earner men are willing to relocate for more money; so amongst the dominant earners, women are significantly more money-driven. The gender gap between equal earner men and women is smaller with 40 percent of equal earner men and 35 percent of equal earner women being willing to relocate for more money. The very large difference between the percentage of dominant earner women and the percentage of equal earner women who would relocate for more money demonstrates that willingness to relocate should not be regarded as a women's issue, but rather as a dual-career couple issue.

Just as children significantly complicate day-to-day life, children also add to the concerns and complicate the logistics associated with relocation. Child care arrangements must be in place before both parents can commence work in the new location. Unlike dominant earners, who are able to move at a moment's notice and leave their spouse to manage the details of relocating the family, it is impossible for both partners of a dual-career couple to pick up and move as quickly. More complex relocation issues along with child care and household responsibilities should be regarded as dual-career couple problems, not as women's issues.

In dual-career couples in which one or more of the partners has children from a prior relationship, the child custody agreement can create greater barriers to relocation than the dual-career couple relationship. Relocation may jeopardize divorced parents' ability to comply with their joint custody arrangements or to exercise their visitation rights. Divorced parents may have to choose between being part of their children's lives and advancing their careers.

WHAT DIFFERENCE DOES IT MAKE?

The balance of power and the division of labor in domestic relationships is rapidly evolving. Similarly at work, the ability to work from anywhere at any time is gradually altering expectations and requirements as to when and where we work. Transitions are difficult. When patterns are static, roles and relationships are well-defined. When things are in flux, we must be more proactive to craft a winning strategy for ourselves.

Understanding that household chores and child care are not women's work when the woman is also employed full time makes it a shared challenge to create a solution that fits the family's budget, lifestyle, and priorities. Couples can discuss which chores they will split and which they will outsource by hiring help or other ways to substitute money for one member of the couple's time and energy.

One of the most sensitive points in couples' discussions may be how much personal time each person wants or is taking. Everyone needs time to relax, but our personal preferences may be to use those precious minutes in different ways. For example, for those with young children who want to exercise, investing in an expensive running stroller may be worthwhile, but you also should come to an agreement on whether it is always the same person pushing the stroller or if there are other trade-offs. Having an acceptable division of "free time" is essential to avoiding conflict and resentment.

At work, women may benefit by anticipating the prejudices of older men in traditional marriages. If they think that they may miss out on opportunities, because of mistaken assumptions on the part of their management, they should volunteer information that they believe might improve their chances of getting what they want. Women who would like to be relocated should not be shy about asking for where they would like to go and what type of experience they would like to acquire.

In contrast, both women and men, who don't want to relocate, should avoid going on the record as being completely unwilling. For the right opportunity, you might agree to sacrifice and undertake a commuting marriage. You want to be able to have a choice of accepting a good opportunity. If you have stated that you are completely unwilling to move, you will never learn what might be offered to you.

CHAPTER 4

Whose Career Takes Precedence?

MIND THE GAP

Lifestyle differences can lead to misunderstanding. The differences in the daily lives of dominant earners and members of dual-career couples are effectively a cultural divide. There is a huge understanding gap between "dominant earners," who provide most of their household's income, and dual-career couples.

The percentage of dominant earners, who provide 70 percent or more of household income, is higher in older generations. In many organizations most of the managers are the dominant earner in their family. In contrast, a large fraction of the younger workforce is part of a dual-career couple.

Members of "equal earner" couples, in which each partner provides between 40 and 60 percent of the household income, are living and working under very different constraints than these dominant earner managers. If you are part of a dual-career couple, your daily life is different from that of a person with a partner providing full-time domestic support. This lifestyle difference can lead to misunderstandings about the younger person's work ethics, commitment, and career ambitions.

Many older dominant-earner supervisors have false impressions of younger dual-career employees. This can limit the dual-career employee's opportunities for advancement and result in members of dual-career couples, especially women, being underrepresented in assignments that are on the fast track with better opportunities for advancement.

MANAGERIAL PERSPECTIVE

One day at work, I encountered a young woman crying in the bathroom. I didn't know her well, so she didn't choose to confide in me. Later when I had the opportunity to speak with a female friend, I learned why the young woman was in tears. The young woman's supervisor's supervisor (let's call him Ralph) had demanded that she relocate with or without her husband, saying, "When are you going to make your career come first?"

The young woman's work group was being relocated to another company facility almost 2,000 miles away. All of the young women had graduate degrees in science and/or engineering with some of them holding doctorates. Ralph assumed that since there were no other similar employers nearby, the women's only choice if they wanted to continue their careers was to move. Ralph had similar sessions with all five of the young woman who had been asked to relocate. Bad move!

Asking that question puts the domestic partners in competition with each other and positions the manager as a bully. No one wants to work for a bully.

Not a single one of the five young women chose to stay with the company and move. A young woman with an engineering doctorate decided to apply her skills to financial modeling. Others joined small start-up companies. All of them continued working, but not for the company at which Ralph tried to bully them.

When I was the age of these young women, my management didn't ask me if I was willing to relocate to corporate headquarters; they found a chance to discretely ask my husband. The messaging my husband heard was so obfuscated that he didn't realize what he was being asked. Now, over a quarter century later some employers have advanced from acting as if the woman was her husband's property to leaning on her to take steps that could jeopardize her domestic relationship.

These old-fashioned supervisors and executives do not understand how to manage a workforce that is increasingly composed of members of dual-career couples. The response that the careers of both partners are equally important is incomprehensible to executives and managers who think that to be a high flyer you must have a partner providing domestic support.

I wondered if many managers were making similar demands that young women go on the record about how important their career was relative to their partner's. Casually checking around my company, I found that many young women had been asked. To find out whether or not my company was unusual, I worked with the Society of Petroleum Engineers (SPE) to conduct a survey.

I discovered that both men and women get asked. However, the results (Table 4.1) clearly showed women, especially women with children, are more likely than men to be asked.[1] If both members of a couple work for the same employer, the odds are even greater that they will be asked. But, overall women are much more likely than men to be asked. Making matters worse, women are far less likely than men to say that their career comes first (Table 4.2).

A man's chances of being asked are not significantly increased if he has children unless he works for the same employer as his partner. Even then, he is only about half as likely to be asked as a woman with children (Table 4.2).

Sadly, the situation may be even worse if the manager doesn't ask the question as assumptions made about the employee's preferences can be more damaging than the truth. The odds of being asked suggest that many managers assume that a male partner's career is more likely to take precedence, especially if there are children.

Table 4.1 Who Is Asked Whose Career Is More Important?

Have you been asked by your employer, "Whose career is more important?"	Percentage of females responding that they have been asked	Percentage of males responding that they have been asked
Dual-career couples	12	8
Equal earners	12	12
Member of dual-career couple with children	18	9
Member of dual-career couple with children and partner working for the same employer	29	17
Member of dual-career couple with children and partner working for a different employer	14	7

Note: Data from the December 2011 SPE survey of members under age 45 (Eve Sprunt, Susan Howes, and Maria Angela Capello, "Bridging the Generation Gap," *Journal of Petroleum Technology* 64, no. 5 (May 2012): 80–81).

Table 4.2   Responses to "Whose Career Is More Important?"

Whose career is more important?	Percentage of all dual-career women	Percentage of equal earner dual-career women	Percentage of all dual-career men	Percentage of equal earner dual-career men
		Now		
My career	13	4	39	16
My partner's career	11	10	3	4
Equally important	76	86	58	80
		In the long run		
My career	14	5	46	34
My partner's career	20	19	3	2
Equally important	66	76	51	64

Note: Data from the December 2011 SPE survey of members under age 45 (Eve Sprunt, Susan Howes, and Maria Angela Capello, "Bridging the Generation Gap," *Journal of Petroleum Technology* 64, no. 5 (May 2012): 80–81).

When both partners work for the same employer, the temptation is to rank the couple relative to one another instead of with respect to their entire peer group. This puts the members of the couple in direct competition with each other and undermines the family unit.

About 80 percent of equal earners consider both careers to be equally important. However, a larger percentage of men than women put their career first even when their partner is making about as much money (Table 4.2).

Women, even if they are outearning their partner, tend to be more protective of their partner's career (Table 3.2). Women are more concerned than their male counterparts that if they relocate, it is to a location where their partner can find work. When asked about relocating, 50 percent of equal earner women but only 37 percent of equal earner men thought that this was an important factor. Surprisingly, 41 percent of dominant earner women also thought that this was important, while as one might expect a far lower percentage, 21 percent, of dominant earner men did. Women independent of their income contribution to the household may feel a greater need to protect their partner's ego. This may be a legacy of the traditional culture of women supporting and flattering the male ego.

One of my goals in conducting the surveys was to gather data to prove to management that dual-career couples were a large and growing fraction of the workforce. I wanted them to better understand what was involved in attracting and retaining this important group. Unfortunately, some of the people whom I hoped to influence refused to believe the results.

When I discussed the results of my surveys with a corporate vice president, he disputed the validity of the surveys. He tried everything he could to discredit the results even though the surveys had collected over 10,000 responses and were very consistent. He ended our final discussion by blurting out, "Well, people don't stay married anymore."

This executive was unwilling to accept that there was a major shift in workforce demographics with dominant earners a shrinking minority. As far as he was concerned there was no need to alter career development practices to increase the representation of members of dual-career couples in management.

To try to convince me that I was wrong, the vice president shared his personal story. Presenting himself as a role model, he described how early in his career his wife was also employed. When he received an international job assignment, his spouse quit her job and followed him. He said that she never regretted ending her career and found greater fulfillment in her volunteer work. His wife assumed the role of providing full-time support for her hubby. Not surprisingly, this executive tended to see all women as playing support roles.

Unfortunately, the vice president is far from alone in his opinions. A 2011 SPE survey on corporate policies for the management of dual-career couples received the following responses as to why managers asked about the relative importance of a couple's careers[2]:

- "This is an appropriate question so that we know the couple's desire."
- "Always, one career has to lead and the other follow."
- "It is a must for one of them to accept being the second one or relegated employee."

The fact that multiple people from different companies provided similar comments shows that the problem extends beyond a single employer.[3] Whether they know it or not, many members of dual-career couples are adversely impacted by this insidious bias.

Executives and managers have explained to me why they think that it is important to ask, "Whose career takes precedence?" They are unwilling to invest in those who are known to be part of a dual-career couple with equally important careers. They do not envision that members of dual-career couples, especially women (as shown by who gets asked in Table 4.1), will work as hard and be as productive as dominant earners. Even if both individuals are highly talented and motivated, these managers think that one career must be sacrificed.

This perspective was hammered home to me when I spoke with a vice president of human resources about the survey results. He shared what he considered to be the best method of ensuring that promising women in dual-career couples were positioned to succeed. He would have someone take the woman's husband aside and explain to him that he should sacrifice his career for his wife, because she was the one with greater potential to attain a high-level executive position.

The vice president of human resources did not view the situation as symmetric for both genders. He did not mention ever needing to counsel a man's wife about sacrificing her career for husband.

When this vice president said that he could stop the practice of employees being asked, "Whose career takes precedence?" I realized that would not solve the problem. Old-fashioned managers would continue to assume that competition between the careers of members of a dual-career couple was primarily the woman's problem. This company and many others are trying to increase the number of women in management, but they insist that the women adopt the lifestyle that was prevalent when men were the breadwinners and women couldn't earn a living wage.

A female executive, who enjoyed having mentoring talks with subordinate women, would lose her audience when she described how her husband quit his job to take care of their children and to provide support for her. Most women do not expect or want their partners to sacrifice their career for them. The majority of women don't consider this female executive's approach to be a viable alternative for them. Today, young couples do not see their careers as "either-or," but as "and."

IMPACT ON UPWARD MOBILITY

If a woman does not declare that her career takes precedence over her partner's and that her career is her highest priority, she risks being thrown off the fast track. Once off the fast track, it is very difficult to claw your way back. Promotions and key assignments go to those who are perceived to be upwardly mobile.

Experience is cumulative. Every opportunity you miss or each time you are passed over puts you further behind.

Age matters. For tenure-track academics, the rules are explicit. It is up or out on a specified timeline. In academia, tenure-track faculty either get tenure or must find a new job. In the business world, there is also a timeline, but the rules are not as explicit or well known. Those without a knowledgeable mentor may not be aware of the often unwritten rules for being selected and staying on the fast track. Unlike their academic equivalents, businesspeople may not get terminated when they are bumped off the fast track. However, those not on the fast track frequently find themselves languishing as they move through a series of lateral staff positions.

Midcareer, after horizontal moves through a wide variety of staff as opposed to line roles, many women are sidelined with little chance of getting promoted. Companies recommend crosswise moves to get breadth of experience. But without a sponsor, people who move laterally to avoid relocation are unlikely to advance. Broadening assignments without promotions do not build the history of a "series of positions of increasing authority" that is frequently cited in executive résumés.

At executive levels of corporations there are few dual-career couples. However, that is not a good excuse for asking employees whose career takes precedence. A large percentage of women in the workforce are part of a dual-career couple. If employers want more women to be in the running for top positions, they should offer women specific opportunities for consideration, not ask women for blanket loyalty oaths. Couples should not be forced to decide which career takes precedence until there is an offer on the table that requires a decision on relative career priority. When there is a specific opportunity, couples can weigh their alternatives and make an informed decision.

If someone's performance is good enough to make them a strong candidate for a position, management should trust that person to make the right decision about accepting added responsibilities. Promotions provide greater financial resources to employees that they may choose to spend on more child care and other household assistance so that they have more flexibility to work extended hours and travel.

Current restrictions on access to fast-track career development have stranded many talented women in dead-end staff positions. When companies look around for talented women who can be promoted into upper management positions, women who have languished in staff positions are deemed unqualified, because they lack essential line management experience. Even if these women have demonstrated leadership abilities in other ways, for example by leading charitable and professional organizations, their management skills go unrecognized and underutilized by their employers.

Companies that fret about the scarcity of female management talent tend to focus attention on the entry end of the pipeline. The emphasis on developing management talent from scratch makes the time to significantly change the gender and ethnic composition of management ridiculously long. In many industries there are few women in upper management despite decades of having significant numbers of women in entry- and middle-level positions. Increasing female and minority representation at higher levels of management can be accomplished more expeditiously by identifying and leveraging people with equivalent experience.

While the "grow your own" approach provides benefits in uniformity and deep knowledge of the organization, that same uniformity of thought and experience can lead companies into the trap of failing to recognize and react to disruptive changes that threaten the organization's fundamental business model. These loyal, homegrown, good implementers and leaders are often not as adept at challenging the status quo. Groupthink and overreliance on common experiences may diminish an organization's ability to innovate and thrive in a changing business environment. To have a robust management team, organizations should have a mix of both "good soldiers" and open-minded innovators.

The leaky management talent pipeline has been hemorrhaging women to staff roles for decades because of screening processes that are biased against members of dual-career couples. Women and men, who have faced challenges because they do not fit the corporate mold, can contribute a resilience and broader perspective that enhances decision making and improves competiveness. Homogeneous management may be less likely to recognize important emerging trends that threaten the organization's competitive position.

Successful organizations understand their markets and quickly recognize new trends. Dual-career couples are a large and growing component of the workforce. A much higher percentage of millennials than baby boomers are part of dual-career couples. Companies with members of dual-career couples in their leadership will be better positioned to know what this growing segment of the population wants and needs, so they will be better positioned to thrive.

PASSED OVER FOR PROMOTION

Here is an example of how someone's career can be limited, when management is unwilling to "waste" resources on developing people they don't think are willing to go anywhere and do anything for their employer. This is a case of what can happen if a person places any restrictions on mobility or availability. They may be denied opportunities for advancement even if those opportunities are completely compatible with the mobility restrictions that they have shared with their management.

Julie works for MegaCorp in Metropolis, where the company has extensive operations. Julie prides herself on being very honest and straightforward. She doesn't like to play games and to deceive people. With so many opportunities to advance with MegaCorp in Metropolis, Julie thinks there is no harm in telling her supervisor that she is not willing to relocate, because her husband, Jack, has a successful local law practice.

Julie applied for the position as widget manager, which would be a major promotion for her. She is convinced that she has a good chance of getting the position, because she has received top ratings in all of her performance reviews.

The committee evaluating the candidates for widget manager agrees that that Julie is clearly the best-qualified applicant for the position. However, even though the company is trying to increase the number of women in management, the committee hesitates. Widget manager is a key stepping stone to the manufacturing general manager role. The current manufacturing general manager is based at company headquarters in Hamletville in another state. The committee wants to use the widget manager position to groom someone for upper management. After mulling over whether to choose Julie, the committee picks Paul, who is clearly less qualified but has not shared any mobility restrictions with the company.

Julie is sorely disappointed when she doesn't get the position. She asks her supervisor why she wasn't picked, but he doesn't tell her that the mobility limitation was the deciding factor. Julie doesn't guess that the mobility restriction was a problem, because it was not a factor in her ability to do a great job in the widget manager position.

If Julie had kept her mobility limitations to herself, she would have been selected as widget manager and could have dealt with the relocation issues several years later. Down the road, when she might be under consideration for manufacturing general manager, many things may have changed. Julie's children could all be older, so that she might have been willing to live separately from her husband during the week. Her marriage may have soured, so she could be divorced when relocation became a reality. Or, her husband might be tired of practicing law and want to do something different. Many things can change in a few years.

Frustrated by her lack of advancement, Julie may quit and take a position with one of MegaCorp's competitors. If she can't find a suitable position with another company in Metropolis, she might simply stop working so hard. In either case, MegaCorp has lost a valuable employee.

Meanwhile, Paul could encounter problems of his own, before being promoted to the manufacturing general manager role. He could be recruited away by a MegaCorp competitor or develop serious medical problems. Succession planning is important, but many unanticipated events occur.

In selecting between two people, subjective arguments can always be made for one person rather than another. Yes, you can argue that the widget manager role is a training position, but that could be said of almost any promotion. Too often discrimination occurs because of assumptions based on preconceived ideas about what another person of an underrepresented group is likely to do. For example, women of child-bearing age are sometimes not promoted, because management believes the woman is likely have a child and therefore slack off. People should be judged on their accomplishments. Discrimination occurs when decisions are based on stereotypes, not objective evaluation of individual performance.

Numerous separate decisions pile up to form statistical trends. Statistics show that women are underrepresented at executive levels. Implementation of policies that better manage dual-career couples can play a significant role in improving women's chances of rising to upper levels of management.

EXAMPLE OF SUCCESSFULLY MANAGING DUAL CAREERS

A good example of two high-powered people navigating the poorly charted waters of being a dual-career couple and not just surviving but excelling is Meg Whitman, who was CEO of eBay from 1998 to 2008 and has been CEO of Hewlett Packard since 2011, and her husband,

Griff Harsh, who is a neurosurgeon at Stanford. Meg Whitman's autobiography, *The Power of Many: Values for Success in Business and in Life*, describes how they juggled both careers and two children without identifying one career as taking precedence.

Meg Whitman wrote about her life in the early 1980s: "I enjoyed my job at Procter & Gamble [in Cincinnati] and I learned a lot, but my commitment to Griff required a change. For his neurosurgical residency, Griff had to pick between two excellent programs: Massachusetts General Hospital in Boston and the University of California, San Francisco . . . I eventually landed a job with Bain & Co., based in San Francisco."[4]

Meg Whitman provided another example of following her husband, "When Griff took a job in Boston in 1992, we moved and I left Disney."[5]

When Meg Whitman accepted the position as CEO of eBay [in the San Francisco area], she described her husband as being "happily ensconced as executive director of the Brain Tumor Center at Massachusetts General Hospital."[6]

She also shared the challenges of being a working mother, "Now, here is some math that every mom understands: two kids are more than twice the work of one, especially when one is a toddler. I will not try to pretend that there weren't moments that made me wonder if I really could make it all work. It's never easy to find balance in life."[7]

She credits her partnership with her husband. "Griff is a wonderful father and, as I have said so many times, I never could have managed a decade at eBay if, despite his own extremely demanding career, he hadn't shouldered a big share of the load keeping our family running smoothly while I was at the office until the wee hours of the morning . . . Both of our jobs are the sort that can invade and erode family life."[8]

Sheryl Sandberg, the chief operating officer of Facebook, had a similarly successful dual-career marriage that was cut short by her husband's death in an accident. Sandberg shared in her book, *Lean In: Women, Work, and the Will to Lead*, her juggling act with her late husband, Dave Goldberg, CEO of Survey Monkey: "My career and marriage are inextricably intertwined. During the first year Dave and I were parents, it became clear that balancing two careers and two cities was not adding up to one happy family. . . . I loved my job at Google and he felt enormously loyal to his team in L.A. We struggled through the commuting for another long year of marital less-than-bliss. By then, Dave was ready to leave Yahoo. He limited his job search to the San Francisco area, which was a sacrifice on his part."[9]

Finding and retaining two satisfying positions within acceptable commuting range is an ongoing challenge for many couples. Even the most successful dual-career couples like Sheryl Sandberg and her late husband, Dave Goldberg, and Meg Whitman and her spouse, Griff Harsh, have been faced with tough decisions. Life is a balancing act for all of us.

DETECTING BIAS

Being part of a dual-career couple is a form of invisible diversity. Unlike gender and race, which are visible forms of diversity, just by looking at a person, you can't guess whether or not he or she is the dominant earner of the family or an equal earner. However, just as people with a form of visible diversity may assess their chances of success in an organization by looking for people like them in leadership, members of dual-career couples would be wise to investigate how many members of dual-career couples are in their organization's leadership team.

If you are considering a position with a new employer, you should do your homework to understand how the corporate culture impacts members of dual-career couples. Checking on the company's success with people with invisible diversity issues is more challenging than verifying how members of visibly diverse groups are doing. The names and pictures of the company's leadership do not reveal if there are barriers to the advancement of members of dual-career couples. You have to dig deeper.

Use LinkedIn, professional society directories, and alumni networks to locate people who work for the company and contact them to see if they are willing to answer some questions. Be respectful of their time. Asking a busy stranger to take the time to meet you for coffee is not the best way to gather the information you want. Don't ask for a lot of their time. Make your inquiries short. Ask if they prefer to respond by e-mail or would like to call you or have you call them at a mutually agreeable time.

In approaching a stranger, be honest about what you want to discuss. Don't use the gimmick of asking them to tell you about their career, if what you really want is a job referral to their company.

Do not seek to have sensitive questions answered during a job interview. You want to convince the employers that they want you. The sell yourself part of the interview is about what you can do for the employers, not how they will treat you or what they can do for you. However, have the questions in the back of your mind and keep your eyes and ears open.

As a job applicant, wait until you have a solid job offer, before beginning negotiations about the terms of employment and asking about conditions including flexibility and family-friendly policies. If your skills are in great demand, you may be able to get a better deal than if you are one of many easily interchangeable candidates.

After accepting a job offer, you should continue your efforts to uncover unwritten rules that can constitute bias so that you can avoid sharing information that could limit your opportunities. A good source of information is the administrative assistants, who often know far more about the leaders and their personal history than anyone else. They might share what they know about their boss's work patterns, preferences, and personal life. "Water cooler" chitchat is not necessarily idle chattering. Use it for information gathering.

If your organization has employee networks for various demographic groups, join them and attend the functions. While the formal programs may be sales pitches for the company, the side conversations can be very revealing. You may also meet people who are willing to advise and mentor you.

TACTICS FOR INDIVIDUALS

Let's look at three cases: (1) interns with a summer job at Gr8Co, (2) job applicants, and (3) employees of Gr8Co. In each case we will look at a woman and a man: two interns (Anna and Adam), two job applicants (Barbara and Bob), and four employees (Carole, Charles, Dawn, and Don).

Two of the biggest challenges for dual-career couples are child-rearing and relocation. My experience is that women are more likely than men to disclose that they are unwilling to relocate because of their partner's career. Also, even though the burden of child care is becoming more equally shared, on average, women still carry more of the load. The behaviors with respect to these issues and other situations can for many people be gender-neutral, but management still tends to view them as being of greater concern to women.

INTERNS

An internship is like an extended interview. The employer is evaluating you, and you are evaluating the company. At the time of their internship with Gr8Co, both Anna and Adam had completed their sophomore year of college. Both of them expect to intern with another employer before seeking a permanent position or applying to graduate school.

Gr8Co has a formal internship program. The interns spent most of their time working on a project, but there were also special events for them. The events were designed to tout Gr8Co as an industry leader and to convince the interns that Gr8Co was one of the best places to work. The interns were told about Gr8Co's employee networks and employee benefits.

Anna was interested in the Gr8Co women's network. Luckily for her there was a women's network luncheon early in her internship. Following the event, Anna e-mailed several of the women she met to ask if they could spare some time to talk with her about their careers. Anna asked them, "What do you like best about Gr8Co?" and "What do you wish Gr8Co did better to support your career?"

Her discussion with a woman in her late thirties who had children was particularly valuable. During that meeting, Anna felt comfortable asking about maternity leave, flexible hours, and relocation. Following the meeting, Anna e-mailed her thanks to the woman for being so generous with her time.

Throughout her internship, Anna seized opportunities to chat with coworkers about their experiences. She tried to find out whether or not her coworkers had to relocate for their career, and if so, how that had impacted their family. By talking with a lot of people, she was able to get a sense of the logistics of coordinating her career with a partner.

After Anna returned to college, she maintained contact with the people she worked with during her internship. She compared notes with her friends as to how Gr8Co compared with the companies with which they interned. The following summer, Anna interned with another organization to broaden her experience beyond one company.

Adam did a lot of checking before his internship started at Gr8Co. He took the internship, because his fiancée had an internship nearby. Adam was an officer of the student section of the professional society in his discipline. Before he started his internship, he checked the membership of the professional society to see who worked for Gr8Co and made initial contact with them. He also checked to see if anyone who had been a member of his fraternity was working there. During his internship, Adam and his fiancée were invited to dinner at the home of fellow fraternity brother. At that dinner, Adam and his fiancée learned a lot about issues associated with using Gr8Co's paternity leave policy and flexible working arrangements.

Job Applicants

Job applicants should be careful about the questions they ask during an interview. Questions that might adversely affect your candidacy are best saved until after you have a firm job offer and when you are deciding between multiple offers.

Barbara was very pleased to get an invitation for an onsite interview with Gr8Co. Her academic record was not as strong as it might have been, because she got married to an attorney and had a child while working on her MBA. She wanted to be sure that she made a good impression, so she didn't want to ask a lot of questions about work–life integration during her interview.

Before the interview, Barbara read as much as she could about Gr8Co and its leadership. However, she couldn't find much. From the financial documents filed with the Securities and Exchange Commission, Barbara learned that only two of the members of its board of directors were women, and that none of the top five most highly compensated employees were women.

Barbara was applying to Gr8Co for a finance position. At the beginning of her interview, a representative from human resources, Gladys, described Gr8Co's two-year developmental program in finance. A new MBA would have four 6-month assignments in different aspects of finance in business units across the country. After the rotational assignments, she would receive her first permanent assignment.

Barbara asked, "Can all of the assignments be in one location?"
Gladys responded, "Selection for the assignments is competitive. We can't guarantee that you will get one of your top choices, so you don't know in advance where you will be going."
Barbara responded, "Are there other entry paths for finance MBAs?"
Gladys answered, "Oh, you wouldn't want those, they don't have as much potential for advancement. Getting into the finance rotation program is a huge jumpstart for your career. We are trying to get more women into the program to help women advance into executive positions."

Barbara knew that making new child care arrangements every six months could be a big headache. She would probably be handling the child-rearing by herself, because her husband would not be able to move around with her. On top of that, after two years, she might not get an assignment near her spouse.

The last person Barbara met with that day was a woman, Zoey, who had recently finished the two-year finance rotation program.

> Zoey opened, "It was a fabulous experience. I got to meet so many people and learn about so many different parts of Gr8Co."
>
> Barbara asked, "Did you relocate during your four rotations?"
>
> Zoey responded, "Yes, twice. My first and last assignments were at headquarters. I loved it."
>
> Barbara followed up, "How much assistance did Gr8Co provide with the relocation logistics?"
>
> Zoey, replied, "I didn't need much help. I travel light. Gr8Co put me in touch with an agent who helped arrange a short-term apartment rental."
>
> Barbara swallowed hard and decided to risk asking, "How did the relocations impact your personal life?"
>
> Zoey laughed, "I was engaged before I joined Gr8Co. My fiancé, Zeke, took a job with a start-up and didn't follow me around. We ended up growing apart."
>
> When Barbara got home after her interview, her husband asked her about it. She said, "It would be a great opportunity, but I'm not sure it is for me."

Barbara's next interview was with a small local accounting firm most of whose employees and managers were women. When she was done interviewing, Barbara had several offers including one from Gr8Co and one from the accounting firm. Gr8Co offered more money and a chance for a very high-powered career. Thinking about her baby and her husband, Barbara decided to go with the accounting firm.

Both men and women may feel the same way as Barbara about multiple short-term assignments in different locations. A young mother might be willing to temporarily separate from her partner if she had someone who could relocate with her and help with child care. This could be a relative, usually one of the baby's grandmothers, or a hired nanny. Depending on your personal priorities and the cost of hired help, a separation from your partner may be acceptable.

For the first two years of my marriage, I lived separately from my husband. I knew what was involved, because he didn't propose to me until shortly after he began a three-year enlistment as an officer in the National Oceanic and Atmospheric Administration Uniformed Officers Corps and was assigned to a research ship based in Miami. The first 18 months of our marriage he was at sea for 3 months at a time.

I was finishing my master's degree at MIT and had applied for PhD programs at Stanford, CalTech (California Institute of Technology) and MIT. I had my pick of all three PhD programs, and was leaning toward CalTech. My husband persuaded me to go to Stanford, because he planned to apply to business and law school there and had declined an offer to get a PhD at CalTech.

Five months after getting married, I finished my master's degree. Then, my husband took leave and drove with me from Massachusetts to Houston, Texas, where I was working for the summer. At the end of the summer, I drove alone from Texas to California to start work on my doctorate at Stanford University. I hardly knew anyone in California, so I spent a lot of time by myself, because my husband could only visit a few times a year. In hindsight, I got a huge head start on my PhD, because I spent so much time studying. If my husband had been there, I would not have had so much time to devote to preparing for my qualifying exams. By the time, my husband and I were able to live together full time, I was well into the research for my PhD thesis.

Like Barbara, our other job applicant, Bob, was married with a young child. Bob's wife was a dentist, so she didn't have flexibility to handle last-minute crises. If there was a last-minute problem such as their child getting sick at daycare, Bob knew that he was the one who would have to manage those types of emergencies.

Bob was interviewing for an entry-level engineering position at Gr8Co. During his interview, Bob learned that flexibility including daily work hours, travel, and relocation requirements varied greatly between the different engineering assignments. After the first couple of years of training, many research engineers were given a field assignment that could involve long hours and travel on short notice. Bob expressed interest in research, but didn't tell the interviewer that his preference was based on the greater control people in research had over their schedules and the lower probability that they would be relocated.

When Bob looked at all of his offers, he accepted the one with Gr8Co, because it offered the most money. He recognized that lack of geographic mobility could be a problem in the future, but he wasn't about to tell Gr8Co that he wouldn't relocate. Even if he only stayed with Gr8Co a couple of years, Bob figured it would be excellent experience and look good on his résumé.

A woman might make the same decision as Bob, but often women are probed more deeply about their relocation restrictions than men. Barbara's situation was in some ways similar to that of Bob. Most large companies such as Gr8Co have many attorneys working for them. Her husband might have been willing to work for Gr8Co. However, even if he worked for Gr8Co, arranging six-month assignments for him to live with her during the two-year finance rotational program would have been difficult if not impossible.

EMPLOYEES

Carole had always been a top-rate performer. With women a large fraction of the entry-level workforce, Carole assumed that although Gr8Co had few women in upper management, midcareer women like herself who had made it into middle management would continue to advance. Her geographic mobility was limited not so much by her children, but by her husband who was a tenured professor at a local university. Carole knew that Gr8Co placed a huge emphasis on geographic mobility, so she thought that she could get the necessary experience to advance when her husband had his sabbatical.

About a year before her husband's sabbatical, Carole started hunting for an international assignment. She contacted everyone she knew, but couldn't get what she wanted. Instead of a résumé-building year abroad, Carole ended up moving from a line management role to a staff management role. After that to avoid relocation, she shifted into a technical role.

Carole didn't realize that Gr8Co was not just after the experience associated with relocation. It wasn't a case of "getting your ticket punched at a time that worked for your personal schedule." Relocation was in effect a "loyalty test." To continue on the fast track, you had to be continuously geographically mobile.

When someone like Carole has been sidelined to a staff role, it can be very difficult if not impossible for her to revive her career unless she switches employers. Carole should be able to leverage her Gr8Co experience, because it is a well-respected company. However, Carole might decide that the risks of switching to an unknown employer do not outweigh the disadvantages of continuing with Gr8Co.

A man might make the same decision as Carole. However, as in the case with the job applicant, Barbara, women tend to be questioned more closely about their relocation preferences than a man. Sadly, I have known too many women like Carole who end up trapped in dead-end staff jobs at midcareer, because they flunk the relocation loyalty test. They can be outstanding performers and valuable assets without relocating, but their talents are underutilized, because of the unwritten rule that upper management must be geographically mobile.

Our other employee example, Charles, also had a couple of children and his wife was a physician, who was board-certified in internal medicine, and worked with a small local medical group. Like Carole, Charles was a middle manager and was well aware of the importance Gr8Co placed on geographic mobility. Unlike Carole, he did not share any geographic restrictions with Gr8Co.

When Charles's boss offered him a management position in London, he was ready. He said, "I'd love to go to London, but my wife is a physician." Charles asked, "Is there any possibility that I could go to a location in which we have a company medical clinic and that Gr8Co could hire her too?"

His boss, William, said, "Let me check into that and get back with you."

Charles knew that his wife was frustrated with the declining medical reimbursements from Medicare. She told Charles that she was willing to join Gr8Co and relocate if she had sufficient time to gracefully exit from her practice.

Not long after, William called Charles. "The development committee was really surprised that you didn't want to go to London, but they are happy to offer you Tanzania. There is a Gr8Co medical clinic there and we can start the process to hire your wife. We will also pay your children's tuition at the local international school."

Charles said, "That sounds great, when would I need to be there?"

William responded, "How about three months?"

Charles asked, "Could we make that six months? If that is not possible can we have my wife start there three months after me so that she has time to arrange for her replacement?"

Charles and his family took the assignment in Tanzania. It was an adventure for the whole family and they used the opportunity to take a couple of safaris. When it was time for his kids to apply to college, their international experience was a differentiator that helped them secure admission to highly selective schools. For Charles, it turned out to be a good career move, because operations in Tanzania were in the formative stages and rapidly growing. He continued to advance, taking assignments both at corporate headquarters, which had a medical clinic, and in other developing countries.

Charles could equally well have been Charlotte. Ease of relocation is the reason most often given for why members of dual-career couples want to work for the same employer. Many couples thrive on the expatriate lifestyle, which in developing countries can mean that low-cost household servants are readily available, so a couple can afford a staff that might include a nanny, a cook, a gardener, and a night watchman. Other couples are more worried about security in countries in which watchmen and fences topped with barbed wire or broken glass are necessary.

Some couples want to work abroad before their children are in school, because they feel that the logistics will be easier. Others because of concerns about health risks to young children want to wait until their children are older. However, health risks can be ever present and everywhere.

I knew a man whose 12-year-old son died while he was working in Nigeria. The child went from playing baseball to death in just three days. His son died from sepsis, which is also known as blood poisoning and occurs when a bacterial infection enters the bloodstream from an infection in the lungs, urinary tract, skin, abdomen (such as appendicitis), or other part of the body. He told me that it made no difference that he was in Nigeria. His son would have died if he had been in the United States. Indeed, according to the U.S. National Institute of Health, more people die every year in the United States from sepsis than from prostate cancer, breast cancer, and AIDS combined.[10] However, I always wondered if his son caught the underlying infection because of the poor sanitation in Nigeria and whether the medical care he received was as good as he could have gotten in the United States. As a parent, I think those doubts could be devastating. If you take your children to live in a developing country, you should ask yourself how you would feel living with that kind of doubt.

Some companies have operations in sites to which they only send employees, not families. The issue may be security risks that make it unwise to have anyone but essential personnel in residence. Or, the problem may be that acceptable living accommodations are very limited. Also, families are usually not posted to places where appropriate school facilities are not available. When families are not permitted, employees often work on rotational assignments.

For example, Dawn had a couple of grade school age children and her husband had a small contracting business. Her boss asked her if she was willing to work a rotational assignment in which she would work for 28 straight days in a country halfway around the world and then be home with time off for 28 days. Her husband said that it was fine with him and that he could take care of their children.

The project was an important one. Working closely with the top management of the project, Dawn built very important relationships with several key leaders, who became her mentors and sponsors. Thanks to the support of these sponsors, Dawn received many important promotions to become a powerful executive.

Like Dawn, Don took 28–28 rotational assignments. Previously, he had worked other 28–28 rotations around the world, and he and his wife enjoyed the extended time off together. Then Don accepted a rotational position in a country that had been part of the former Soviet Union (FSU). Many of the young women there viewed the expatriate men as a way to escape poverty. These women aggressively flirted with the lonesome men. Don and several of his colleagues ended up getting divorced and marrying a younger woman from the FSU country.

Men seeking a way out of an impoverished country may also target lonely women. However, I knew of more men whose marriages ended as a result of rotational assignments, perhaps because I worked in a male-dominated industry. One man I knew, who had worked rotational assignments and had divorced and remarried a fellow expatriate (who was also working on a rotational assignment), was convinced that rotational assignments broke up marriages.

As the vice president told me, when he was trying to discount the importance of dual-career couples, "Many marriages don't last." You are the best judge of what you think will strain your relationship with your partner. Also, you are the one who must decide whether the risk–reward balance associated with the separation is worthwhile from your perspective.

PLAYING CORPORATE POKER

Never admit to your employer that your career does not take precedence over your partner's. Life has many twists and turns. You want to see what the company is offering before you make a decision.

Once you have an offer, you should be ready to negotiate. What compromises are you willing to accept? Are you willing to live apart from your partner for the right experience? Under what circumstances would your partner agree to relocate with you? How can the company's offer be modified? Is the timing of the relocation hard and fast? Often there is room to negotiate. If you don't ask, you certainly won't get what you want. Develop the attitude that it never hurts to try to negotiate. And ask for what you want. Don't be shy.

CHAPTER 5

Why Share an Employer?

LOVE IN THE OFFICE

We spend a large fraction of our time at work, so it is not surprising that many people meet their mates while on the job. In 2013 Career Builder conducted a survey of 3,008 workers in private-sector companies of varying sizes in different industries. A total of 38 percent of the participants had dated someone else who worked for the same company. The Career Builder survey, which was conducted by Harris Poll, also found that of those with an office romance, 31 percent ended up marrying their office sweetheart.[1]

The results of a survey that I led in 2013 for the Society of Petroleum Engineers (SPE) are consistent with the Career Builder survey.[2] In the SPE study, 15 percent responded that they currently worked for the same employer as their domestic partner. Another 20 percent said that previously they had shared an employer. Combining those who worked for the same employer in the past with those who currently do, in total 35 percent reported sharing an employer with their partner at some point in their career.

A 2014 survey by Vault.com found an even higher percentage of people in office romances than the survey by Harris Poll for Career Builder.[3] Vault.com reported that 56 percent of business professionals said that they had participated in some type of workplace relationship. However in the Vault.com study, a lower percentage of the romances turned into long-term relationships than in the Career Builder survey: 17 percent of the women but only 11 percent of the men said that the office romance led to a long-term relationship.

Office romances are a fact of life, but participants should be aware of the possible consequences. The Career Builder–Harris Poll survey noted that 7 percent of those who dated a coworker reported having to leave their job when the relationship went sour. Short of losing your job, there are many other ways in which sharing an employer with the same person with whom you share a bed can impact your career and your finances.

A friend divulged that when he joined a new company, he was surprised by the very low salary of a young woman, who reported to him. The woman in question was vibrant and dynamic—a clear leader. When he checked with his fellow managers, the male colleagues explained, "She's female, and she dated a technician." My friend added that his fellow supervisors thought the woman's ultimate display of poor judgment was that, "She married the technician."

Of course this is also a prime example of the double standard to which women are held. Countless men, including those who have risen to the highest levels, have married their secretaries.

Romantic partners may have drastically different perspectives on the level of commitment and the anticipated duration of the relationship. If you are involved with someone at work, it is essential to confirm that you and your lover are in agreement about the nature of the relationship before factoring the relationship into your decisions about your career. You may not like your lover's answer, but it is better to know before you take actions that may negatively impact your career.

The 2013 SPE survey explored the advantages and disadvantages of sharing an employer with your domestic partner.[4] In that survey, 34 percent of the women and 25 percent of the men in dual-career couples said that they would prefer to work for the same employer as their partner. Those responding in the affirmative included 65 percent of the women and 55 percent of the men who currently work for the same employer as their partner and 40% percent of the women and 22 percent of the men who previously worked for the same employer as their partner. Overall, women in a dual-career couple are more likely than men to see advantages in working for the same employer as their partner.

EASIER RELOCATION

"Ease of relocation" was, by a wide margin, the main reason women responding to the SPE survey gave for wanting to share an employer with their domestic partner.[5] In that survey, 58 percent of the dual-career couple women cited coordinating relocation as being the "most important" factor. In contrast, only 26 percent of dual-career couple men picked that factor as being the "most important," putting it in second place slightly behind "coordination of daily schedules," which was picked by 29 percent of the men.

It is tempting to speculate on this big gender difference. One possibility is that more women than men anticipate that they will be the trailing spouse in a relocation and think that they will be better positioned to protect their career if they work for the same employer as their partner. Another possibility is that women want the ability to relocate to advance their career, but are less willing than men to negatively impact their partner's career for the benefit of their own career. In the December 2011 survey of SPE members under the age of 45, 81 percent of equal-earner women but only 64 percent of equal-earner men would *refuse* to relocate if it meant their partner could not work.[6]

These gender differences may diminish with the passage of time and the evolution of gender roles. Many men still feel threatened if their wives are more successful than they are, and women may anticipate that their husbands will do at least as well as themselves. When the traditional pecking order is overturned, the relationship may be negatively impacted.

Traditionally women have been indoctrinated to protect the male ego, but men are not equivalently trained to be as supportive of women's self-esteem. Hence, women tend to be more protective of their mate's career than vice versa.

Even though many women want to share an employer with their partner to minimize problems with relocation, it does not always work as well as they hope. One woman I know had to take a leave of absence while her husband worked overseas even though they shared an employer.

Those employers that handle relocation of dual-career couples well can create a cadre of very loyal employees. The following story comes from an anonymous comment provided in response to the 2013 survey by the SPE.[7] To make her comment easier to follow, the woman, her spouse, her company, and his company have been given fictitious names. Janet's experience is an example of how good management of relocation of dual-career couples can build lasting loyalty. Janet described her employer NLiteN as having put "golden handcuffs" on her. "It would take a pretty bad work environment to get me to quit now. I don't know that any amount of money could entice me away to be honest."

When NLiteN asked Janet to accept an international assignment, her husband, Peter, worked for DiffCo. Janet said that she would not move unless NLiteN provided a job for Peter in the new location. NLiteN was a relatively small company, so it wasn't easy for the company to find a place for Peter. Janet described herself as being, "forever in the debt of the two people who made it work. I know who they are. That's what I like about the company. It's small enough that relationships are what make it work well. Yet it is big enough to provide job satisfaction and security to a dual-career family with two small kids."

Another anonymous comment to that survey shows that not everyone enjoys the company support that they want. Again the names of the individuals and their employees are fictional. Emily's experience was that when her skills were in demand by a business unit in Smallville, her employer, Dino Corp, tried to find a position for her partner, Bobby, in the location. When that didn't work out, Dino Corp did not attempt to identify a different assignment that fulfilled both Emily's and Bobby's career needs. Instead, Dino Corp "just recommended that Bobby go to the external group jobseekers to find employment outside of the company."[8]

Between the tremendous support that Janet received from NLiteN and the brush-off that Emily got from Dino Corp, there is a lot of middle ground. Sometimes, part of an employee's relocation package is access to "outplacement services" for the trailing partner. Outplacement services can supplement headhunter services, by providing coaching and training in résumé writing, interview preparation, and networking as well as guidance on changing careers. Outplacement training on becoming an independent consultant could be especially useful for trailing partners, who may find themselves following their mate through a rapid series of relocations. If outplacement services are offered, they should be provided for a sufficient length of time for the trailing spouse to have a reasonable opportunity to find another position before the benefit expires.

NEGOTIATIONS

Some people who work for the same company as their partner believe that it provides them with extra influence. In a comment in response to the 2013 SPE survey, a man responded, "It brings some potential additional leverage in negotiations with the employer." Similarly a woman noted, "The company knows they need to look after both of our careers—if one person is unhappy and resigns, the other is more likely to follow (to two new jobs at the same company ideally)."[9]

Another good example of negotiating with an employer for what you need is the case of Dick and Jane. As in the prior examples, the names and company are fictionalized. For many years, two geologists, Dick and Jane, who were citizens of the European Union and worked for different employers, moved around Europe together without being married. When Dick was transferred by Big Oil to the United States from Europe, Jane was unable to secure a work visa unless they married and she was also employed by Big Oil. To persuade Dick to move, Big Oil offered Jane a position in the same group reporting to the same manager. They married and relocated.

While Dick and Jane were working in the United States, oil prices plummeted. Petroleum companies including Big Oil reacted by terminating large percentages of their staff to reduce overhead. Jane was given notice that she was to be terminated. However, Dick was the most highly valued geologist in their work group and was not on the list to go. Jane explained to their common manager that because her U.S. visa restricted her to working for Big Oil, she and Dick would return to Europe. In that "downsizing" thanks to her strong negotiating position, Jane was the only person who was able to get her termination reversed. Many years later, Dick and Jane are still working for Big Oil.

NEPOTISM CONCERNS

People tend to meet their mates in school or at work, so dual-career couples are frequently in the same profession and often in the same narrow specialty. Thus, antinepotism rules can be a significant impediment for some legally married couples working for the same employer. Rules against nepotism can make it difficult to hire family members, especially if one of them is in a position of authority. Other employers are willing to hire family members, but have restrictions that prohibit family members from working in the same department or on the same project.

As in the case of Dick and Jane, both members of a couple may be allowed to report to the same manager. However, usually there are rules that prohibit one spouse from being in a position of authority over the other. If one partner is a rising star with a large and rapidly expanding span of responsibility, the trailing spouse may have difficulty finding an acceptable position that is outside of the portion of the organization reporting to his or her mate, but still in the same geographic location.

If the couple is good at negotiating, creative solutions can be devised and implemented to accommodate the trailing spouse of a high flyer. For example, Global Corp wants Sally to lead a new business unit in Ulan Bator, Mongolia. Everybody in the new Mongolian office will report to Sally. What will her partner, Jack, do? Depending on the nature of Jack's skills and desires, they can ask for a variety of accommodations. Jack might be able to be physically located in the office in Ulan Bator, but work on projects that report to the Asian business unit director or to headquarters. If relatively short separations are acceptable to Sally and Jack, Jack might be able to work in Global Corp's Beijing office. That would enable Sally and Jack to get together every week or so.

In approaching Global Corp about negotiating acceptable terms for the new assignment, Sally and Jack need to know their priorities. Which conditions must be met and which are not essential? Start by asking for what you as a couple want. If Sally has credentials that make her uniquely valuable to Global Corp, Sally and Jack (like Dick and Jane) are in a strong negotiating position even when their industry is experiencing a recession. Be creative and be ready to offer multiple alternative solutions. Even if Sally feels vulnerable, she should try asking for a variety of accommodations. At worst, Sally is comparing the original offer with her opportunities outside of Global Corp.

SECURING A FAIR DEAL FOR BOTH PARTNERS

If both members of the couple want to work for the same organization, employers may try to take advantage of the situation. Let's look at Bob, who is an experienced college professor, and his partner Edith, who just finished a postdoctoral fellowship. If Bob is determined to accept a position at rural Ivy Walls College, which is a long distance from any other institution where Edith can find employment, her ability to negotiate with Ivy Walls College is severely limited. However, if Bob has other offers and does not reveal that he will accept Ivy Walls's offer even if Edith has to take another poorly paid postdoctoral position, they might be able to negotiate a better deal for her.

Relatively few employers have rules that prohibit offering trailing spouses less compensation or a lower-ranking position than the spouse would have received being hired independently. Commenting to the 2013 SPE survey about the trailing person being hired at a discount relative to their market value, one person said of an enormous, international company, "It is why several couples have left the company or did not join it."[10]

CAREER DEVELOPMENT COMPETITION

The main reason women do not want to share an employer is that for career development purposes, many employers compare partners with each other as opposed to with their entire peer group. Many of those responding to the 2013 SPE survey complained, "Employers require one career to lead and the other to follow."[11]

In that survey, in the anonymous comment section, women voiced their objection to this approach to managing dual-career couples.

- I want to be evaluated on my own work without the additional influence of a partner at the same firm.
- I am a professional, not the wife of X. It does not help me at work if I am considered a spouse, female, or X's wife. It invites questions as to who does the domestic chores at home; who is "in charge" at work vs. at home . . . I would like to be considered for my skill-sets, not who I am with.

In response to that survey, men anonymously shared similar concerns about being compared with their domestic partner:

- Your own work strengths or weaknesses apply to both parties resulting in less fair reviews.
- May end up competing for promotion/seniority.
- The reality is that one career must be deemed the priority.

Thus, many couples decide that the disadvantages of working for the same organization outweigh the advantages. Being treated as a "trailing spouse" or compared to their partner can be career limiting. One of the anonymous comments summarized that perspective, "Career planning within one company is difficult, since the influence on each other is very high. It is much easier if the company doesn't know that you are a couple."

UNSUPPORTIVE MANAGEMENT

A detailed response to the 2013 SPE survey highlighted multiple problems that dual-career couples encounter when working for the same employer.[12]

My husband and I work for the same company. Despite joining the company independently and working in positions that are compatible with working in the same locations, we have been repeatedly informed by various managers and human resources representatives that "dual-career couples are very difficult."

Dual-career status is definitely something that is generally viewed as being detrimental to our respective promotion prospects. The company has an official policy not to duplicate certain salary benefits for dual-career couples, so in many cases, one partner is financially penalized. This is despite the fact that a dual-career couple costs less to transfer and house on international assignments than two employees with non-working spouses.

During our last transfer my husband was asked during an informal job interview whether I was planning to "get pregnant during the assignment" because this "could be a problem."

In a separate interview I had a manager try to bully me into accepting a lower position than the one that I'd applied for because my husband was the preferred candidate for another position in the same location. I was informed in no uncertain terms that I was "being fussy" and that we should be "grateful for being able to find two jobs in the same location."

Not only managers, but also colleagues may make inappropriate inferences. Another woman responding anonymously to the SPE survey described the trade-offs.[13]

My husband and I currently work for separate companies. The expectation I feel from my managers and peers is that my husband can easily join me if I transfer to another business unit, but he makes an equivalent salary and is equally driven and dedicated to his career.

We've mostly worked for separate companies, but did once work together in a medium sized company. All I ever heard was "Oh, you're so-and-so's wife." (Eyebrow lift, I can see them thinking, "Is

THAT how you got your job here?") Honestly, I got there because I worked hard and I was the right person for the job. I couldn't stand that stigma. Based on my experience, I think it is easier to work for different companies.

COORDINATION OF BENEFITS

Coordination of benefits when both partners are legally married and work for the same employer can be a sore point. Some dual-career couples think it is unfair if they do not get double of every kind of benefit when they are working for the same organization. They point out, "Working in two companies, we can get double benefits. Yes, it is double, but we are two workers."[14]

Employer policies for coordination of benefits differ drastically, even within a single industry. When both partners work for the same employer, certain types of benefits may be per family or per couple, not per employee. Other companies allow the couple to choose if they wish to be treated as a family or as independent employees for benefit purposes.

Even the U.S. government combines the benefits of couples who work for the same employer. Under Section 825.201(b) of the U.S. Family and Medical Leave Act of 1993 (FMLA), couples who work for different employers have greater benefits than those who share an employer.

§825.201(b) Same employer limitation. Spouses who are eligible for FMLA leave and are employed by the same covered employer may be limited to a combined total of 12 weeks of leave during any 12-month period if the leave is taken to care for the employee's parent with a serious health condition, for the birth of the employee's son or daughter or to care for the child after the birth, or for placement of a son or daughter with the employee for adoption or foster care or to care for the child after placement. This limitation on the total weeks of leave applies to leave taken for the reasons specified as long as the spouses are employed by the same employer. It would apply, for example, even though the spouses are employed at two different worksites of an employer located more than 75 miles from each other, or by two different operating divisions of the same company. On the other hand, if one spouse is ineligible for FMLA leave, the other spouse would be entitled to a full 12 weeks of FMLA leave. Where the spouses both use a portion of the total 12-week FMLA leave entitlement for either the birth of a child, for placement for adoption or foster care, or to care for a parent, the spouses would each be entitled to the difference between the amount he or she has taken individually and 12 weeks for FMLA leave for other purposes. For example, if each spouse took six weeks of leave to care for a parent, each could use an additional six weeks due to his or her own serious health condition or to care for a child with a serious health condition. See also §825.127(d).[15]

Following the Supreme Court's decision on June 26, 2015, on same-sex marriage in *Obergefell, et al. v. Hodges*, eligibility rules for family and medical leave were retroactively revised to March 27, 2015. As of that date, all legally married couples, whether of opposite sex or of same sex, or couples married under common law have the same federal family leave rights regardless of where they reside. The "definition of spouse expressly includes individuals in lawfully recognized same-sex and common law marriages and marriages that were validly entered into outside of the United States if they could have been entered into in at least one state."[16]

The change in the family and medical leave definition of a couple impacts both homosexuals and heterosexuals in common law marriages. A common law marriage is a legally recognized marriage between two people, who have not purchased a marriage license or had their marriage solemnized by a ceremony. The rules for common law marriage vary from state to state.[17]

Some of the criteria used to determine if two people have a common law marriage are:[18]

- Did you live together?
- Did you sign contracts together to buy a home or a car?
- Did you have joint bank accounts?
- Did you share household duties and expenses?
- Did you have and raise children together?
- Did you each refer to each other as husband and wife?
- Did you file joint tax returns?

Once the government makes changes in eligibility rules, other organizations often change their rules to be consistent. Couples who work for the same employer and who did not obtain a marriage certificate but who could be considered to be in a common law marriage may wish to consult an attorney.

In the United States, one of the biggest benefit coordination issues is health care. Some companies require both employees to carry their own insurance with specifications as to who can claim the children. Other employers have health care claims filed first to one person's coverage with anything that is not covered then filed against the other person's benefits. Another variation is to allow one person to opt out of health care coverage and be covered as a dependent by his or her partner and get a credit. Depending on individual circumstances, these alternatives may have a significant financial impact and create an incentive for people to work for separate organizations.

Companies, even within the same industry, may handle the benefits associated with an international assignment very differently. Some companies only allow the leading partner to be employed on expatriate terms. The other partner is engaged on local terms and doesn't receive the same benefits. This drastically reduces the benefits provided to the family. However, working for the same employer may still be in the couple's best interests, if it is virtually impossible to otherwise secure a work visa for the trailing spouse.

In some locations employers provide expatriates with a house, subsidized schooling for the children, a car, and tickets "home" for the family one or more times a year. If one partner is employed as an expatriate and the other as a local hire, the local hire does not get the international bonus, airline tickets, and extended home leave. The couple may consider it unfair if they receive the same subsidy that is provided to a single individual for housing, schooling, and transportation, because their organization has two people working for them, while for benefits purposes they are being treated as one.

If the company treats expatriate benefits as "family" rather than "individual," the dual-career couple working for the same employer will not get double benefits. They may both receive an overseas premium and extended home leave, but under this type of policy, if one employee is entitled once a year to get tickets home for the entire family, the family is not entitled to two sets of tickets home for the family. How benefits are coordinated can create considerable resentment.

At the other extreme, some companies treat both members of the dual-career couple as if they were individual employees. Instead of providing only one housing allowance, some organizations add the salaries of both partners together, calculate an equivalent pay grade and provide the family benefits based on the equivalent pay grade, which is higher than either individual pay grade. However, this approach may not be as generous as doubling the benefits of someone of their pay grade and still leave the couple feeling dissatisfied.

Despite the issues around coordination of benefits, most couples who wish to work internationally find the logistics to be much easier if they both work for the same company. In international moves, obtaining a work visa for the accompanying partner is often one of the biggest headaches. If you share an employer, who is moving you both as employees, usually obtaining a work visa for the trailing spouse is not a problem.

Sometimes, those working for the same company never have the opportunity to benefit from the logistical advantages of being moved as a couple. One woman explained, "I was told I could not be promoted, because my husband would not transfer, even though a transfer was never offered. I left the company and we transferred."[19]

If companies want to be attractive to members of dual-career couples, they should not stint on paying the same amount for benefits for each member of a dual-career couple as they would for two separate employees. Compensating both members at their fair market rate is important in building a good reputation as an attractive employer for couples who want to work for the same organization.

Unlike the traditional dominant earner with a spouse in the support role, dual-career couples do not want to be a "two for the price of one" deal. If two qualified people in a dual-career couple work for the same employer, the compensation of one partner should not be discounted to less than his or her market value. It is a case of "equal pay for equal work."

TENURE COMPLICATIONS

Coordination of two careers can create difficulties in some unexpected ways and places. When I visited the women's studies group at "Prestige University," to discuss dual-career couples, I learned how tenure complicated their ability to hire talented young female faculty. My host explained that the university had been unable to make sufficiently attractive offers to three high-potential women, because Prestige University did not want to provide tenure to the trailing male spouses.

These female candidates were all married to older male academics. The trailing spouses did not qualify for any open positions at Prestige University. Although the candidates' spouses had tenure elsewhere, these trailing male spouses either duplicated existing faculty or were not of the caliber that Prestige University wanted. The young women were promising, but did not have proven track records. Prestige University was not certain that any of these women would ultimately be given tenure. If the women proved to be unworthy of receiving tenure, Prestige University did not want to be stuck with the older male partner. Without a tenured position for their partners, all three women chose to accept positions elsewhere.

JOB SECURITY

In the 2013 SPE survey, we did not include "job security" as one of the factors we asked people to evaluate with regard to whether or not they wanted to work for the same employer.[20] However, so many of the comments mentioned job security as a reason for not working for the same employer; it was obviously a major consideration for many dual-career couples. In a significant fraction of the comments about sharing an employer with their partner, people said that doing so was like having "too many eggs in one basket."

Since the 2013 SPE survey included people in the petroleum industry as well as in other fields, we looked to see if the concerns about job security were industry specific. For women, regardless of whether or not the women were working in the petroleum industry, 28 percent of the women's comments on the pros and cons of sharing an employer mentioned job security. Men were even more concerned about job security, with 37 percent of the comments from men in the petroleum industry mentioning it and a greater percentage of the men in other fields. Since the survey did not prompt people to comment on job security, the data indicate that, for dual-career couples, job security is a significant factor in deciding to work for a different employer, with men more concerned about job security than women.

Many couples see having both partners in the workforce as providing a financial safety net, because if necessary, they can limp along on one salary and a single set of benefits. People are worried about a shared employer hitting hard times and both partners in the dual-career couple losing their jobs simultaneously. These couples see themselves as actively diversifying their family finances by working for separate employers.

QUESTIONS TO ASK YOURSELF

- Do you mind being compared with your partner?
- How would you feel if your employer decides that your partner's career is more important than yours?
- How would you feel if your employer without consulting you in advance asked your partner to make decisions that will impact your career?
- Do you enjoy discussing office politics and your work with your partner?

QUESTIONS TO DISCUSS AS A COUPLE

- Do you think sharing an employer is a serious financial risk for your family?
- Are you worried about your employer knowing too much about the family's combined financial resources?
- Do you expect to relocate to advance your careers?
- Are you and your partner eager to work in other countries around the world?
- Are you willing to accept receiving fewer benefits as a couple, then you would receive as two individuals?
- Do you think that working for the same employer will improve communication between yourselves?
- Do you enjoy discussing your work at home with your partner?
- Will working for the same employer improve your quality of life by easing coordination of daily logistics including commuting and child care?

QUESTIONS TO ASK A POTENTIAL EMPLOYER

Do not ask the following questions until you have a firm job offer from the potential employer. You do not want to raise prematurely any issues that might adversely impact the hiring decision. Once you are deliberating on whether or not to accept an offer, you should make these inquiries if the issues are applicable to you.

- What policies does the company have regarding employing both members of a married couple?
- How is career development of the members of a couple managed when both people work for the company?
- How is relocation of married couples handled when both work for the company?
- How does the company coordinate the benefits of two employees, who are married to each other?
- How do the benefits of a couple compare with the benefits of two individuals?
- Can you put me in contact with some of the couples who work for the company?

CHAPTER 6

How to Balance Opportunity with Sacrifice

FRATERNITY HAZING

When complaints are raised about work–life balance, attention tends to be focused on the life issues. However, the key word is *balance*, which is distinctly different in this case from work–life integration. The issue is whether people are being offered opportunities that entice them to forgo current enjoyment to secure a future reward. For the right incentives, people will give up many things.

Some employers concentrate their investment in career development on the top 10 percent or so of their employees. There is the implicit assumption that a person on the "fast track" will compromise his or her personal life for the opportunity to advance through a series of positions of "increasing responsibility." The unstated message is that, "You have been chosen and you must prove your loyalty by following orders that push you to the limits of your mental and physical abilities." This approach is similar to fraternity hazing. It is designed to create a management cadre with similar values and loyalty to the organization.

People who have been inducted into the executive ranks through this hazing often believe these sacrifices are essential to acquiring the experiences necessary to be a leader. Furthermore, the veterans of this process may have the delusion that they are much smarter and knowledgeable than those who were not offered the fast-track opportunities or those who opted out. The net result can be leadership that is out of touch with the rank-and-file workforce.

Members of dual-career couples are often eliminated early on, because they are not willing or able to work ridiculously long hours and/or relocate frequently. If members of a dual-career couple go into the hazing process, they may end up separated or with one of the partners sacrificing his or her career for the other.

Those who have been through this corporate hazing may fail to appreciate that everyone needs a sense of opportunity. Opportunities can't be reserved for just those who are willing to sell their soul to the organization. If you want an engaged workforce, everyone must feel that they have opportunities, challenge, and career potential.

CHANGING JOBS

Reserving the sense of opportunity for only those on the "fast track" turns the bulk of employees into wage slaves. When few opportunities come our way, we lose interest in our work and mentally disengage. In large bureaucratic organizations, people who lack opportunity either look for it elsewhere, often in volunteer groups, or become work zombies, who have retired in place.

In the 2013 Society of Petroleum Engineers (SPE) survey, "insufficient opportunity" was the most commonly given reason for changing employers, and correspondingly, "opportunity, challenge, career growth" was the top factor cited for staying with an employer.[1] Women and men, regardless of whether they are part of a dual-career couple, a dominant earner, or single, are attracted and retained by a sense of having a bright future with rewarding career opportunities.

This does not mean other factors aren't important in attraction and retention, but having opportunities to develop skills and acquire valuable and/or enjoyable experiences are for most people the most alluring "carrots." Factors that create an unpleasant, hostile, or unsafe work environment are among the many "sticks." When we talk about "work–life" balance, we are talking about the balance between the "carrots" and the "sticks." The more painful the "sticks," the more enticing the "carrots" must be to keep people fully engaged.

FAMILY EXCUSES

When women quit midcareer, frequently they tell their employer that it is because they want to spend more time with their family. In general, people avoid telling the truth in exit interviews, because they don't want to burn bridges. Wanting to spend more time with your children or to take care of other family members is a convenient excuse that avoids burning bridges.

Someone who is frustrated with their opportunities at work may even think that the "life" as opposed to "work" side of the equation is the real problem. When a friend, "Whitney," was about 40, she told me that she quit because she wanted to have a child and go back to school. I was surprised by her decision, because it appeared to me that Whitney's career was going well. She had an impressive track record including an engineering degree.

Several years later, I again asked Whitney why she resigned. She said, "I no longer felt promotable or that I had the opportunity to do the type of things I could when I was younger. There was constant pecking at everything I had done. I would have stayed if I had gotten an international assignment, but I decided, I'll just travel on my own, and I have."

When someone exits the workforce, they have come to the conclusion that the ongoing pain associated with working outweighs the benefits. Accordingly, when a woman quits to spend more time with her family, she is really indicating that the opportunities and rewards that she thinks she will receive by continuing to work do not justify the sacrifices.

What a person shares during an exit interview can impact his or her chances of being rehired by that employer. To be on the safe side, people often provide an excuse for quitting that doesn't suggest any dissatisfaction with their employer or with their job. In contrast, those responding to the SPE survey on attraction and retention could be confident that the results were anonymous and their responses could not come back to haunt them.[2] Thus, they were more likely to be honest about their motivations for leaving than they would be in an exit interview.

In the 2013 SPE survey, women who had left the petroleum industry were offered a choice of 20 drivers for exiting. The top reasons are ranked below based on the number of positive responses with number 1, the most common. It was noteworthy that the top five factors these women selected had nothing to do with traditional female responsibilities.[3]

1. For more interesting work
2. Insufficient opportunity, challenge, career potential

3. To live in a location I like better
4. For a position that was a better fit to my core competencies
5. Opportunity to develop new competencies
6. To take care of my child/children

The top two reasons, for "more interesting work" and "insufficient opportunity, challenge, career potential," indicate deficiencies on the work side of the balance, not on the life side. Of the top five, only the third most frequently selected factor, "to live in a location I like better," involved work–life balance. The classic female excuse, "to take care of my child/children," was relegated to sixth place. For most of the women surveyed, lack of opportunity, not the burdens of motherhood, prompted them to drop out of the petroleum industry.

The 2013 SPE survey also asked individuals who had exited the workforce to identify which of 20 factors might motivate them to return.[4] "A chance to make a difference" (which is a form of "opportunity") came in second overall. The other two of the most alluring incentives to return to work were ways of reducing the sacrifice associated with employment (part-time work and telecommuting). In effect, those who had made the decision to quit would return for a more acceptable pain–gain balance.

Hewlett et al. reported that between the ages of 25 and 30, 41 percent of the technical workforce is female. However, between ages 35 and 40, attrition spikes with 52 percent of women in technical careers exiting.[5] The sense of opportunity that motivated these women to endure years of grueling training in science and technology was not sustained through midlife. Despite the tremendous investment women made in their careers, lack of opportunity led them to the decision that continued sacrifices were not justified.

When I was in my mid-thirties, I was frustrated at work due to lack of opportunity. I felt that my career was in a rut. However by that time, both of my children were in elementary school. I thought to myself, "How could I justify dropping now, when I have already survived working full-time the entire time my kids were preschoolers?" If they were toddlers, I am not sure that I would have stayed the course. However, in hindsight, despite all of the pain, I am glad that I did.

Let's look at a hypothetical example of a mother dealing with insufficient opportunity. Frances recently returned to work after having her second child in three years. Her mother stayed with Frances to help for a few weeks immediately after the new baby's birth, but left after a month. Now, it's just Frances and her partner, Norm, splitting the evening and weekend child care and household chores. Frances is swamped. Her three-year-old, Mason, is jealous of the attention the baby is getting and has been having tantrums. Both Frances and Norm are exhausted.

Frances works for TrainingCo whose business is booming. Frances was responsible for much of that success. A year earlier, Frances persuaded her supervisor, Bart, that TrainingCo should offer a series of one-hour webinars as an alternative to their one- and two-day classes. The webinar series was a winner and is now yielding more revenue than the short courses. There was interest in creating a separate webinar business unit and Frances thought that she had a good chance of being selected as its manager, after her maternity leave was over.

When Bart called Frances into his office and shut his door, Frances hoped that it was to inform her that she would be the manager of the new webinar division. Instead, Bart said, "Have a seat. Before I tell the rest of the group, I wanted to share with you that we have hired a talented new fellow, Fred. He interviewed while you were out and is very impressive. Fred wasn't willing to join us unless it was for a management position, so I have decided to make him manager of the new webinar division. I'd like you to show him the ropes and brief him on our current portfolio of webinars."

Frances was devastated. She mumbled a few things and exited Bart's office as quickly as she could. Using the excuse of having to pump breast milk, Frances disappeared for half an hour to think.

That evening after she and Norm had gotten Mason to sleep, Frances sat down to nurse the baby. She told Norm that they needed to talk about making some major changes.

> Frances began, "It just doesn't seem worthwhile to continue with TrainingCo. I'm just pooped, and I feel as if I am going in circles at work."
>
> Norm asked, "You seemed so happy and upbeat when you left today. What happened?"
>
> Frances groaned, "I didn't get the promotion to run the webinar business and Bart expects me to train a new guy to be the manager."
>
> Norm responded, "You had such a great idea with the webinars and did such a fantastic job, why don't we start our own business?"
>
> Frances was silent for a few minutes and then replied, "How can we afford to do that?"
>
> Norm answered, "I'll keep working at my job. In the evenings, I'll help you with the new business. If we start the business from

home, you can stay home with the baby. That will save the time you spend commuting and the cost of infant daycare. I'll take Mason to and from preschool."

Frances answered, "Let me think about it."

The next few days she was so distracted thinking about the pros and cons of starting her own business that she hardly got anything done. When Bart asked her if anything was the matter, she mumbled, "The baby is waking up every couple of hours at night and I'm worn out."

After mulling the situation over for a couple of weeks, Frances knew that she needed a change. She went to see Bart and explained that she was resigning so that she could spend more time with her baby.

That night, she told Norm, "I felt so trapped. Quitting was a relief, but I don't want to fritter away my time. We need to come up with a viable business plan or I should start networking to find another job. We can't simply clone the webinar business that I developed for TrainingCo, because it could lead to legal problems. We must develop a webinar product line that is distinctly different from what I did before. I'm thinking about targeting professionals, who have annual continuing education requirements for their profession. The webinar program could incorporate testing and certification."

In telling her boss, Fred, that she was quitting to spend more time with her family including her new baby, Frances was not burning any bridges. Traditional dominant breadwinner managers think it is natural for women to want to stay home with their children.

In this example, Frances was leaving, because her boss didn't recognize her accomplishments and failed to provide appropriate rewards. In the 2013 SPE attraction and retention survey, "lack of recognition" and "conflict with your boss" are some of the most common reasons people quit.[6] There is an old saying, "People don't leave jobs; they leave bosses."

Frances's story illustrates the impact on retention of insufficient opportunity, conflict with your boss, and lack of recognition. Not only was Frances's work not satisfying, but with a new baby, she was struggling at home as well. With her husband's reassurances, she felt that she could afford to quit.

In contrast with Frances, in my case, when I was frustrated with an awful boss in the late 1980s, I had survived the relentlessly parenting of the preschool years. Another major factor was that the bottom had dropped out of the job market for technical experts in the petroleum industry, because the oil price had crashed. My husband didn't want to relocate and the positions that I could get without relocating seemed to provide considerably less job security than I currently had. Every time I looked at an alternative, I asked myself, "Would taking this position move me up or down on Maslow's hierarchy of needs?"

MASLOW'S HIERARCHY OF NEEDS

I was introduced to Maslow's hierarchy in the early 1980s, when I was sent to my first management course, when my daughter was barely a year old. I was excited and thrilled to be picked for the week-long training course in another city. I thought that my selection for the course indicated that I might get the opportunity to move up into a management position soon.

Most of the others in the class were more than 20 years older than I was and some were already managers. I was in my early thirties. The discussion of Maslow's work focused on the differences between what types of incentives motivated my generation, baby boomers, and what kinds of rewards appealed to those who had grown up during the Great Depression. In many ways the contrasts were analogous to those that are cited as existing between millennials and baby boomers.

Abraham Maslow was a psychologist, who in 1943 published a paper entitled "A Theory of Human Motivation," in which he postulated that people had five sets of needs that drive their behavior.[7] Maslow grouped together as the most fundamental set of needs, physiological necessities. These are the basics required to sustain life including air, water, food, sleep, clothing, and shelter. His hypothesis was that only after people are confident that they have secure and ongoing access to these essentials does the focus of their desires shift to the next most important set of needs, which are grouped together as "safety" and include freedom from fear, security, order, law, and social stability. Maslow's premise was that individuals successively shift their aspirations to a higher-order set of needs after more basic needs are satisfied.

Since the five types of motivational factors are organized in a hierarchical order, Maslow's theory is commonly represented by a pyramid. Physiological and safety needs form the two lowest levels of the pyramid. After those needs are satisfied, we transfer our focus to love and belonging, which encompasses family, friendship, intimacy, and sense of connection. The next level of the five-tiered pyramid is self-esteem, which encompasses achievement, reputation, status, and responsibility. The top level is self-actualization, which consists of creativity, spontaneity, meaning, and realization of one's potential. Over the years, others have proposed modifications of Maslow's hierarchy and added levels, but the five-level version is most frequently cited.

In my training course in the early 1980s, my course instructor elaborated at length about how my baby boomer age group was focused on esteem and self-actualization. In contrast, he emphasized that my colleagues, who had come of age during the Great Depression of the 1930s, were far more concerned about job security. His message was that management should tailor incentives to appeal to the different generations based on which level of Maslow's hierarchy was important to that cohort.

Now, when I hear people droning on about the difference in values between millennials and older generations, it always makes me think back to that management course and Maslow's hierarchy. That course and the articles I subsequently read about millennials always seem to assume that movement through Maslow's pyramid tends to be upward. However, life can be a school of hard knocks.

When I was sitting in that conference room decades ago, the focus was solely on upward mobility and motivating people who were fixated on esteem and self-actualization. As it turned out, the petroleum industry in which I worked was at the edge of a precipice. I was about to find out what it was like to crave job security. My attitude adjustment was mild compared to someone who gets caught up in a military crisis or prolonged civil unrest. However, it was still a huge jolt and psychological shift.

From the time I started graduate school in 1972, oil company recruiters had been courting me. My technical skills were in great demand, so I had my choice of jobs. The first few years of my career as a research scientist at Mobil, I received large annual raises, was promoted multiple times, and received incentives to stay with the company. Naively, I didn't realize that the job market for my skills was tightly linked to the price of oil.

As the course instructor emphasized in that course in 1982, the need for job security was not on my radar screen. I was primarily concerned with whether or not I was being promoted as fast as the men whom I considered to be my peers in terms of achievement. In my ignorance, the impact of a business cycle on my career was the farthest thing from my mind.

Then the oil price went into free fall. Over the next four years, the price of oil tumbled. Petroleum engineers and earth scientists like myself switched from being highly sought after to not being able to find positions that used their technical skills. New graduates went from receiving multiple job offers to getting none. As a form of petroleum industry gallows humor, people shared the sick joke that with a geology degree, you could get a job selling shoes or in a McDonald's flipping burgers.

Immersed in scientific research, I had paid little attention to the price of oil or the fluctuations in the price of the company's stock. Apparently, many of my colleagues at Mobil's research lab were equally divorced from reality. The president of the business unit ordered that the daily oil and stock prices were to be prominently posted so that we all saw them as we entered and left the facility. My world and sense of security began to crumble.

The opening round of layoffs did not frighten me. The first people who were terminated were those who were widely recognized as "deadbeats." The corporate culture during the boom times was that it was easier to ignore the poor performers than to go to the trouble to document a case for their termination. I was confident that I was a strong player with an excellent record of accomplishments.

However, as one round of layoffs followed another, the personnel cuts grew deeper and deeper. When I saw people whom I respected and thought were valuable contributors terminated, I began to think the selection was more arbitrary and political than objective. I noticed that the groups that lost their incumbent manager either through retirement or by being pushed aside suffered much larger cuts. The decisions as to who was fired and who got to stay no longer seemed fair. Concern about losing my job grew to be a perpetual gnawing fear deep in my gut. It lurked in the back of my mind day and night, at work and at home.

I felt like a participant in a horrible game of musical chairs with the music stopping about every 18 months and more chairs being taken away. For two of the downsizings, I was in a group in which half of the people were let go. Despite my confidence in my abilities and accomplishments, I became increasingly terrified that I would lose my job and not be able to find another satisfactory position.

As layoffs became an all too frequent occurrence, members of my generation slid down to lower levels on Maslow's hierarchy of needs. We were no longer focused on satisfying our desires for self-esteem and self-actualization from our work. Job security (a form of safety) became our overwhelming driver.

When people are afraid they will lose their job, the environment is ripe for abuse and bullying. For the first time in my life, I fell victim to a bully. I was completely blindsided.

During this dark time, X, who was about 30 years older than I was, became my supervisor. As soon as X became my boss, she morphed from trying to mentor me to seeing me as competition. Previously, when X thought that she had no hope of being promoted, because there were no female managers in the research lab, she had shared stories about her impoverished childhood with barely enough to eat and struggling to get an education. Also, she had explained that because her first husband had a heart condition, she thought it was too financially risky for her to have children. If her husband died at an early age, which he did, X didn't think that she could both work and care for children.

One day after she became my supervisor, X walked into my office, glanced at the pictures of my kids on my desk and declared, "You have had it all." Her statement turned out to be a declaration of war. She found numerous ways to make my daily life miserable. When it became clear that her vindictive behavior was seriously damaging my career, I tried to transfer to another business unit. X was not about to let her victim slip away. She called other managers to blackball me and filled my personnel file with slanderous material. Despite my prior record of outstanding accomplishments, my complaints to X's boss and to human resources fell on deaf ears.

With very low oil prices and a prolonged petroleum industry recession, X's bullying continued for a couple of years. Then, miraculously I had the opportunity to talk with someone from company headquarters. He took action and about six weeks later, X announced her retirement and quickly exited.

The poison that X left in my personnel file continued to haunt me for at least another year. When my next supervisor announced his retirement, he called me into his office and told me he was shredding malicious notes that X had added to my file.

During this bleak time, I sought job opportunities that didn't require relocation, but the job market was dismal. The few options I had didn't seem to be a better alternative. Although some of the other positions offered greater status, they appeared to provide even less job security. I craved job security.

Several times, I tried to persuade my husband to consider relocation so that we could both attempt to secure better jobs. He refused and I wasn't willing to divide the family.

Years later when I publicly mentioned during a panel discussion at a SPE annual meeting that I had been bullied at work, a crowd clustered around me after the close of the session. Several men and women shared that they too had been bullied by their supervisors.

When people feel they must keep their job, they are willing to endure many indignities to stay employed. Workplace bullying proliferates in industries and occupations in which jobs are scarce.

When oil prices began to recover in the current century, a major oil industry service company attempted to persuade my son, who was getting a PhD in mechanical engineering from MIT, to interview with them. He refused saying, "My mom works in the petroleum industry." My son considered employment in the petroleum industry to be unpleasant and unstable, because throughout his childhood, I had been consumed with fear of losing my job. The recruiter didn't attempt to argue with him.

However, just because we give up on satisfying our desire for esteem and self-actualization from our employment, it doesn't mean that we don't seek those forms of gratification from other sources. During the protracted slump in the petroleum industry, I immersed myself in professional society activities. I hoped that through volunteer work I could build my reputation and revive my career. The evenings and weekends that I spent on unpaid projects reaped rewards for me in terms of professional contacts, publications, positions of increasing responsibility within the nonprofit groups, awards, personal satisfaction, and friendships.

The professional society activities turned out to be my key to job security. Through the volunteer work, I built a widespread network of friends, who had firsthand experience with my ability to develop creative solutions and get things done.

Several of the good friends I made through professional society work have also had the need to activate their network to find a new position at times when my industry was rife with layoffs. These fellow professional society volunteers were able to secure excellent positions despite a dismal job market.

A few years ago when I shared my perspective with another active volunteer, "Bill," he said that it was the same with him. Bill confided that the time he spent on unpaid activity varied depending on how frustrated he was at "his day job." When he felt as if he was spinning his wheels at work, he devoted more energy to professional society roles. If high-potential people do not have appropriate channels for their talent and energy in the job, those skills and enthusiasm will be applied elsewhere.

Other volunteer leaders have described their "day jobs" as "the job from hell." Far too many people talk about marking time until they reach a personal milestone and can quit. They may be working and contributing, but their employer is getting less than their best effort.

Although my experiences were only in the petroleum industry, unforeseen factors beyond our individual control can derail any career and send us tumbling down Maslow's pyramid to a lower level. Disruptive technologies can unexpectedly push huge, highly respected companies into bankruptcy. Individual industries can flounder. Business cycles impact many people simultaneously. Economic crises may devastate our savings, or even worse, civil unrest, terrorism, or war can threaten our survival and drag us down to Maslow's lowest level.

During the many decades of a career, the odds are that you will go through several business cycles. Even seemingly recession-proof careers like medicine can be seriously impacted by changes in the compensation provided by government programs. To weather the storms that will come your way, you must develop personal resilience. When you get knocked down, don't let embarrassment about loss of status overwhelm you. Pick yourself up and start clawing your way out of the hole.

Medical crises can be as devastating as financial ones. As individuals, our well-laid plans can be shredded if we or a loved one is seriously injured or ill. Sickness shifts our focus to physical survival. Even if the health crisis is satisfactorily resolved, it may permanently alter our long-term priorities and goals.

When I went in for a routine physical at the beginning of 2007, I sat on the examining table waiting for my internist thinking that I was unusually healthy for my age. The prior year I spent about three-quarters of my time traveling around the world as president of the SPE and had not had any health problems. Everything seemed to be great until my doctor peeked in my ear and noticed a red spot on my ear drum. That red spot turned out to be the tip of a medical iceberg. A tumor had wormed its way from the jugular vein through the mastoid bone into the middle ear. It was barely touching my ear drum, and had not yet affected my hearing, but was probing the cerebral membrane. For months, each new test yielded new bad news. By the end of that year, several tumors had been removed in major surgeries that involved multiple stints in intensive care. The expert on my rare cancer gave me the prognosis of a 45 percent chance of surviving five years. Needless to say, my priorities shifted.

In those days before the Affordable Care Act (or Obamacare), many people including myself felt one of the most important benefits from their employment was access to health insurance. My husband was retired with no health care benefit other than mine. I worried that if I couldn't continue working we might end up without health care or that he would be left alone without coverage.

Once again, I felt highly vulnerable. About a year after my initial diagnosis and only two months after my last surgery and grim prognosis, I got a new boss. In my first one-on-one meeting with him, he harassed me about my health concerns and urged me to retire. He hadn't bothered to figure out that I was not yet eligible for retirement. This time, I wasted no time going outside of the chain of command with my complaints about bullying. Five months later, that boss was no longer with the company.

The time to stop bullying is right at the start. Don't let the situation drag on and become a he-said-she-said battle. Document, get witnesses, and go out of the chain of command with your complaint. If your organization has an ombudsman program, seek help from them. Bullying in the workplace is far too common.[8]

Even without bullying, a major health crisis alters your priorities. Before my diagnosis, with a retired husband and adult children, I had thought that I was finally in a position in which I could spread my wings and see how high I could fly as the dominant earner in my household. Just when I felt the family obligations were no longer a top concern, I found myself on the emotional roller coaster of quarterly monitoring for a recurrence of the cancer. I felt chained to the specialists, who had shepherded me through the illness and knew my complex medical history. I no longer wanted to relocate for better career opportunities.

For about five years the prospect that the next round of blood tests and PET, CT, or MRI scans would find a dangerous new tumor kept me focused on my health. Luckily for me, the expert's prognosis proved to be wrong. No tumors have been found since 2007. When my doctor admitted that his prognosis no longer applied and refused to provide a revised forecast, I discovered that what I wanted to do with the remainder my life had been permanently modified.

Personal crises or widespread cataclysmic events can drastically alter our aspirations and desires. An opportunity that we may consider irresistible at one point in our lives may at other times have lost its allure.

VALUE OF AN OPPORTUNITY

We are constantly faced with choices: work–life, cost–benefit (pain-gain), and risk–reward. In each case, we are mentally weighing the value of one alternative against another.

For millennia, two-pan balances have been used to compare the physical weight of disparate things. The classic statue of the "Lady Justice" is shown holding a two-pan balance. In a transaction whether it is purchasing vegetables, grain, or gold, a known weight is placed on one side to determine the purchase price of the item on the other side. Gold was weighed against the seeds from carob trees, which is why gold is designated as being so many carats. When I visited Burma in 2003, fruits and vegetables in market were weighed against old D-cell batteries. Determination of the relative value of intangible things including justice is much more difficult.

We never really know the value of the elusive opportunity we are chasing nor can we predict the full cost of our choices. As we make countless decisions, we should keep both our personal and professional objectives and priorities in mind.

One rather grim piece of advice that I find worthwhile is to write your own obituary. In other words, think of where you want to end up and work backward from that to devise a path to get there. If it is important to you to accomplish something that takes many years of work, get started immediately. If you keep postponing starting your walk down the path to that goal, you will never get there.

How much is a specific career opportunity worth? A promotion that comes with a raise can involve more work hours, more travel, or a move to a different location. There are many factors to consider:

- While the increase in compensation associated with the promotion can be viewed as one side of the balance, is that really how much more disposable money you will have?
- How important is this promotion as a stepping stone toward your long-term goals?
- If you decline the opportunity, how much will it harm your career?
- How well do you know your priorities and understand the long-term consequences of your decisions?
- Have you discussed the opportunity with your partner or are you assuming that you know his or her perspective?
- Do you care what your partner thinks?

Members of dual-career couples often respond differently to monetary incentives than dominant earners. Family adjustments associated with a lucrative opportunity may make it less appealing to people in dual-career couples. As in the following example, supervisors who are dominant earners may be perplexed by how a member of a dual-career couple responds to an opportunity.

Frank has worked at XCO, a large integrated company, for 30 years. About two years ago, Frank hired Jack, who had just finished his MBA. When he looks at Jack, Frank sees a younger version of himself. They went to the same state university and both majored in finance. Frank enjoys mentoring Jack and thinks that, with his help, Jack's career might be even more successful than his own.

Jack likes his supervisor, Frank, but Jack is not at all certain that he wants to stay with XCO long term. Jack recently married Maria, an app developer, who works for a well-funded technology company. Maria's employer provides unusually generous maternity benefits that are much better than XCO's. They would like to have at least two children and Jack has noticed that some more innovative companies offer far more paternity leave than XCO. Jack has been pondering when or if he should investigate changing jobs.

Both Jack and Maria receive about the same salary, but her compensation also includes stock options if she stays with the company for five years. They both recognize that the stock options might be worth a lot of money if the company has a successful product launch and that could make a big difference to their financial situation.

Frank thinks that Jack should get some experience at XCO's corporate headquarters and has secured a position for him in the strategic planning group. The new position would also mean a 20 percent raise for Jack. From Frank's perspective, this is a highly desirable opportunity. When Frank shares the good news with Jack, he is surprised that Jack doesn't immediately leap to accept the offer, but instead replies, "I'd like to speak with my wife before making a decision."

By the time he gets home, Jack is reasonably certain that he doesn't want to accept the position. Headquarters is located two time zones away, so commuting home over a weekend would be difficult. On top of that, he knows that strategic planning involves a lot last-minute rush work that spills into the evenings and weekends. It would be difficult to squeeze in traveling to see Maria a couple of times a month.

The lure of the position from Jack's perspective is the upward mobility. The position would put Jack on the fast track and could involve multiple relocations over the next few years. While his marriage might survive one short-term relocation, he doesn't think it will if they are working in different cities for multiple years.

When Jack discusses the offer with Maria and explains the implications for his career, Maria reminds him that it would be difficult to conceive a child if they only see each other occasionally. After witnessing the difficulty her older sister had getting pregnant, she senses her biologic clock ticking loudly. Not only is she reluctant to wait, but also she would like to take advantage of her company's generous maternity benefits. Maria suggests that it may be a good time for Jack to check out getting a position with a more dynamic local company or a start-up. They both think it would be easier for Jack to make the switch, before he gets too old.

After they jointly agree that Jack should decline the strategic planning position, Jack ponders how to deliver his decision to Frank. He decides to use the excuse that he doesn't want to be separated from Maria, because they are trying to have a baby.

The conversation with Frank doesn't go as Jack thought it would. When Jack explains why he and Maria don't want to engage in a commuting relationship, Frank counters, "Just take her with you. Although Maria thinks she will keep working after the baby, my experience is that she would rather stay home. My wife loved her job as a nurse, but as soon as we had our first child, we both agreed that it was best for her to quit. She has never regretted that decision. She loves picking out a new house when we move."

Frank is perplexed that he can't convince Jack to accept the position. He is left wondering, "Why did I waste so much of my time mentoring him?" In disgust Frank thinks, "Just let Jack find out how hard it is to get a promotion without a strong sponsor. That will show him what a big mistake he has made."

This example illustrates how differences in lifestyle and expectations can lead to conflict. Jack was in a no-win situation. If he moved to headquarters, he jeopardized critical long-term family plans. In saying no, not only has Jack lost his mentor, but also Frank's misreading the situation could lead to long-term conflict between the two of them. Jack would be wise to either transfer to a position that doesn't report to Frank or find a job with another company.

In other cases a person may be convinced that he or she wants to seize an opportunity that is accompanied by major complications. Suppose that Edith has been offered a promotion that comes with a significant raise and extra responsibilities that are likely to increase both the number of hours that she has to work and the frequency that she must travel. Edith has a one-year-old daughter, Madison. Her husband, Max, also has a demanding job that involves long hours and business travel. However, this is the type of opportunity that Edith has been hoping for and she doesn't want to let it slip away.

Edith investigates the availability of daycare with longer hours and overnight care. Currently, Madison is watched during business hours by Mary, a woman in her neighborhood, who is licensed to offer day-care in her home. Mary is reluctant to extend her hours, because her children are home in the evenings. After spending the day minding other people's children, at night Mary wants to devote herself to her own offspring and to assisting them with their homework. Knowing that Mary will resist a request for caring for Madison in the evenings, Edith offers to pay double the normal hourly rate for the extra time. Edith also persuades Mary to agree to take care of Madison overnight if both she and her husband must be away at the same time. Adding up the anticipated extra child care costs, Edith thinks that she will actually take home less money after expenses than she would if she didn't accept the promotion. However, Edith is confident that the promotion will enable her to continue to advance and is willing to sacrifice both time with her toddler and money to secure the opportunity.

Once Edith has made up her mind to accept the promotion and has the necessary child care arrangements in place, she discusses the situation with Max. Max points out that the extra income will put them into a higher income tax bracket, so accepting the promotion will after expenses yield less money than Edith anticipated. After a thorough discussion of the impact of the promotion on their finances and their discretionary time, Max and Edith agree that it is a good idea for her to accept the new post.

What if the tables were turned and a man, Kurt, is the one with the tantalizing promotion? Kurt comes home and announces, "Great news, Cathy, I just got promoted." Then he mentions that it means he will be working longer hours and that he will not be able to share as much of the child care and housework. Cathy reminds him that she is already stretched thin and sometimes must work late herself.

When Kurt suggests that Cathy negotiate leaving their toddler with Mary until later in the evening, Cathy objects. She retorts that Kurt should be the one to try to work out a deal with Mary since it is his promotion that is upsetting the status quo. Furthermore, because Kurt will be providing less help with the housework, Cathy proposes that they should have the team that cleans their house come twice as often.

After negotiating with Mary, Kurt comes back to discuss the situation with Cathy.

Kurt grouses, "Mary is going to charge so much for the extra hours, my entire raise and then some will be eaten up by Mary's charges."

Cathy points out, "If the promotion is as good as you say, in a year or two, you will be earning more than enough to cover the extra costs.

My career is important too and if we stint on child care, my earnings will suffer."

Kurt grumbles, "Given the extra expense of the additional child care, can't you make do with the existing frequency the cleaning crew comes?"

Cathy argues, "No, I don't like living in a pigsty. Why don't you mow the lawn instead of paying Ralph to do it? If you are working such long hours, you will need some exercise, so you may as well keep fit by mowing the lawn."

Kurt concedes, "Oh, all right, you win, we'll pay for more house cleaning."

Cathy has won. She persuaded Kurt to work out the logistics so that his promotion did not heap more of the domestic burden on her. She made the point that both of their careers are equally important and that she does not have primary responsibility for finding a solution when Kurt can't handle his share of the child care and household chores.

In the first case with Jack and Maria, the couple did not think the sacrifice of living apart was worthwhile for them. In contrast, in other two examples with Edith and Max and with Kurt and Cathy, the couples decided that the opportunity was worth the sacrifices that would result. There are no universal right or wrong answers. Each of us must assess what is right for our personal pain–gain balance.

QUESTIONABLE TRADE-OFF

Whether and when to have children are big decisions. Before fertility treatments and tests for genetic birth defects became readily available, women like myself who wanted to have children knew that their chances of having a healthy child declined with age. In that era, a first-time mother over the age of 35 was considered to be old.

Thanks to modern medicine, the time window in which a woman can expect to have a child has been significantly extended. Some employers offer fertility treatments as an employee benefit to provide their staff with greater flexibility. However, that doesn't mean that postponing maternity to get your career well established is necessarily a good idea.

In 2014, Apple and Facebook announced that they would provide as much as $20,000 for egg freezing as a benefit to their employees including the spouses of male employees. In an article about the new benefit, National Public Radio (NPR) quoted Marcy Darnovsky, executive director at the Center for Genetics and Society, "When you're in a situation of your employer offering you a choice, you really have to be careful that you're distinguishing between something that's an expanded option and something that's actually subtle or even explicit pressure to do what your employer wants you to do."[9]

NPR cautioned that, "While techniques and success rates are improving, there's no guarantee the procedure will lead to a baby down the road."[10]

Comprehensive studies are not yet available on the success of having babies born from frozen eggs. USC Fertility advises, "If 10 eggs are frozen, 7 are expected to survive the thaw, and 5 to 6 are expected to fertilize and become embryos. Usually 3–4 embryos are transferred in women up to 38 years of age. We therefore recommend that 10 eggs be stored for each pregnancy attempt. Most women 38 years of age and under can expect to harvest 10–20 eggs per cycle."[11]

USC Fertility notes, "To date, USC Fertility has cryopreserved the oocytes of more than 150 women. Of those who have returned for their eggs, 15 of 21 (65%) have delivered babies."[12]

How would you feel if you were in the 35 percent of those women, who have not been able to have a baby?

Women who are concerned enough about their future fertility to go through the invasive medical procedures entailed in egg freezing may be devastated if, for the sake of their career, they postpone attempting to have a baby beyond their normal fertility range and are subsequently unable to give birth. Accepting the offer of payment for egg freezing is like a Faustian pact with the devil. Your career may not be as successful as you dreamed and you could end up with no biological children of your own.

Some people who should be most aware of the risks are opting to postpone motherhood until midcareer. A female endocrinologist mentioned to me that many female doctors freeze their eggs, because their training, internships, and fellowships can last through their thirties. She said that because of the extended period of training in medicine, "midcareer" for doctors was their forties, not their thirties.

Women who delay childbirth and subsequently undergo expensive and difficult enhanced fertility procedures take maternity very seriously. Often the fertility procedures produce twins or greater multiple births that complicate pregnancy and make parenting even more daunting. Older parents are also more likely to have a special-needs child.

Although an older woman may have more financial assets to invest in hiring help to assist with parenting, she may feel that it was pointless to have children only to have little contact with them. Energy and physical resilience also decline with age, so if you postpone being a parent for the sake of your career, you may have more difficulty dealing with the sleep deprivation that bedevils the parents of infants and toddlers.

RELOCATION

In some organizations, geographic mobility is essentially a requirement for being on the fast track. Current management "paid their dues" by moving around the world in a "series of positions of increasing responsibility" and expects anyone who aspires to fill their shoes to do the same. Thus, advancing up the management ladder may involve multiple relocations including assignments in foreign countries. Equivalent experiences acquired without living in another area are deeply discounted when candidates are compared.

In organizations that prize geographic mobility, dual-career couples can be cut off from opportunity in various ways. The manager may assume that the person in a dual-career couple will not be willing to relocate, because of his or her partner's career. Alternatively, the company will ask people to make an open-ended declaration that they will be geographically mobile. Without the precommitment for an unknown opportunity, employees will not be considered for assignments that involve relocation. Individuals' careers can be impaired, because they are never given the opportunity to decide for themselves on specific opportunities unless they say yes to relocation in general and then veto a move that they find unacceptable.

A 2013 survey by the Society of Exploration Geophysicists (SEG) asked, "Would you be willing to accept a job that required relocation if your partner had to take a position that was less satisfying to them than their current employment?"[13] In that survey, there were negligible differences between equal-earner men and women with 43 percent of the women and 41 percent of the men willing to accept a relocation if their partner would have to take a less satisfying position. While the majority of the equal earners are not willing to force their partner to make sacrifices so that they could relocate, over 40 percent of them are.

When those in dual-career couples were asked in a SPE survey what their employer could do to make it easier for them to relocate, more than half of women and about 40 percent of men mentioned assistance with their partner's employment.[14] Despite the problems that can arise when both partners work for the same employer, about 15 percent of the women and 7 percent of the men in dual-career couples want their company to offer employment to their partner as part of the relocation assistance.

Dual-career couples who are willing to relocate should endeavor to negotiate additional employment assistance for the trailing partner. Large organizations often employ people in a wide range of occupations. To facilitate relocation, either when someone is first recruited or in conjunction with a subsequent relocation, the employer may be willing to hire the accompanying partner. Alternatively, employers can cover the cost of outplacement services (which can include career counseling, résumé writing workshops, interview skills training, and job search guidance) and headhunter fees for the trailing spouse. Outplacement provides training to the displaced person. A retained headhunter's role is to actively seek out job opportunities. Ideally, if your organization does not hire your trailing spouse, you want the cost of both outplacement and headhunter fees included in your relocation package.

International relocations can be far more stressful than domestic ones. Accompanying partners may have a lot of difficulty securing a visa that permits them to work. In many countries, the partner may be unable to secure a work visa. Language, cultural, and religious differences can be daunting. Living a long distance from family and friends in an unfamiliar culture can create a sense of isolation and be very stressful. The attitudes of every member of the family have tremendous impact on whether a foreign assignment is a positive and productive experience for the employee.

Male trailing spouses, who cannot find employment, may have a much more difficult time dealing with an international relocation than their female counterparts. "Expat" wives are not new or unusual, so often social networks exist for them. There are usually not comparable social groups for male trailing partners. This can increase the isolation and unhappiness of a male partner, who may also be struggling with the emotional issues associated with putting his career on hold.

In 2011, the Permits Foundation conducted an "International Mobility and Dual-Career Survey of International Employers" of 177 organizations that employed about 7.5 million people in both the private and public sectors.[15] That survey found that:

- 66 percent of employers report that dual-career and partner issues are becoming more important to their organizations;

- 51 percent of employers report that employees have turned down international assignments due to their partners' career or employment concerns;

- 21 percent of employers report that assignees have returned home early from an international assignment within the last three years because of concerns over their partners' career or employment.

Some organizations have joined alliances to provide mutual assistance in offering employment to trailing spouses in international relocations. Partnerjob.com was created by a group of companies to enhance international mobility of dual-career couples by providing a worldwide database through which partner organizations can contact potential candidates and where job seekers from those organizations can look for positions.

Even if both partners share an employer and are transferred together, they face more hurdles than an employee with a stay-at-home spouse, who can manage the move logistics. Dual-career couples, especially those with young children, do not have much spare time to research a new area. Child care is essential the first day both members of a dual-career couple begin working in a new location. Unfortunately, relatively few employers provide information or help arranging child care. Assistance with personal logistics including daycare, locating housing, and selecting health care providers could greatly reduce the stress of relocation.

If the level of support offered through standard policies does not meet your needs, try requesting more. It doesn't hurt to ask. If your employer highly values your experience and skills and/or you are difficult to replace, you are in a stronger negotiating position and can push harder for what you want.

People have drastically different perspectives regarding the circumstances under which they are willing to uproot their family. I have known many men and women who refuse to uproot their children during high school. It depends on you and your children whether or not a drastic change is a great or a terrible experience.

I went to public schools in Brooklyn until early in my senior year of high school and had never been west of eastern Pennsylvania. At the beginning of my senior year, there was protracted teacher's strike that I feared would never end. I complained so much that on just a few days' notice, my mother shipped me off to live with my aunt and uncle in Los Alamos, New Mexico, for the remainder of my senior year. It turned out to be a fabulous experience that I have always treasured.

In contrast, we didn't relocate from Texas to California until spring of my daughter's freshman year in college. Even so, she was very upset, because visiting her family in California during college breaks meant that she could not also see her childhood buddies in Texas. The summer following her freshman year, she insisted on working in Dallas and staying with some old friends.

For many people, the impact of relocation on the health and welfare of their children can be of paramount importance. "Zack" refused a promotion and transfer to company headquarters, because he had a special-needs child. In his current location, Zack's family had a doctor, who they felt was providing excellent care for their child. The new location also offered access to excellent health care, but Zack didn't want to switch doctors. Zack quit rather than move. Subsequently, he joined another company that offered advancement without relocation.

Other families relish the adventure and thrive. One woman, "Julie," with two young children and a husband who also worked for the same company felt that the inexpensive household help available in the remote camp where she lived in Indonesia enabled her to continue full-time employment and professional society activities when her children were toddlers.

I met Julie when I visited the camp. I flew into the camp on a helicopter and left the same way. Helicopters were used because the alternative was a long drive over hazardous roads to the nearest city with a commercial airport. During my two-day visit, I never left the camp.

Julie and her family lived within the camp fence. Her commute was negligible. She could work long hours, because she had a full-time nanny, a cook, a houseboy, and a gardener. Her family was thriving in the remote camp environment.

Julie may have been much happier than the nonworking spouses, because she had a very busy work schedule. In some remote locations, isolation and boredom lead some people to become alcoholics, even in countries in which alcohol is officially banned.

Employers can support dual-career couples and encourage employees to pursue preferred career paths by providing mentoring, role models, additional logistical support, and extra time. The unknown is both terrifying and tantalizing. We seek out adventure travel to locations that offer what are for us exotic cultures and sights, but we want guide books to explain what we will encounter and human guides to smooth our path and protect us from harm. Role models and mentors are the tour guides of the business world.

If you have been asked to move to a new location, talk to others in your company who have transferred there from your current location or from a similar area. If you have school-age children you should talk with a person who is familiar with the schools and/or child care options. If you don't know anyone in the new area or someone who has lived there, ask human resources or your new supervisor if they can put you in touch with someone whose family situation is similar to yours.

A dual-career couple needs more time than a dominant earner couple to make a decision on whether or not to accept relocation. The person being transferred and his or her partner must understand the partner's employment opportunities in the new location, the impact on both partners' careers, and the financial consequences.

A relocation package that provides an economic incentive for a family with a sole breadwinner could be an economic disaster for a dual-career couple, because the other partner's current and future income is adversely impacted. For equal-earner couples, a raise is unlikely to make up for the loss of the partner's job. If both partners are earning the same amount of money and the relocation means the trailing spouse will lose his or her job and be unable to work for the duration of the assignment, the wages of the relocating employee would have to be doubled to make up for the loss of the spouse's income.

You have a lot to consider. Ask yourself:

- How will your career benefit from the relocation?
- What are the job opportunities like for your "trailing spouse" in the new location?
- Does the new location offer the medical and educational services that your family needs?
- If your partner can't or won't move, is some form of a commuting marriage feasible and acceptable?
- How would maintaining two residences impact your relationship, your children, and your finances?
- Is the offer so good that your spouse is willing to take time off or give up his/her career to follow?
- What are the consequences of saying no to the relocation?

If a person thinks an opportunity provides sufficient upside, he or she is often willing to accept conditions that he or she would avoid in the abstract. More than half of equal-earner men and women are willing to relocate for valuable experience. Men and women whether an equal earner or a dominant earner are about as likely to be willing to accept an international assignment. People in dual-career couples who are willing to relocate should make it very clear to their management that they are interested, so that they don't miss opportunities as a result of their boss making false assumptions about their mobility.

LIVING APART

A 2013 survey by the SEG (that polled individuals, not couples) found that 40 percent of equal-earner men and 46 percent of equal-earner women have lived apart for work-related reasons.[16] However, 52 percent of those responding to that survey said that they were not willing to separate for work-related reasons.

In that survey, willingness to separate varied. For an opportunity to earn more money, 16 percent of the equal-earner men and 11 percent of the equal-earner women were willing to live apart. Rotational assignments that involve living apart for about half of the time were acceptable to 21 percent of the equal-earner men and 11 percent of the equal-earner women. Even more equal earners, 27 percent of the women and 22 percent of the men, responded that they would live apart if they could easily commute to be together on weekends.

Sometimes, the only way both members of a couple can find acceptable employment is to work in locations that are too far apart for daily commuting. In other instances, a deliberate decision is made to have a commuting marriage so that one or both partners can take advantage of an attractive opportunity. Either way the separations can be a strain on the relationship.

Organizations offer 14- or 28-day rotational assignments in places in which it is difficult or prohibitively expensive to provide facilities to support the families of staff members. The time it takes to reach the work location, which can be more than 24 hours, is part of the time-off period, so that there is always a person in the role on site.

People may take on rotational work within their own country or as expatriates. When I flew more than a thousand miles from Santiago to the Atacama Desert in northern Chile, the plane was full of people on 14-day rotations to the remote mines. In Canada when the heavy oil projects were under development in northern Alberta, people went there on rotational assignments from all over the country. I spoke with women from Newfoundland, who rotated to Fort McMurray to work in administrative and medical positions. All around the world, people take on periodic, long-distance commutes that may involve living in communal housing.

A friend of mine, "Steve," met his current wife when they were both working 28–28 rotations in Nigeria. Steve had previously been married and never told me why he got divorced. However, he was convinced that rotational assignments destroyed marriages.

Certain locations acquire a particularly bad reputation for breaking up marriages, so that may be a factor in a couple's decision as to whether or not to accept a specific opportunity. In some impoverished countries, local women view unaccompanied expatriate men as a way out of poverty. When the Soviet Union fell apart, Western companies sent numerous unaccompanied people to look for new business opportunities there. Many long-term marriages that had survived previous separations ended, because the local ladies focused all of their charms on expatriate men. A couple's willingness to separate may depend on the reputation of the location.

It wasn't just the former Soviet Union that was a problem. I once had a boss, "George," who met his wife when she was his secretary in Indonesia. George was personable, but I didn't think he was particularly handsome, so I was surprised when friends cautioned me that George's Indonesian wife was insanely jealous. I heard that George had to be relocated from his former posting, because of his crazy wife. His wife had smashed her car into the front of an office building, because she thought that the reason George claimed to be working late was actually another woman. Friends warned me that George's wife had threatened every woman who worked for him. His wife thought he was such a desirable prize that he had to be closely guarded. Sure enough, I got a call from her, asking to speak to him. I just pretended that I didn't know George and she never called again.

What types of family separations you find acceptable is a highly personal decision. For some, the motivation is a "carrot." It is the attraction of an opportunity, whether to earn more money, gain valuable experience, or have adventures. For others, the separation is more painful and is driven by a "stick." Accepting an undesirable position could be a financial imperative, because of lack of locally available jobs.

PERSONAL CHOICES

Once when I was flying from San Francisco to Houston, I sat next to a "dead heading" female pilot, who was traveling home to Florida from San Francisco after working flights back and forth across the Pacific. We talked about what it was like being a woman in a male-dominated profession. She was married to another pilot and they had raised three sons. They chose to coordinate their shifts and have a nanny care for their children while they were both away. Their preference was to be together as a family when they were off duty rather than to alternate shifts so that one parent was always home. Her children were grown and she was very pleased with how the situation had worked out.

Other people may think that it is more important that one parent always be home with the children. In some ways leaving teenagers in the care of someone other than a parent can be at least as risky as hiring caregivers for infants and toddlers.

When my daughter was in high school, both my husband and I had to be away at the same time. While I was away for over a week, he was gone for only a few days. I returned home first and was surprised to find our daughter at home, when she was supposed to be staying with friends. I was gullible enough to believe her cover story, but when my husband got home, he called the police and got the details on the party they had broken up at our home.

My daughter swore up and down that it was the only time she ever had a party at our house while we were away. However, when you tell lies, you must have a very good memory. My daughter's recall wasn't good enough. At her graduation from Dartmouth, she shared a story about her misadventures in high school, but the story was about a different party than the one we officially knew about. When she realized the discrepancy between the party that I knew about and the one she described, she said, "In high school, I managed information so that you wouldn't worry too much," I decided that it was appropriate that she was starting law school in the fall. The takeaway is that even a "good kid" (as she often described herself in high school when I interrogated her on some aspect of her behavior) can get into a lot of mischief if a parent isn't at home.

Although people in dual-career couples share many of the same challenges, they also have different hopes, dreams, priorities, and preferences. What constitutes an irresistible opportunity varies from person to person and often changes with time for a single individual. The dream job before becoming a parent can turn into the job from hell when the person becomes a parent.

One size does not fit all. A good analogy is clothing that is labeled, "one size fits all." These garments often fail to fit anyone well. For opportunities to be alluring, they need to fit the individual.

Benko and Weisberg of Deloitte LLC recognized the benefits of making individual adjustments to standardized career paths and presented the case for what they termed "mass career customization" to "align the workplace with today's nontraditional workforce." They wrote about the need to better accommodate nonlinear careers and argued that greater flexibility is required to promote greater diversity in leadership.[17]

More and more people around the world are part of dual-career couples. Greater diversity means increased variation in the types of opportunities people want. Even for the same person, the opportunities that excite and motivate him or her evolve and change as he or she progresses through different stages of life.

The fact that different people crave different types of opportunities is what makes negotiations possible. If everyone placed the same value on everything, negotiations would be extremely difficult if not impossible. Fortunately, one person's dream job is another's job from hell. Therefore, we can afford to pay someone to do a task that we prefer not to do.

If people felt more secure in sharing their goals and aspirations, it would be easier to match people to the best and most rewarding use of their talents. However, when a manager doesn't consider it feasible for both members of a couple to pursue high-powered careers, it is unlikely that the manager can have honest and constructive career development discussions with a subordinate who is part of a dual-career couple. The situation can easily deteriorate into an unpleasant conflict. If you are faced with that situation, find another position with a more congenial boss either in that organization or elsewhere. Alternatively, you can carefully manage what you say to avoid limiting your opportunities. The odds of changing the manager's mind are low.

COMMUNICATION

If your boss thinks that people in dual-career couples must mimic the lifestyle and work patterns of sole breadwinners to advance, discussions can go in circles or be confrontational. You can't wait for traditional, dominant earner superiors to see the light. You must make the extra effort required to devise a constructive way to communicate.

If you don't explain to your supervisor what you want and ask politely, your chances of getting it are vanishingly small. Be prepared to have a reason for your request that you think has a chance of resonating with your manager. Even if you are initially refused, your request may linger in the back of your boss's mind. Let me share what happened to me when I tried this approach.

I was not getting good vibes from my new boss, "Hank." My prior supervisor had retired and half of the people in his group had been terminated as a result of a reorganization and downsizing. Seeing respected, hard-working colleagues fired had left me terrified that I would lose my job in the next round of layoffs.

In my first post-reorganization meeting with Hank, he volunteered that since I was assigned to a different type of work than I had done in the past, it was highly unlikely that I would be able to earn an above average rating for that year. When Hank gave me that forecast, I thought that I was trapped. No matter what I did, I could not win. I worried that Hank was not going to give me a good rating and therefore I would be doomed in the next cycle of staff reduction.

Years earlier when Hank was my boss's boss, he told me, "You can't have a younger woman supervising older men." This time he gave me an equivalent message. Hank informed me that I would be working on a team headed by a younger man. He said, "Jeff is going places. You should call him, 'sir.'"

To make matters worse, I was convinced that Jeff's team was over-staffed. I was afraid that I was trapped in a no-win situation with a bull's-eye on my forehead. I wracked my brain as to what I could do. My husband was refusing to relocate. With two kids, I didn't want to split the household.

Since my high school days, I had dreamed of being a research scientist. With little work in the technology niche to which I was assigned, I asked around and found an empty niche. My cultivation of new internal clients was successful in bringing in work, but I was still anxious. Given Hank's attitude, I realized that my best chance of surviving was to leave research.

I had served as a technical consultant for the new business development group that was located about 10 miles across town. I decided to ask for a transfer and made an appointment to talk with Hank. The conversation did not go as I had hoped. In response to my request, Hank bounced the responsibility for finding another position back to me, saying that I would need to develop contacts myself to see if an opening was available. You can imagine my surprise when a week later with no advance warning Hank showed up and introduced me to my new boss in business development, "George."[18]

Subsequently, I learned that to balance headcount, Hank and George were trying to arrange a swap of people between the two groups. New business development was required to shift a specific individual to research to provide ongoing engineering support following an acquisition. Hank refused to relinquish the engineer that George wanted in exchange. Someone had to be move, so, because I had asked, I got picked. I didn't have many of the skills required for the position, but I started learning as fast as I could. The first six months were terrifying, especially because it was a period of downsizing, but it was worth it.

Six years later when my employer, Mobil, was in what turned out to be a year-long process of obtaining government approval to merge with Exxon, I decided that it was a perfect opportunity to investigate job opportunities. I didn't know what the precise timing of the merger would be, but I knew that the status quo was not an option. I anticipated that I could not remain employed with the merged company without relocating, so it would be my choice as to whether or not to accept the severance package. I wanted to have evaluated all of my alternatives, by the time I had to make a decision.

My career shift from research to new business development turned out to be invaluable. The chief technology officer (CTO) at Chevron told me that since I had demonstrated the ability to reinvent myself, he would give me the opportunity to do so again. The lure of that opportunity was so enticing that I grabbed the severance package as soon as I could and quit before finding out what ExxonMobil would offer me. Subsequently, the CTO gave me several opportunities to take on radically different roles with steep learning curves.

SPONSORS

Unless you just get lucky the way I was when I got transferred from research to business development, it can be very difficult to get the position you want without a well-placed sponsor. Being good and motivated is not sufficient. Beyond entry-level "social promotions," sponsors become increasingly important in determining who is selected for a highly competitive position. You rarely can break into the executive ranks without a sponsor.

A sponsor is different than a mentor. Many people can mentor you by providing advice. Peers can mentor each other. In contrast, a sponsor is an influential person, who can speak on your behalf and support your candidacy for highly sought after positions.

Loss of a critical sponsor can halt a promising career in its tracks. Over my decades in the workplace, I have seen highly talented people have their careers come to a screeching halt when their sponsor leaves or falls out of favor. Ideally, you have more than one sponsor, so that if one leaves, retires, or loses power, you have other allies.

You don't acquire sponsors by approaching people and asking them if they will sponsor you. Sometimes the stars align and you have someone see you in action and decide that you are someone he or she wants to support. This happened to me in my volunteer activities with the SPE. Without my knowledge, several men whom I considered to be casual acquaintances kept recommending me for positions of increasing responsibility.

One of the men, Ed Mayer, had a wife who was a judge. When we first met, Ed was a member of the SPE board of directors. He was the board's liaison at a couple of committee meetings in which I was a participant. Our contact was so fleeting, that I was scarcely aware of Ed's existence, but he began putting my name forward for important society roles.

Another key sponsor, Aziz Odeh, had two daughters, one a doctor and the other a petroleum engineer. Aziz was the senior scientist in Mobil's research lab. His daughter also worked there and was a collaborator with me on several important projects. He was the go-to person for the top people in the SPE. Without my realizing that he was doing it, Aziz would strongly support my candidacy for professional society positions.

Years later, I had a third key sponsor, Andrew, who had a wife, who was a doctor, and three daughters. Andrew overlapped with me for a couple of years the first time I served on the SPE board of directors. About a decade later, Andrew Young became president of the society and called to ask me if he could nominate me for a presidential term.

I never sought out any of these men to ask them to be my sponsor. Ed stayed very much in the background, so it was years before I figured out the key role that he had played. These three men shaped my life by serving as my sponsors. With their support, I was amazingly fortunate in the volunteer organization.

I have always wondered what prevented Aziz from providing comparably valuable support for me within Mobil. Without sponsors at work, I did not fare as well in my paid employment as I did in my volunteer activities.

You should not wait to be discovered. At work, one approach is to make yourself invaluable to a person who is talented and moving up in the organization. You want someone who doesn't see you as competition and understands and appreciates your personal constraints. If you work hard and make that person look good, you have a chance of progressing behind him or her as he or she advances.

There is a natural tendency for people to support someone like them. Dual-career couples are an invisible form of diversity and face discrimination from those who think that high flyers must have the dominant career in their household. Until members of dual-career couples make greater inroads into upper management, it will be difficult to find an executive in a dual-career relationship to serve as your sponsor. However, as in my case, although relatively scarce, there are some well-placed dual-career couple people, who can be in a position to help you.

Even if you don't share a lifestyle with a sponsor, you may be able to leverage other affinity factors to secure a sponsor. Downplay your differences, and leverage any similarities that you have whether it is an alma mater, a home town, a particular professional society, or a common hobby. Over the course of your career, you benefit if you have multiple supporters.

BALANCING PRIORITIES

One of the most difficult things can be really knowing what you want. I have often felt that it is easier to look at a specific opportunity and decide whether or not it satisfies my priorities and is a good fit, than to describe what I want. In the instances in which I have identified an opportunity and asked for it, I have had good luck.

In assessing what you want, I have found it valuable to look at the implications of that opportunity in terms of Maslow's hierarchy of needs. Would the opportunity be a net advance overall or would it undermine my need for love and belonging? Would I be comfortable with the job security risks associated?

There is an old saying that, "No one on their deathbed ever wished that they had spent another day in the office." Nonetheless, we want the things that the money we earn from working can buy. Often even if we have plenty of money, we tend to want more. But money doesn't buy happiness. The key is balance.

CHAPTER 7

How to Secure Necessary Flexibility

When I was working for Chevron as a corporate venture capital executive, I'd often hear the question about an investment opportunity, "Is it a vitamin or an aspirin?" The reason for the question was potential backers want to know if the start-up company's product is a "nice to have" or a "must have" item. Vitamins can be beneficial, but unless someone is suffering from a serious vitamin deficiency, they are merely nice to have. On the other hand, if you have a throbbing headache, the need for an aspirin or other painkiller is urgent.

Employers often regard flexible work arrangements as nice to have, but not essential. They may have family-friendly benefits in theory, but the organization's culture is such that people are reluctant to make use of them, because they think that doing so will damage their careers. When only a few people take advantage of the options, management may mistakenly believe that paternity leave and flexible work arrangements are not important for the majority of the workforce—just "vitamins."

For members of dual-career couples, especially those with children, work schedule flexibility is often indispensable, like getting an aspirin for unrelenting pain. Flexible work arrangements are a crucial tool that can enable members of dual-career couples to create a sustainable integration of their work and life and achieve an acceptable pain–gain balance. Having choices puts them in greater control over how they allocate their time.

Studies on the "sense of control" indicate that merely having a choice of alternatives can make a critical difference.[1] The need to feel in control is deeply ingrained in human nature as a mechanism for survival. We are programmed to be more willing to take risks if we feel that we are in charge of the situation. The classic example is that when something is to be cut, if you have control of the knife, you are willing to position your hand much closer to the blade than if someone else holds the knife. Another example is pain control. If you are confined to a hospital bed and have control over the administration of your pain medication, you feel better and may use a lower dose than if you must wait for a nurse. For those suffering from an adverse work–life balance, access to flexible work arrangements is a cherished form of pain relief.

New parents, who are overwhelmed with infant care, lack of sleep, and work stress, can find comfort in knowing they have choices of leave, part-time, and telework. They can actively make decisions as to how to achieve better balance. Ultimately, even if you chose not to exercise any of the options available to you and to stick with the status quo, you have the satisfaction of being in charge. A sense of control helps us to survive hard times.

WORK–LIFE INTEGRATION

In the absence of hired help managing the home front, work–life integration is a major challenge for people in dual-career couples. In Chapter 6, which explored the importance of "opportunity," the focus was on the "carrot" or "gain" side of work–life balance and what entices us to make personal sacrifices. In contrast, in this chapter the focus shifts to the "stick" or "pain" side and how to manage the challenging logistics that arise when both adult members of a household work.

The Families and Work Institute reported that, as of 2008 in the United States, both people were employed outside of the home in 80 percent of couples.[2] Furthermore as of 2010, 71 percent of women with children were part of the workforce. On average the women in these dual-earner couples provided 45 percent of the household income, making the members of those couples what I refer to as "equal earners."

The increase in families in which both parents work full time has coincided with an escalation in the time fathers spend engaged in child care. From 1977 to 2008, the average number of workday hours fathers spent with their children increased from 2 to 3.1. Not surprisingly, the Families and Work Institute found that 49 percent of the fathers in dual-career couples complained about work–family conflict.[3]

According to the Pew Research Center, about 60 percent of two-parent households with children under age 18 have two working parents.[4] Overall 53 percent of working parents with children under age 18 report that it is difficult for them to balance the obligations of their job with their family responsibilities. Fathers spend an average of 7 hours per week on child care and mothers spend twice as much, 14 hours per week. Worrying that the increased time with their kids was still insufficient, 46 percent of the fathers and 23 percent of the mothers criticized themselves for not spending sufficient time with their children. The Pew Research Center (consistent with the findings of the Families and Work Institute) determined that balancing work and family is difficult for 56 percent of the working mothers and 50 percent of the working fathers.

Fathers are much more engaged than when I was a child in the 1950s and 1960s. My father worked late, so I rarely saw my father on weekdays. My father's stress came not from being torn between household duties and work, but from the burdens of his work. He would get headaches every Sunday afternoon, because of the tension of having to show up in court on Monday morning as a defense attorney, not because he was worried about who would get us to the dentist or handle other household anomalies.

Although my mother had worked as a fashion illustrator for many years prior to marriage, she stopped working after her third child was born. She found that after having three children in four years, she could not even handle working part-time from home. She did not return to working professionally until the youngest of my four siblings was about seven years old and then she worked from home reinventing herself in a new career as a children's book illustrator and author.

Although my mother was not in paid employment when I was young, she provided less supervision than is expected now. We were shooed out of the house to play, but with some strict instructions. Notably, we were forbidden to play in the street in Brooklyn, New York, which prevented us from joining in the stickball games. I would hunt for empty bottles in the shrubbery and take them to the corner candy store to exchange for pennies. Then I used my pennies to buy chewing gum and candy that was prohibited by my mother. By the time I was eight years old and in third grade, I was responsible for walking two of my younger siblings to and from school. In grade school, I was riding the New York City subways and buses by myself. In those days, it was completely acceptable. Now, I suspect it would be frowned on as inadequate adult supervision.

Today, parents are living in a pressure cooker world. Not only are parents expected to ensure that their elementary school–age children are constantly supervised, but also they are supposed to spend more quality time with them. Children's time is increasingly structured with parents feeling obliged to transport their offspring to numerous activities. Adding to all of that, with modern communications, work intrudes into the home 24/7.

Many parents barely have time to breathe and may argue about who will be more penalized by making use of available work flexibility if home repairs or child care issues require one of the parents to be available during business hours. With virtually no disposable time, competition for precious personal time to recharge is another potential source of friction between the overextended parents of young children. For these working parents, flexibility is not a luxury; it is essential to survival.

According to the Families and Work Institute, 71 percent of non-professionals and 56 percent of professionals think that using work flexibility options to handle personal or family needs will negatively impact their careers.[5] That study found that employees, both professional and nonprofessional, who believed that they could be flexible, experienced much greater job satisfaction, greater business engagement, and better physical health and were more likely to stay with their current employer than those with less workplace flexibility.

Many companies offer various forms of flexibility, but the trick to making such programs work is that they must provide flexibility without long-term penalties. Everyone should be convinced that they can make use of the flexibility without damaging their career. If employees think using flexible work arrangements will damage their career, they will avoid using the benefits.

The Pew Research Center reported that 70 percent of working mothers and 48 percent of working fathers with children under age 18 say that having a flexible work schedule is extremely important to them.[6] Furthermore, of those with no minor children, 43 percent of the working women and 36 percent of their male counterparts say that a flexible work schedule is extremely important. Everyone wants access to flexibility.

Working Mother concluded that, "When flexibility is positioned as a working mothers' issue, it can wreak havoc on employee attitudes. Colleagues may see working mothers as having special status, and feel that they are left to pick up the slack."[7] Furthermore, Working Mother concludes that "flexibility has progressed from being a 'nice to have' to a necessity for millions of workers—whether male or female, parents or not."

Flexibility can come in myriad forms including the following:

1. Standard-length workdays with flexible starting and ending times
2. Compressed workweeks
3. Reduced work or part-time work
4. Job sharing
5. Telecommuting
6. Family leave—time off for care of sick family members
7. Extended paternity leave and maternity leave
8. "Stop the tenure clock" for academics
9. On-site child care

Jobs that do not require full-time presence at specific times in a specific location allow for greater flexibility. Mobile phones, computers, and the Internet have cut the chains that required many people to work on-site. Conference call systems allow workers at multiple sites including those working from home to collaborate. On-site presence is no longer required for many types of work. People want the discretion to adapt their work schedule to optimize integration of work and life, while preserving future opportunities to advance.

The first six forms of flexibility can be worthwhile for someone of any age or gender. Of those alternatives, the first four may be utilized even if physical presence at the business site is required. The fifth choice, telecommuting, is more applicable to some occupations than to others. The seventh, eighth, and ninth options are all parental benefits, but apply whether or not the parent is part of a dual-career couple, a dominant earner, sole breadwinner, or a single parent.

From an employer's perspective, paid leaves can be among the most costly and disruptive form of flexibility. Leaves create staffing discontinuities that can be difficult to bridge. However, for the individuals impacted, time at home can have a huge impact on their subsequent relationship with their family and their enthusiasm about work. In the detailed discussion of different types of flexibility, I will start with the various types of leave and then return to the workstyle alternatives.

PATERNITY LEAVE

In her bestseller, *Lean In: Women, Work, and the Will to Lead*, Sheryl Sandberg exhorted women to "lean in" at work. Far fewer people remember her equivalent call for men to "lean in" at home, but that advice is at least as valuable. She wrote, "We all need to encourage men to lean in to their families."[8]

Sandberg emphasized, "As women must be more empowered at work, men must be more empowered at home. I have seen many women inadvertently discourage their husbands from doing their share by being too controlling or critical."[9]

Furthermore, Sandberg advised women: "Whenever a married woman asks me for advice on coparenting with a husband, I will tell her to let him put the diaper on the baby any way he wants as long as he is doing it himself. And if he gets up to deal with the diaper before being asked, she should smile even if he puts the diaper on the baby's head."[10]

I'm a generation older than Sandberg. My husband, who "drove ships" when he was a National Oceanic and Atmospheric Administration commissioned officer fulfilling his equivalent of military service, likes to say that, "the man has to be there for the laying of the keel, but not the launching of the ship." In other words, after conception, the man's role is optional. Men of his generation viewed that any portion of the child care they assumed was a sign of being incredibly "liberated."

When our children were born, we had no relatives nearby to assist. Still, there was no question of him taking any more time off than was needed to take me home from the hospital. Although my husband was much more involved than my father, it wasn't until I saw my son in action as a new parent that I realized how engaged a father could be.

My son took off two weeks after his first daughter's birth. He was the one who demonstrated to me his wife's methods for diaper changing and baby bathing. Even a couple of weeks of paternity leave can help the father overcome many of his inhibitions about the more daunting aspects of child care. The patterns initiated during a paternity leave tend to continue throughout the child-rearing period.

My son and daughter-in-law are both employed full time as PhD engineers. However, despite my son's active role in many aspects of child-rearing, it is clear that my daughter-in-law is still carrying more than half of the load in terms of feeding and soothing the children.

They both need to travel for their work. When my son is gone, my daughter-in-law manages all of the child care alone in his absence. In contrast, when she travels, my son asks for assistance from his mother-in-law or myself. I kidded him about it, but he admitted that if he carried the full load by himself for three or four evenings, he would be a wreck.

Studies confirm my personal observations about the importance of paternity leave in the long-term engagement of fathers in child care. Rehel conducted interviews with 50 fathers working for a single financial firm in Chicago, Toronto, and Montreal and 35 of their female partners. She perceived a big difference between fathers who took an extended leave of three weeks or more and the others. "Extended leave challenges the perceived naturalness of women's superior parenting capabilities by providing men with time to develop a similar sense of parenting through hands-on experience. Being present provides insight into what needs to be done, while extended exposure enables participation and practice. Fathers, then, are able to move from the helper role to that of co-parent."[11]

The Canadian fathers in Rehel's study had access to state-supported leave that could be supplemented by the company to provide six weeks at 90 percent of their salary. Even so, 70 percent of the fathers in Toronto and 30 percent of those in Quebec chose not to use the generous leave. "The most commonly cited reason for not taking more extended time off was a concern for how this would be perceived by supervisors, colleagues, and, sometimes, clients."[12]

Having taken two weeks off after the birth of his first child and a week after the second, my son is much more of a co-parent than my husband was. However, he has not reached the level of parenting expertise that Rehel observed for fathers who took longer parental leave.

Huerta et al. analyzed data from four countries—Australia, Denmark, United Kingdom, and the United States—to determine how leave policies affect father's engagement with their offspring. They concluded that, "Fathers who take leave, especially those taking two weeks or more, are more likely to carry out childcare related activities when children are young."[13]

In a workforce that has a large percentage of women, paternity leave may pay off for the employers through reduced attrition of mothers, because of greater support at home from their male partners. The International Labour Organization conducted a detailed study of paternity and maternity leave policies around the world that concludes, "In order to achieve both women's and men's full potential in all realms, policies need to change traditional social attitudes and behaviours by recognizing men's right to parenthood and actively encouraging a shift towards a model in which men act as active co-parents rather than helpers of their women partners. This is crucial for the development of a more equitable division of labour in the home, which is the premise for gender equality at work."[14]

In most developed countries, men have access to paid paternity leave; Scandinavian countries are amongst the most generous with Finland offering 54 days, Iceland providing 3 months, Norway reserving 14 weeks of parental leave for fathers, and Sweden granting 10 days of paternity leave plus 2 months of paid parental leave reserved for each parent.[15] Australia provides 14 days. The United Kingdom allows two weeks and nine other European countries provide at least 10 paid days. In contrast, the Society for Human Resource Management reported in 2014 that only about 14 percent of U.S. companies offered any paid paternity leave and that percentage had not improved since 2005.[16]

In the United States, employers that offer the most generous policies tend to be in technology, finance, and professional services. Netflix proclaimed in 2015 that it planned to offer unlimited paid paternity leave in the first year after a child's birth or adoption. Facebook gives employees four months. Goldman Sachs and Morgan Stanley fund 16 weeks. Bank of America, Dow Jones, Google, and Microsoft allow 12 weeks and Twitter provides 10 weeks.

It is wonderful that these companies have taken such an impressive lead in providing paid paternity leave. However, there is still the key issue of whether or not male employees feel that using some or all of the leave will damage their career. Ron Lieber, a columnist for the *New York Times*, shared in August 2015 that he was planning to take his second paternity leave this year. Mr. Lieber emphasized that Mark Zuckerberg, CEO of Facebook, "may have the biggest opportunity to help members of the paternity fraternity by using every last day of his leave. Without prominent men in high-performing organizations making parental leave the default choice, the mainstreaming of paid leave for fathers will take a lot longer."[17]

Mark Zuckerberg took two months of paternity leave. He stayed away from his office, but how much time he worked during that time is subject to speculation[18].

A 2011 Society of Petroleum Engineers (SPE) survey of people in the petroleum industry revealed that men in Norway took longer paternity leaves than other men.[19] Most Norwegian men reported taking between 9 and 12 weeks, which is slightly less than the amount of paid parental leave reserved for them, but 15 percent of the Norwegian men took more, which is consistent with using the entire amount of leave to which they were entitled. In the United States, 46 percent of men took one to two weeks, which is more than men from other countries (excluding Norway), but less than the three weeks that Rehel thinks are required to advance from helping to co-parenting. However, 39 percent of the American fathers recounted that they took no paternity leave.

Women should encourage their partners to take paternity leave, because of the long-term benefits in shifting men from helping to co-parenting. When fathers are in the helping mode, they tend to participate more in the "fun" aspects of child care, leaving mothers to handle the more labor-intensive tasks such as preparing children's meals, feeding, and bathing. A few weeks of fathers' engagement at the outset can have long-term payoff in the form of more equal division of labor.

Rehel observed that some fathers did not utilize any of the time that could be shared by the parents.[20] Several of these men informed Rehel that their female partners wanted to use as much of the shared leave as they could get. If mothers want their mates to more equally bear the burden of feeding, bathing, and soothing their offspring, they should not hog the family leave. Men need the family leave time to become engaged in the nitty-gritty-poopy of child-rearing.

If more men make use of the paternity interlude available to them, women benefit from more than just increased co-parenting. When both men and women suspend their careers to take family leave, discrimination against women will decline, because the expense and disruption of parental leave will be more gender-neutral.

Gradually men may be becoming less worried about a stigma attached to using paternity leave. In California in the first 10 years after the inauguration of paid family leave, claims filed by men increased by more than 400 percent. In 2013, just over 30 percent of all of the family leave claims were filed by 65,513 men.[21]

A quote in the California program's tenth anniversary report reveals how one man's positive experience encouraged other men to make use of the program.

A few months before our son was due, I researched my options for spending the most amount of time at home with my family. It was vital for me to help with our transition from the hospital to our home, and support my wife in any way possible. Paid Family Leave was invaluable to me as a new father, and my wife, as she delivered via C-section and needed a lot of help with the baby while she recovered. Once I returned to work, many of my coworkers who were also soon-to-be fathers heard about my time off and used Paid Family Leave to support their spouses and spend time with their newborns.[22]

Men can prepare themselves for taking paternity leave by talking with other men who have done so. Mentors are especially important when you are dealing with the unknown and feel that you are taking significant risks. Coaching from a man in a similar situation, who has taken time to care for an infant and suffered no negative consequences, can prepare you for the experience and provide you with tips to minimize any collateral damage.

If you know that you want to be a father and hope to take time for bonding with your newborn, compare family leave policies when you consider job offers. Discrete inquiries about the corporate culture can determine if people routinely use the benefits. If the company is inhospitable to using paternity leave, the odds are that employees are uncomfortable leveraging other types of flexibility.

MATERNITY LEAVE

Parenthood is a newborn sprint that is followed by a marathon. Mothers who return to work after only six to eight weeks of maternity leave may still be physically exhausted. In the absence of support of extended family, working mothers need the support of their partner and their employer to stay the course.

All developed countries except the United States offer 13 or more weeks of paid maternity leave.[23] In most of those countries, the cost is covered by "social insurance." The United States is the only industrialized nation in the world that does not provide any government-guaranteed, paid maternity leave. According to the Department of Labor, only 12 percent of employees in the private sector in the United States have access to any paid family leave.[24]

In the United States, women with short-term disability insurance generally receive six weeks of sick leave for a simple vaginal birth. A cesarean delivery or other complications may add a few additional weeks.

The U.S. Family and Medical Leave Act (FMLA) of 1993 entitles employees to use up to 12 weeks of unpaid, job-protected leave for specified family and medical reasons if certain qualifications are satisfied. You are eligible if you work for the federal, state, or local government, or for a company that has 50 or more employees working within 75 miles of your work location and you have worked for your employer for at least 12 months and for at least 1,250 hours during the previous year (an average of 25 hours per week for 50 weeks). However, your employer isn't required to save your job for you if you are among the highest paid 10 percent of workers at your company and your employer can demonstrate that your absence would cause substantial economic harm to the organization.

If you and your partner work for separate qualifying employers, you each are eligible for the full 12 weeks. However, if you and your partner share an employer, you share the time allotted for FMLA leave and must split the 12 weeks if you are using it to care for your child. This is one of those situations in which parents with the same employer should consider splitting the leave if the mother is physically able to return to work after six or eight weeks. While the mother may not wish to return to work so soon, in the long run she will benefit if her partner becomes a better co-parent.

Some of the qualifying reasons for taking the unpaid FMLA leave are:

- for the birth and bonding with a newborn child;
- for the placement with the employee of a child for adoption or foster care, and to bond with that child;
- to care for an immediate family member (spouse, child, or parent—but not a parent "in-law") with a serious health condition.

Federal guidelines require you to submit your request for leave at least 30 days in advance. If you're planning to use unpaid leave, think about reserving some time in case your child gets sick after starting daycare. Toddlers and preschoolers frequently exchange germs, so upper respiratory illnesses and contagious conditions like conjunctivitis are common amongst children in group care environments. Since federal leave is unpaid, you should also consider the impact on your finances of forgoing your salary at a time when you will have many additional expenses associated with new child.

About 60 percent of U.S. workers are eligible for the FMLA leave. Sadly, many new mothers do not have access to even unpaid leave that protects their ability to return to their job.

Only three states currently offer paid family and medical leave: California, New Jersey, and Rhode Island.[25] The state of Washington passed a paid family leave law in 2007, which was to have gone into effect in October 2009, but the law was never implemented and subsequent legislation has postponed it indefinitely.

California was the first state to offer paid family leave with the law passing in 2002 and the first payments were made in 2004. People participating in a company or state disability plan are covered. In the first

10 years of the program, approximately 90 percent of claims filed were for parents bonding with a new child. The California paid family leave does not protect your job, but it provides partial wage replacement to men and women. In 2013 the benefit amount was about 55 percent of earnings up to a maximum of $1,067/week.[26]

Given the lack of federal paid maternity leave and only a few states with any paid leave, it is not surprising that a SPE survey found that American women tend to take less time off after childbirth than women in other countries.[27] In the United States almost half of the mothers surveyed stayed home for only about the time that they are considered to be medically disabled; 48 percent of the mothers reported taking leave for eight weeks or less with 10 percent of mothers taking only two weeks or less. Elsewhere around the world, only 18 percent of women took eight weeks or less.

As with paternity leave, technology, finance, and professional services employers offer the best maternity benefits. These organizations tend to have long hours and corporate cultures that are not very appealing to many women. Many of these businesses are under pressure to increase the representation of women at all levels. Offering maternity benefits that are much better than normal is a way to attract and retain younger women.

Typically the maternity leave offered by a firm is at least as long as the paternity leave. Disability leave usually can be combined with a maternity/family leave benefit. Thus for example, female Microsoft employees have 12 weeks of family leave like the men with an additional 8 weeks of disability. At Google, women receive 18 weeks of paid maternity leave and 22 weeks if there are complications.

The CEO of YouTube, Susan Wojcicki, announced in the *Wall Street Journal* in December 2014 that she was planning to take her fifth maternity leave from Google.[28] (YouTube was acquired by Google in 2006.) Wojcicki explained that she was entitled to 18 weeks of paid maternity leave like every other female employee and noted that, when Google increased paid leave to 18 weeks, the rate at which new mothers quit declined by 50 percent.

Some companies are offering perks designed to retain new mothers. The private equity firm, KKR & Co., announced that employees (male or female) who are the primary caregiver may travel with their infant and a nanny until the child is a year old.[29] KKR will pay the cost of the additional transportation, lodging, and meal expenses. Also, KKR increased from 12 to 16 weeks the paid leave for new parents, including for those who adopt or use a surrogate, and doubled the leave for parents who aren't a baby's primary caregiver, from 5 to 10 days.

IBM announced plans to launch a program that would enable women to ship their breast milk home when they are traveling on company business.[30] The program would start with domestic travel in the United States, but the intent is to go global. The idea is that women will use a smartphone app to have a temperature-controlled package delivered to their hotel. IBM will pay for the packaging and shipping.

After hearing about the IBM plan, I know a new mother, who is still nursing, who purchased a special highly insulated "traveling refrigerator" so that she could take home breast milk that she pumps on business trips. She lamented that the biotech company where she works was not trying to make life easier for working mothers. While many companies offer lactation rooms, which nursing mothers can reserve to pump breast milk, hers does not. She told me that she was more fortunate than the women in her group who have cubicles. As a manager, she has a door, but she had to use posters to cover the extensive glass wall of her office.

If you are thinking about having a baby, your choice of employer could be influenced by the maternity benefits available. If your organization's benefits are lacking, far in advance of when you might think you would need them, you could collaborate with other women to document what the competitors for your skills are offering. Asking for what you want in the context of attracting and retaining valuable talent might persuade your company to be more accommodating in providing support for new mothers such as comfortable lactation rooms with clean refrigerated storage for breast milk.

Women who are considering having a child and are switching employers may wish to discretely check on the maternity benefits. You should be careful, because overt interest in the policies might cost you a job offer.

LONG VERSUS SHORT TERM

For both mothers and fathers, taking care of an infant is exhausting, especially if the baby wakes up multiple times during the night. When a man slacks off, because of exhaustion from getting up in the middle of the night to feed an infant or to soothe a toddler, the boss may not be watching as carefully for signs of impaired performance as with a new mother. Thus when a father's performance slips slightly, it may be less noticed or more likely to be condoned than an equivalent backsliding by a mother.

When I was in graduate school at Stanford, the machinist in the School of Earth Sciences, Peter, was one of my best buddies. My thesis work involved experiments using pressure vessels at high pressure and temperature. Growing up I was never taught how to use even basic tools such as wrenches and screw drivers, let alone how to operate machine tools. Those were "boy things." Peter taught me what I needed to know about how to build, maintain, and run my experimental equipment. At the same time he told me stories about his life that were relevant to the difficulties that I was encountering.

When my son was an infant and would not sleep for more than a few hours at a time, Peter shared his own tale of woe as a new parent. Peter's first son, who by the time he told me the story was fully grown and a physician, had been a colicky baby, who screamed constantly and never slept. Peter was so exhausted that he would sneak away at work and hide in a broom closet to sleep. From a safety perspective, sleeping in the closet was certainly safer than operating a lathe or a milling machine while overwhelmingly tired.

In hindsight, I wonder if Peter's manager knew what was happening and chose to look the other way, because Peter was an extremely talented and dedicated worker. Accommodating a highly skilled worker for a brief period while he or she is going through a difficult time is much better than enforcing conditions that make the person injure him- or herself or quit. However, lenience varies drastically from supervisor to supervisor even within the same organization. Your relationship with your boss may have a major impact on assessment of your long-term potential and tolerance of short-term declines in performance.

Some women believe that it is better to take the first couple of years off after childbirth. They fear that a temporary decrease in productivity because of the fatigue associated with infant care will result in long-lasting career damage. If this is of concern to you, you may want to consider negotiating a longer unpaid leave or working part-time instead of completely exiting the workforce.

Surveys have found that women who have a job to return to are much more likely to reenter the workforce than those who do not. Rege and Drange observed, "Several studies show that job protection associated with parental leave increases the likelihood that mothers return to the labor market when their children are older, and that it increases the job continuity with the pre-birth employer."[31]

The path back to work is much easier, if a job is held open for you during your maternity leave. The main challenges in that case are arranging child care and the daily logistics of being a working parent.

If you don't have a job, you also have the major effort to find a new job. A new mother may find it difficult to motivate herself to assess and update her skills, write a résumé, search for job opportunities, and arrange babysitting if she secures an interview. When you look at all of the extra steps, it is not surprising that once a mother leaves the workforce, the odds of her returning even when her children are older are significantly lower than if she has a position waiting for her.

Don't rush to quit if you just need to slow down for a while. Whether you are physically exhausted like my machinist friend, Peter, or just wish to spend more time with your baby, try to arrange something that can keep you engaged in some capacity with your employer. Taking advantage of unpaid leave, part-time work, telecommuting, and project-based work can greatly increase the probability of easy and successful reentry.

Unpaid parental leave enables parents to both enjoy the new baby and to more easily rejoin the workforce. After being immersed for months in some of the less rewarding and more onerous aspects of child-rearing, paid work may appear to be an attractive alternative. It can be a relief to return to an adult world and let someone else care for the baby during working hours.

When my kids were young, and there was a lot of pressure to stay home, I realized that I didn't believe those who claimed that having children in daycare was detrimental to their long-term mental ability and future potential. Reports about how harmful it was to have someone else tend my children during the day did not resonate with me. When I looked around, I realized that for generations, the rich and mighty had relied on nannies, ayahs, and other hired help to take care of their children. Despite being raised by minions, the children of the elite went on to become the future leaders. For me, it was about quality time with my children, not about being ever present.

My husband loved to torture me by correctly informing friends and relations that our daughter's first daycare center subsequently became a pet-boarding facility. However, when my daughter was three she was selected as one of only 22 girls who were granted admission to the most exclusive private school for girls in Dallas, The Hockaday School. Many of her classmates were legacies and daughters of wealthy titans, but she was accepted on her own merits despite having spent her days in generic daycare since she was six weeks old.

When my daughter was in high school at Hockaday, she complained that, "Her friends parents didn't care if they got good grades." I made it very clear to her that I did! Somehow, she managed to squeeze in a lot of partying as well as studying in high school and was accepted by Dartmouth under its early admission program.

Don't let relatives, friends, and other stay-at-home mothers try to shame you into quitting to devote yourself to your children. You don't need to be a full-time parent to be a good parent. You can shape your progeny's values by setting appropriate expectations, spending quality time with them, and ensuring adequate supervision.

Short of quitting because of frustrations with child care and working parent logistics, flexible work arrangements may be a good solution if you feel that you are at a breaking point.

FLEXIBILITY

In the SPE survey of people under the age of 45, 9 percent of mothers and 2 percent of fathers wanted to work part-time, while 19 percent of mothers and 21 percent of fathers wished to telecommute, and 34 percent of mothers and 28 percent of fathers desired flexible hours.[32] While relatively few parents want to work part-time, just knowing that it is an option may make it easier for some stressed parents to continue working full time. Staying on the payroll in a part-time capacity retains parents in the workforce, and paves the way to return to full-time work, when the burdens of parenting diminish.

There are negatives to part-time work. Your income and probably your benefits will be reduced. Furthermore, if you opt for part-time work, make sure that you are aware of any barriers to returning to full-time employment. If someone else is hired to pick up the load that you are shedding, you may not have the option to return to full-time status whenever you want.

Access to health care and other corporate plans may be a pivotal factor in deciding whether or not to work part-time. Eligibility for your benefit plans may depend on working a minimum number of hours. If you chose to work part-time, the cost for your health care and other benefits may increase at the same time your income decreases, because of a reduction in the company subsidy.

Another consideration in the decision to switch to part-time status is whether your pay will be based on the percentage of full-time employment you select or on the actual number of hours that you work. Just as salaried staff frequently work more than 40 hours a week, someone on a half-time schedule may find themselves working close to three-quarters or full time. I have known salaried people on part-time status, who end up working far more hours than they planned. If you are paid for all of the hours that you work and avoid having to work 125 percent of full time, you might be happy. But, you don't want to end up being paid for part-time and working full time. Be sure that you understand how working more hours than planned will be compensated and how variability in your work hours per pay period impacts your benefits.

When someone continues part-time instead of quitting, there is continuity both for the employer and for the individual. Recruiting and training can be expensive. From the employer's viewpoint, the person's knowledge of the business and the investment in his or her training is not lost. From your perspective, you can keep your skills and professional network current and will not have to hunt for a new position when you wish to return to full-time work. Part-time work can be a win–win situation.

If the employer is willing to entertain multiple variations on part-time work, new parents can gradually increase their work hours as they get adjusted to new sleep patterns and become comfortable being away from their offspring for a longer time. Gradually returning to work can reduce separation anxiety and feelings of guilt. Parents who are less stressed are more apt to stay in the workforce in the long run.

Some types of jobs are more amenable to being handled by a part-time person than others. Accommodating someone who is in a position that requires physical presence at specific hours may require hiring another person to cover the remainder of the schedule. If you and a colleague work in a similar capacity and are both interested in working part-time, you might collaborate and propose job sharing to your management. If you propose something workable, your organization may be happy to accommodate you.

Having the option to take a leave or work part-time allows people to work the math of whether they want to take a financial hit of staying home or maintain their income and benefits by working full time. Although many people may contemplate part-time work, most elect to continue full time when faced with a reduction in pay and benefits.

COMPRESSED WORKWEEKS

In many organizations, the majority of employees have chosen to work some version of a compressed workweek. The most common schedule of this type is 80 hours worked over 9 business days in a two-week period instead of the standard pattern of 80 hours worked over 10 business days in a two-week period. Another alternative is 40 hours worked over 4 business days in a week period.

Compressed workweeks were initiated in the mid-1980s and were not designed to be a benefit for employees. Employers were under pressure to reduce the number of miles driven to and from work by their employees to decrease traffic congestion and auto emissions. Despite subsidies for riding public transit and carpooling, most people persisted in driving alone to work. The concept behind compressed workweeks was that if people drove one less day to work, there could be a reduction in air pollution.

In the 1980s California suffered from some of the worst air pollution in the country. Cities in Los Angeles County began testing unconventional work schedules in 1984, when local governments were urged to do something to reduce traffic congestion and improve air quality during the Los Angeles Summer Olympics. The initial target was to eliminate one day of driving a week. Since the goal was emissions reduction, not employee satisfaction, the first trials involved working 10-hour days (40 hours in a 4-day week). There were mixed reactions to the very long workday. People without children enjoyed having three-day weekends, but the 10-hour days created child care problems for parents and also complaints from employees about fatigue. A 1984 survey found that workers were opposed to a permanent four-day workweek.[33] To address the child care and fatigue complaints, employers gave up trying to eliminate one day of driving a week and shifted to eliminating one day of commuting in a two-week period.

The idea of compressed workweeks spread across the country to other areas that suffered from air pollution and expanded from summer programs to year round, because some regions experience their worst air quality in the winter. Ultimately, while many organizations continue to offer compressed schedules with either 9- or 10-hour days, most people opt for 9-hour days, which are more compatible with daycare arrangements and less tiring.

Since one of the goals of the compressed work weeks was to relieve traffic congestion, employers also introduced flexibility in starting times. The concept of being in the office for "core hours" and scheduling meetings during those times evolved. No longer was everyone expected to be in the office at the same time.

The compressed workweek came to be viewed by many people as an employee benefit. If someone had a very long commute, they tended to opt for the 10-hour days instead of the 9-hour version. Personal business that had to be conducted during working hours could now be handled on the 9/80 day instead of having to take time off from work.

Parents could send their kids to daycare on the 9/80 day and have personal time to recharge or for a lunch date with each other. Especially for those with only two weeks of annual vacation, a 9/80 work schedule was like a gift of an additional 25 days off per year.

Compressed workweeks may be a factor in your decision to accept a job or to stay with a company. In 1999, when Mobil and Exxon were merging, I had been enjoying a 9/80 schedule for a couple of years as a Mobil employee. Exxon did not offer compressed workweeks, but Chevron did. It was not the top factor in my decision to switch employers, but it was a consideration.

TELECOMMUTING

Technology has liberated many of us from having to be in the office to work effectively. Indeed, there are situations in which telecommuting is more effective. A huge amount of time is wasted and fossil fuel expended to transport people to offices in which they just sit at a computer in a cubicle and talk on the telephone. If they need to speak to a colleague, they pick up a phone instead of walking down the corridor. When a document is shared, it is done with an attachment to an e-mail. The office is not paperless, but reports are transmitted electronically. The day is spent focused on a computer monitor.

Why can't staff members commute only when their presence is required for face-to-face discussions? Unlike with compressed workweeks, there hasn't been a widespread environmental campaign in support of telecommuting. Compressed workweek schedules were created not to benefit employees, but to reduce air pollution. It is unfortunate that we don't have an equivalent push to eliminate unnecessary commutes with the goal of reducing greenhouse gas emissions and minimizing climate disruption.

Companies could earn credits for reduction of emissions. Telecommuting can reduce not only CO_2 discharges (which have been implicated in climate change), but also NO_x emissions (which contribute to smog and acid rain). In addition, elimination of unnecessary commuting would diminish traffic congestion and reduce travel time for those whose presence at work is mandatory.

Purging unnecessary driving is a win–win–win solution for the environment, for those commuting to work, and for those working from home. Everyone saves time. Those staying home save the most time, but those driving to and from work have shorter travel times, because the telecommuters are not taking up space on the road.

According to Lister and Harnish, as of 2011, 45 percent of the U.S. workforce held a job that was compatible with at least part-time telework., and "If those with compatible jobs worked at home 2.4 days a week (the national average of those who do), the reduction in greenhouse gases (51 million tons) would be equivalent of taking the entire New York workforce off the roads."[34]

According to Global Workforce Analytics, in the United States habitual work-at-home (excluding those who are self-employed) has swelled by 103 percent since 2005. As of 2014, 3.7 million employees (2.5 percent of the workforce) now work from home at least half the time. The employee population as a whole grew by 1.8 percent from 2013 to 2014, while telecommuter population increased by 6.5 percent.[35]

Employers have benefited from 24/7 access to staff. Employees are in effect "on call" around the clock. Business calls chase us on cell phones. Evenings, weekends, and vacations are spent catching up on e-mails and on reading and writing reports. Time pressure has escalated for people imperiling their fragile work–life balance. The boundaries between work and life have blurred, amplifying pressure to respond rapidly to business issues and creating constant work stress. Stressed people are more likely to get sick and to make mistakes.

In reaction to e-mail intruding into the home, in April 2014, labor unions and corporate representatives in France agreed on an "obligation to disconnect from remote communications tools" that would apply to 250,000 employees of consulting, computing, and polling firms, whose contracts stipulate an annual number of workdays, not daily working hours. The pact if approved by the French Labor Ministry would require that employers verify that the 11 hours of daily "rest" time to which all workers are legally entitled was spent uninterrupted.[36]

Most employees have not benefitted as much as their employers from modern communications that enable many people to work from anywhere. These people are stressed by work pursuing them 24/7. We need reciprocity. When possible, a sense of balance should be restored by using the 24/7 connectivity to allow employees to work at home.

Working from home can be an attractive alternative for the following groups:

- for dual-career couples, who are unable to find attractive positions for both partners within reasonable commuting distance of a single residence, telecommuting can minimize family separations;

- for couples who are stretched thin, who can more productively use the time that would otherwise be wasted on commuting;

- for parents with child care concerns, working at home can facilitate breast feeding and alleviate worries about an unsupervised nanny, even though they will still need to enroll their kids in day-care or hire a nanny;

- for couples who prefer to live in a location that is too far from their worksite to commute on a daily basis.

Telecommuting can be a win–win for both the employer and the employees. In her March 2015 TED Talk, Dame Stephanie Shirley described how in the 1960s, she founded a software company, Free-lance Programmers, in the United Kingdom with women working part-time in their homes.[37] Dame Shirley's company grew to employ about 8,500 people and ultimately was valued at over $3 billion. The success of her company made millionaires of 70 of her team members.

Dame Shirley explained, "I recruited professionally qualified women who'd left the industry on marriage, or when their first child was expected and structured them into a home-working organization. We pioneered the concept of women going back into the workforce after a career break. We pioneered all sorts of new, flexible work methods: job shares, profit-sharing, and eventually, co-ownership when I took a quarter of the company into the hands of the staff at no cost to anyone but me."[38]

Unfortunately, telecommuting doesn't always work out so well for everyone involved. The productivity and success of telecommuting workers was compared with office workers in a controlled study conducted under the auspices of the National Bureau of Economic Research.[39] The senior management of CTrip, a 16,000-employee travel agency, was interested in allowing call center employees to work from home, because they saw potential benefits in the form of reduced office rental costs and reduction in the high attrition rates. Those participating in the study worked from home four days a week and spent the fifth day in the office.

That study found a 13 percent improvement in productivity of the call center employees working from home versus the control group. Those working from home reported greater work satisfaction and experienced 50 percent less attrition than the control group, but their promotion rate fell by about 50 percent. The disadvantages of telecommuting from the employee's perspective were the loneliness of working at home and the lower rate of promotion despite higher productivity.

The second author of the report on CTrip's experience with telework, James Liang, was at the time of the study a doctoral student at the Stanford Graduate School of Business.[40] Mr. Liang was also the first CEO and current chairman of CTrip. Having the company chairman as an active member of the study team should have ensured strong management support for the study and unbiased treatment of the participating employees, but it didn't.

After adjusting for performance, lower rates of promotion were found for those telecommuting despite documented higher productivity. As a result, even though many CTrip employees strongly preferred working from home, some decided to continue working in the office, because of their concerns about reduced rates of promotion. Employee awareness of the mismatch between performance and promotion rate hindered CTrip's ability to fully leverage the reduced rates of attrition and the $2,000 savings per year per capita associated with telecommuting personnel. The lower rate of promotion of telecommuters existed in spite of top management's involvement and the adverse business impact of not appropriately rewarding those working from home. In this well-controlled study with full management support, supervisors' enhanced personal relationships with those with whom they had daily contact undermined reward for performance and negatively impacted the company's ability to reduce overhead costs.

Independent confirmation of advancement and loneliness issues associated with telecommuting came from a friend, "Jasmine." She also raised the issue of teleworkers receiving inadequate career development opportunities. Jasmine disclosed that her trailing spouse, "Matt," had worked exclusively from home for four years. After Jasmine took a new job in a different location, Matt quit his job to follow her. Matt's company decided that they needed him and offered to let him work remotely. From Matt's perspective, the major disadvantages of telecommuting were lack of face-to-face interaction with his peers as well as limited personal and career development. Jasmine said, "This was not intentional on his management's part. It was just one of those out-of-sight, out-of-mind situations."

Even though Matt was disciplined and did not do housework during his working hours, his working from home was beneficial from Jasmine's perspective with regard to child care and other household issues. Jasmine's work was not interrupted if her kids became ill at daycare, because Matt had the flexibility to rush to pick up the kids. Also, when Jasmine was transferred again, Matt was able to follow her without additional disruption to his career.

Not all work is compatible with telecommuting. The Society for Human Resource Management advises, "Telework is best suited for jobs that require independent work, little face-to-face interaction, concentration, a measurable work product and output-based (instead of time-based) monitoring, but it may be used in other jobs as well."[41]

The telework policy template of the Society for Human Resource Management specifies, "Individuals requesting formal telecommuting arrangements must have been employed with [Company Name] for a minimum of 12 months of continuous, regular employment and must have exhibited above-average performance, in accordance with the company's performance appraisal process. Any telecommuting arrangement made will be on a trial basis for the first three months, and may be discontinued, at will, at any time at the request of either the telecommuter or the organization."[42]

Lister and Harnish observed that, "The biggest barrier to telecommuting by a wide margin is management fear and mistrust."[43] Securing the option to telecommute often requires negotiation by the employee because of the distrust issues. If you are a long-time, strong performer, it will probably be easier to convince your supervisor to trust you than if you are a marginal worker or relatively new.

Although employers tend to be reluctant to take on a new employee on a telecommuting basis, you may still be successful. My daughter, who has unusual legal experience that is very valuable to some organizations, was hired by a large and well-established law firm to begin working on a telework basis. Also, my brother-in-law was employed by Oracle on a telework basis as a new employee. If an organization is having difficulty acquiring someone with your skills, it will be more willing to accommodate your requests.

Before approaching your boss about telecommuting, you should seriously evaluate whether you would be happy working from home. For strong extroverts, working alone even a few days a week to avoid a long, expensive commute or to spend more nights at home might be difficult. Ask yourself:

- Will I mind not having daily, face-to-face contact with coworkers?
- Do I have sufficient self-discipline to work from home?
- If I work from home, how will I keep my personal life from interfering? Children? Pets? Personal logistics?

- What space can I dedicate for my home office?
- What equipment will I need?
- Am I willing to travel for work? How often? For what duration?
- How will my work be evaluated?
- How will I document my productivity?

If you will be telecommuting full time, you also need to find out:

- How will I get training to maintain and enhance my skills?
- How can I maintain visibility with my supervisor?

Organizations that allow telecommuting may have strict rules if you are doing it on more than an ad hoc basis. You may be required to:

- demonstrate for risk management purposes that your home work space is as ergonomically correct and as safe as your employer's normal office space;
- document with photographs that your home office meets company safety standards;
- periodically reassess your work space and document the findings with photographs;
- sign a statement pledging that you will not allow children, family members, or pets into your home work space;
- sign an agreement affirming that you understand that you will be covered by workers' compensation laws only if you are injured during the course of performing job-related activities;
- log into a time-tracking system, to prevent fraudulent overtime and hours claims.

You should provide your boss with suggestions on how your performance can be quantitatively and qualitatively evaluated. Reaching agreement with your supervisor on deliverables and a communication plan is essential. You should also have a visibility plan so that you are not overlooked when raises, bonuses, and promotions are distributed.

If you are hoping to get promoted, you should be aware that out of sight can be out of mind. You may or may not decide that the benefits of working from home outweigh the potential downside of career stagnation.

Daily face time with your supervisor is not necessary for business or career advancement. Face time can be rare even if your boss's office is right down the hall, because of perpetual travel and meetings. Furthermore, as professionals advance, they may work in a different location than their manager. But, everyone should have a communication plan to keep their boss informed about their accomplishments, progress, and any delays or problems they encounter and a visibility plan to avoid being out of sight and out of mind.

Frequent, regularly scheduled calls with your manager to discuss progress, performance, metrics, and expectations are essential for communication and visibility plans. Telecommuters should also participate in group meetings by phone or videoconferencing. A videoconference provides a higher level of engagement than an audio-only call. Periodic face-to-face meetings are advantageous for telecommuters, but the frequency will depend on cost and logistical barriers to getting together.

If you are a telecommuter, you should ask to be copied on all e-mails that are sent to the team, so that you are aware of the group news. You ought to engage with other members of your team by e-mailing or calling people. Both your manager and you must make it a priority to interact on a regular basis.

Some telecommuters lament that they can't simply drop into a colleague's office to pose a question. In effect, you can. If you want to query someone, send a short concise e-mail or pick up the phone and ask if they have a minute. If the answer is more involved than they want to explain in an e-mail, ask if there is good time to schedule a call.

My experience is that you can build strong friendships remotely. Early in my career, I began working with people remotely around the world both for business and for professional society activities. I developed good rapport with people long before I met them face-to-face and maintained those connections even though I have rarely had the opportunity to meet with them in person. I started doing this decades ago, when intercontinental phone calls were outrageously expensive with long lag time and distracting echoes. It is great if you can meet with people around the break area and go to lunch together, but face-to-face contact is not essential in building rapport. Frequent phone calls and e-mails with personal tidbits intertwined can build long-lasting relationships.

Just because you are telecommuting doesn't mean you cannot ask for training and to attend professional meetings. Training and meetings are as important if not more so for telecommuters than they are for people working in the office. If you are a full-time employee, you should have equal access to training. Speak up and request what you think you need. Ask your manager to recommend training that would be beneficial. Don't be shy (and forgotten)!

People working at home should develop a business routine and stick with it. Having a separate place dedicated to work is a good way to create the division between work and life. Your commute may only be down the hall or to the basement, but you are shifting into another mode and focusing on work. Go to work on time.

NEGOTIATING FOR FLEXIBILITY

The key to negotiations is to know what you want and to understand the other side's goals, in this case your management's key concerns. Do your homework. Talk with colleagues and friends who have experience with different types of flexible work arrangements.

Before starting discussions with your supervisor, ask around to discover as much as you can about what other people have been able to do. Precedents that work in your favor are always good to have in your pocket. Don't volunteer the ones that aren't. For example, you may be relatively new to the organization, but you know that some long-term employees have been allowed to telecommute. If an older man who has worked for the organization for many years has been granted the right to work from home to take care of his ailing wife, use that as a reason why you should also be allowed to telecommute. Ignore the difference in age and years of employment and stand on the precedent that has been established.

In some ways, it can be harder to understand your own desires and priorities than those of your management. Make sure that you understand the advantages and disadvantages of the work arrangement that you are considering. Assess the impact on your benefits, your income, and your upward mobility. Find out what barriers may exist to returning to normal, full-time status. If you are considering telecommuting, think through how good a fit that would be for you either full time or part-time. If possible talk with people from your organization, who have used that type of arrangement and probe them about the pluses and minuses involved. Ask those who have used different types of flexible work arrangements what they would do differently if they had a chance to do it over again.

If you are expecting a child, explore your alternatives prior to the baby's birth. When you are out of the office and caring for an infant, it is much more difficult to gather the information on the workstyle alternatives. Think about how much you have invested in your career. Yes, you have also invested a lot in your new baby. And like many women, you may feel "career limited" by the time you give birth and believe that being a mother further impairs your potential to advance. But, don't rush into quitting! Instead, negotiate for the flexibility that you want. If you are convinced that you want to stay at home with your child, ask for an extended leave without pay instead. If at the end of the leave you still don't want to return to work, you can throw in the towel then.

A new parent who yearns for time with her or his infant may find that being a full-time, stay-at-home caregiver is a relentless grind with insufficient mental stimulation. When you tire of being a full-time parent, you may welcome the opportunity to return to work full time or part-time. Returning to the workforce after taking time off to be a full-time parent can be very difficult.[44] Resuming your career will be much easier if you have a position to which you can return.

By the time they have children, many professional women are highly experienced and their employers have invested a lot in their training. Many well educated women delay having children until they are in their thirties. In the United States, first births to women aged 35 or older increased from just 1 percent in 1970 to 8.2 percent in 2010. Of those responding to the worldwide 2013 SEG survey, 57 percent of the women had their first child after the age of 30.[45] Similarly, in the 2011 global SPE survey, 45 percent of the women reported having their first child after the age of 30.[46] With the worldwide trend for women to delay motherhood until their thirties or later, many organizations are concerned about midcareer attrition of female talent. This might make your employer more willing to customize a schedule that works for you.

Many employers are hesitant to allow employees to telecommute on a regular basis because of lack of trust. Old-fashioned managers, who have been accustomed to visually taking attendance, managing by walking around, and dropping in unannounced on their subordinates, hate to approve working outside of the office for the majority of the time. However, they may be under pressure to reduce attrition of midcareer women, so you could be in a more favorable negotiating position than you think. The better you understand in advance the concerns your supervisor has about the flexibility you are requesting, the more prepared you can be to refute the objections.

Don't begin negotiations with concessions. Ask for what you want first and wait for a response. If you want to telecommute, focus the discussion on how your performance will be monitored and appraised. Be prepared with your personal hierarchy of what to concede first. For example, if you want to telecommute, you could negotiate the number of days of a week or the duration of the period of telecommuting. If all works well and you like working from home, you could try again later to negotiate an extension or fewer days in the office.

Don't be afraid to look for a better deal. If your current employer refuses to accommodate requests for flexibility, look elsewhere. Telework allows you to work from anywhere anytime, so even if you aren't willing to relocate, you may have more job opportunities than you have ever imagined.

CHAPTER 8

Documenting Competency and Achievement

Keep your résumé up-to-date. It is infinitely easier to capture accomplishments real time than to sit down at a blank screen and attempt to recreate a record of your career. Capture your accomplishments real time while you are still enjoying the warm glow of success. If you have lost your job, getting yourself in a good frame of mind to create a résumé can be very difficult.

Maintain a long version of your résumé or as Europeans would say curriculum vitae. Then when you need a biographic sketch or career summary for an announcement, for an internal job application, to respond to a headhunter, or to find a new position after you have been terminated, you can respond rapidly. A résumé or short biographic sketch should always be customized to emphasize the skills and experiences that are most applicable to the position that you are seeking or are most applicable for the audience.

Take a close look at your résumé. Would you hire yourself? Given the job market for your skills, how desirable a candidate do you think you are? Do your positives outweigh the negatives from an employer's perspective? What actions can you take to enhance your marketability?

If you place restrictions on where and how you will work, you can make it more difficult to find employment. The less flexible you are, the more attractive you must be relative to the competition. Coordination of two careers and child-rearing or other family obligations often introduce limitations.

Geographic constraints are common for equal earners. Finding two positions within reasonable commuting range of a residence is more difficult than securing a good job for one person with geographic flexibility.

Another complicating factor for members of dual-career couples is time. When a person in a dual-career couple receives a job offer or a transfer that involves moving to a new location, that individual often wants additional time to make a decision, because he or she does not wish to commit without knowing whether or not his or her mate can find acceptable employment in the new locale. In business, time is money. Time restrictions impede an organization's ability to quickly deploy staff to where they want them. Postponing acceptance of an offer can lead to its loss, if you are not an outstanding applicant.

Yet another constraint can be work style. If you aspire to telecommute, particularly as a new hire, you must be a very strong competitor. Requesting part-time work, when the employer needs a full-time staffer, adds the complication of finding another person who is willing to pick up the remaining load. Every limitation on your flexibility makes you slightly less attractive to an employer.

I know a woman, "Lucy," with unique and in demand skills. However, Lucy was unwilling to relocate because of her husband's situation. A couple of companies offered Lucy a fabulous salary and benefits, but were not prepared to entertain her request to telecommute. One of those companies approached her a second time months later offering to let Lucy work remotely if she was willing to travel as needed. She was told that the position was still unfilled and that she had always been its top candidate. In the interim, Lucy had become pregnant. As soon as the hiring manager heard that she was expecting, the job offer evaporated. From the hiring manager's perspective, there were now more complications than he was willing to accept.

BATTLING UNCONSCIOUS BIAS

Bias exists when there is prejudice either for or against people with certain distinguishing characteristics. Characteristics that are immediately observable to a casual observer such as race, gender, physical disability or pregnancy, body weight, age, appearance, speech can all provoke positive or negative impressions that are independent of the person's abilities. In contrast, invisible characteristics, such as parental, marital, or relationship status, may escape detection.

Subtle personal predispositions or biases have a way of blindsiding us and subverting our impressions. We may think that we are not prejudiced, but we all harbor hidden biases that despite our best intentions influence our decisions. Unconscious bias is particularly difficult to avoid.

I am as guilty as anyone else. I have spent over 35 years working in the male-dominated petroleum industry and strive to support other women. I'm a member of the Society of Women Engineers, the Association for Women in Science, the American Association of University Women, and other groups advocating for women. Yet, when I read the following vignette by Susan Clancy, an experimental psychologist, I made exactly the type of biased assumption that I am constantly fighting.

"A boy and his father are involved in a car accident. The father is killed, but the boy is taken to the hospital and into surgery. Upon seeing him, the surgeon says, 'I can't operate on this boy because he's my son.'"[1]

My automatic assumption that the surgeon was male shows how deeply ingrained bias can be. Of the doctors whom I regularly consult, most are women. Throughout my career I have fought for recognition as a female scientist. Yet, I was guilty of the stereotypical biased assumption. My mental image of the surgeon was of a man. We don't think or like to admit that we are biased, but we are.

Clancy explains that, like me, the majority of people instantaneously leap to the conclusion that the surgeon was a man. She points out that we do not formulate our mental image because of an intent to evaluate men and women differently. The mental image occurs spontaneously without conscious thought. Unfortunately, we have been conditioned to associate certain roles with men. That ingrained, unconscious bias shades multiple decisions and provides people with various characteristics including gender, race, physical attractiveness, and so on with an inherent advantage that impacts who gets hired and promoted.

Extreme measures may have to be taken to combat bias. Here's a good example. As recently as 1970, the top five orchestras in the United States were less than 5 percent female. Then orchestras began using blind auditions in which the candidates were hidden behind a screen on the stage, so that the selection panel could not see them. The evaluators' biases were so ingrained that the auditioning musicians had to be instructed to remove their shoes before they walked across the stage, so that the distinctive sounds of a woman's shoes would not influence the selection.[2]

After this corrective action to focus the judges' evaluation on musical talent, the percentage of women increased. By 1997, 25 percent of the orchestra musicians were women. Now, some top orchestras are more than 30 percent female.

Multiple studies have demonstrated that the presumed gender of the name on a résumé can impact selection.[3] In studies in which the gender of the name on résumés is switched, both men and women rate the male applicant as more competent and hirable than the identical female applicant. It is the old trap in which a woman has to be twice as good as a man to be considered to be as half as qualified.

In a study with over 600 participants, Tamar Kricheli-Katz observed that when women compete for high-status positions, they tend to be held to higher standards than men.[4] Her theory is that women who compete for high-status positions pose a male "identity threat." When male managers were told that a high-status occupation was hiring more women, they tended to evaluate women as less competent and to offer them lower salaries. Men who were not in high-status occupations and women managers did not share the bias of the male managers.

Avoiding gender bias is difficult for women. Compounding the gender discrimination, it is also more difficult for women than it is for men to avoid bias against members of dual-career couples. When a traditional manager sees a wedding ring on a woman's finger, he tends to automatically assume that her husband's career takes precedence. If the position for which the woman is applying involves travel and possibly relocation, unconsciously the interviewer may discount her relative to male candidates and single women. Even if the woman is not wearing a ring, the interviewer may probe to determine her marital and parental status.

Men are more likely to escape casual discrimination against dual-career couples and working parents during interviews. They are not usually probed about their plans to have children or how their current children might impact their ability to travel on business. Typically, the problem doesn't come into play until the men are working and they want flexibility to handle child care issues or refuse to relocate.

A woman I know was denied a promotion, because her management assumed that she would be unable to travel. She was widowed with an eight-year-old son and tried to convince her employer that she was mobile. Frustrated, she accepted a position with another firm that also required extensive travel and took her son with her everywhere.

People with a form of invisible diversity can try to "pass." However, whether it is a homosexual passing for straight or a light-skinned black passing for white, "passing" will increase your stress. There is a perpetual requirement to hide your personal life. Some people in dual-career couples attempt "to pass" as the person in their household with the "dominant career" by working for different employers. This is much easier for men than for women, because traditional managers automatically assume that men are the breadwinner in their family.

When couples share an employer, envy can also become a problem. Knowledge of how much a subordinate's partner earns can make a traditional single-earner boss jealous, if the combined income of the couple is greater than his. The jealousy can color the supervisor's evaluations and recommendations.

Even if you work for different employers, envy can be an issue. If for any reason your household income is higher than that of your boss, avoid displays of greater affluence at work. Everything you do from the clothes you wear, the car you drive, and your casual chitchat makes an impression. At work we are ceaselessly under scrutiny.

Members of dual-career couples want to be judged on their own individual competencies and merits. They prefer to be compared with their peer group, not with their partners. They do not want their partner's career to be a factor in their employer's decisions about raises, promotions, and transfers. However, we are judged by the company that we keep, so for better or for worse, the more our employer knows about our domestic partner, the bigger a factor it may unconsciously be in management decisions.

Much of your performance assessment is subjective and tends to be based upon your supervisor's perception of your performance rather than actual results. Unfortunately, impressions can be swayed by personal prejudices, so sometimes we are fighting an uphill battle. In those cases, complaints may get you nowhere and it may be better to vote with your feet. This is especially true if your boss is biased against you because of something you can't change such as being a woman, or don't want to change such as being a member of a dual-career couple. Even if you are in a "protected group" (against which overt discrimination is legally prohibited), lawsuits can be futile and cause more harm to you than good. Pick your battles carefully. If your supervisor is hopelessly biased against you, find a greener pasture and get out before too much damage is inflicted.

Previously, I mentioned my career shift to get away from a boss, "Hank." At the beginning of the performance evaluation cycle, immediately after he became my supervisor as a result of a downsizing reorganization, Hank predicted what my performance appraisal would be at year-end. He informed me that because I had been assigned to a technical specialty outside of my previous experience, I would be unable to earn an above-average rating for that year. Hank emphasized the tight squeeze I was in by adding that, even though I was a fast learner, others in his group had too much of a head start for me to catch up. I was convinced that the team was overstaffed and Hank was setting me up to be terminated in the next round of layoffs.

Hank had a chip on his shoulder, because he had been demoted a level in the "right-sizing" process. In that layoff, half of my prior group had been terminated and my boss retired. I felt trapped between a rock and a hard place. I got out of Hank's group as fast as I could, even though it involved a major career shift and leaving my chosen career in research.

I had learned not to run to "human resources" to complain that my supervisor was prejudiced. The human resources group exists to maximize employee performance in support of the organization's strategic objectives. While you may get help from human resources on benefits and payroll issues, HR is not there to help you as an employee. The primary function of HR is to serve and protect the company.

Disputing management decisions is difficult and often unsuccessful. Ellen Pao's 2015 gender discrimination lawsuit against Kleiner Perkins, a renowned San Francisco venture capital firm, illustrates how tough it is for an individual to win in court. Ellen Pao had the advantage of a Harvard Law School education and a couple of years of working as an attorney for a noted New York City law firm, Cravath, Swaine & Moore LLP. Her lawsuit alleged that she was fired because of workplace retaliation by a male junior partner with whom she had a romantic affair. The defendant, Kleiner Perkins, claimed that she was dismissed for performance reasons unrelated to the lawsuit. During the trial, there was intensive examination of Ellen Pao's behavior and attitudes. The jury decided against her on all counts after a 24-day trial with intense media coverage. Legal action is expensive and time-consuming and can destroy your career.

Filing a discrimination lawsuit is a step that should not be taken on lightly. If a lawyer will not accept your case on a contingency basis, that is an indicator that your chances of winning are not good. In a contingency fee arrangement, an attorney agrees to represent you and to get paid with the fee a percentage of what you are awarded if the lawsuit is successful. Law firms may be more willing to take on your cause if you are part of a group that will file a class action suit. When you are part of a group, the focus is not on demonstrating that the problem is a result of your personal character flaws and performance. The emphasis is on the relative performance and treatment of the protected class versus the overall population.

PATERNALISM

Prejudice can also be a problem when someone is trying to be supportive. Incorrect assumptions can lead to misguided attempts to help that can be career limiting. Sometimes the manager is trying to protect you from situations that he or she thinks would not be good for you or your domestic relationship.

For example, the 2013 Society of Petroleum Engineers survey found that 25 percent of both men and women in equal-earner dual-career couples were willing to live apart from their partners to gain valuable experience.[5] However, only 15 percent of the dominant breadwinners were willing to live separately from their partners for that reason. If a manager does not think it is good or appropriate for people to temporarily separate from their domestic partners to gain work experience, he may never offer some opportunities to subordinates who are in dual-career couple relationships. This is unintentional discrimination, because of paternalism.

Here's a possible scenario. Joe is Mike's manager at Tech Corp in Los Angeles. Joe likes Mike and has met Mike's wife, Ashley. There is a chance for someone in Joe's group to go to Austin for a year to work as an assistant to the CEO. This is a high-visibility role and many of those who have held that position have advanced rapidly afterward. Joe also knows that Ashley works full time in her dream job, creating special effects for movies. Mike and Ashley have a two year old. Joe thinks of his daughter Becca when he sees Ashley. Becca's marriage failed because of the strain of struggling to take care of two small kids while her husband served in the army in Afghanistan. Joe fears that a separation could destroy Mike's marriage and doesn't want to negatively impact Ashley's career, so he never mentions the opportunity to Mike.

Joe was paternalistically trying to do what he thought was right for Mike. However, in doing so, he hindered Mike's upward mobility. We don't know what Mike and Ashley would have decided if Joe had been offered the opportunity to work in Austin. However, Mike should have had the chance to consider the opportunity. Variations on this type of career-limiting paternalism play out all of the time.

Articles have been written about people not pursuing promotions and other career opportunities, because they are concerned about how long days and heavy travel schedules will impact their family.[6] We don't hear about the opportunities that are missed, because the person never had the chance to consider the opportunity. Be careful if you have a well-meaning supervisor to make it crystal clear if you want to travel on business or relocate.

Sometimes an opportunity is missed, because the question is asked very subtly and posed to the wrong partner in a dual-career couple. Early in my career, I was given opportunities to present my research when top management from New York was visiting the research lab where I worked in Dallas. On one occasion, all of the speakers were invited with their spouses to a very expensive restaurant, the Mansion on Turtle Creek. During dinner, the vice president of research turned to my husband and asked, "How does Eve like New York?" I knew that, in effect, the VP was asking if I would like an assignment at headquarters. My husband, without thinking of what the question meant responded, "Eve hates New York." I was helpless to do anything about it at the time and was never offered the opportunity.

Asking the spouse what the employee thinks is a variation of the practice of taking the spouse aside and suggesting to him/her that he/she should let his/her partner's career take the lead. The opportunity is being presented to the wrong member of the domestic partnership in an inappropriate way. Company representatives should not ask a male partner to make a decision for his wife or what his wife thinks. That in effect positions the female as the male's property. The male is being given the decision-making authority instead of the woman. It is extremely inappropriate behavior. However, there is very little you as an individual can do about that. If you think it could be a problem, attend the business social functions alone.

Over the years, I have grown more cautious about when I include my husband in business-related events. He isn't immersed in my professional activities, so there is no way that he can catch all of the nuances and subtleties. I have learned that it is better to go solo than to "cry over spilled milk" after my husband unintentionally responds in a way that undercuts what I am trying to accomplish.

PERFORMANCE EVALUATION

Dan Ariely, a professor of psychology and behavioral economics at Duke University, wrote, "Human beings adjust behavior based on the metrics they're held against. Anything you measure will impel a person to optimize his score on that metric. What you measure is what you'll get. Period."[7]

Unfortunately, many of us do not push our management to clarify exactly what they want and the timing. Whenever you get a new supervisor, schedule a one-on-one meeting to discuss what is expected from you and how your work will be evaluated. The conversation may focus on what is considered acceptable, but you should press for more information. You need to know what you must do to be promotable. If your boss can't describe that, you may be stuck in a dead-end position.

If you are telecommuting or working a part-time schedule, reaching clear agreement on performance metrics is especially important. Arrange frequent updates with your supervisor to minimize the "out-of-sight, out-of-mind" problem. If possible, the discussions should be booked well in advance, before your boss's calendar becomes overcrowded. The chats don't need to be long or formal. However, if they are frequently skipped because your supervisor is too busy, that is a potential red flag. For telecommuting to work well, both sides must commit to making the effort to communicate.

Tailor memos on your progress to your superior's preferences. Some managers want a level of detail and frequency of reporting that others find to be a waste of time. Ask for examples of the type of communications desired that you can use as a template. After your first submission verify that you are providing the information in a satisfactory form. Periodically probe your boss on how your responses can be improved.

No one likes negative surprises. Your supervisor is supposed to know what is going on, so that she or he can keep her or his superiors appraised of any exceptions. Often any kind of surprise whether good or bad is viewed as a problem. As soon as you know that something unanticipated has occurred or is likely to happen, let your boss know.

Whether or not your employer requires formal annual performance appraisals, it is essential to know your manager's opinion of your work. Even in the absence of official reviews, you are being compared with your peers. It is far better to get bad news while you have time to take corrective action than to find out the hard way by getting laid off or receiving a less than average increase in salary.

SOFT SKILLS

While part of your supervisor's assessment of your performance depends on your specified deliverables, other factors come into play. Unwritten rules can trump the known metrics. Your perceived dedication to the organization, communication skills, teamwork, and ability to avoid and resolve interpersonal conflict are very important.

Organizational culture is important and there can be a lot of differences in what is considered to be a preferred or even an acceptable communication style. Past experience in another organization or an outside mentor cannot provide insight into aspects of your work group's culture that can have a major impact on how your behavior is perceived and on your effectiveness. You need an internal mentor with whom you can have honest discussions. To be effective, you and your mentor should be able to discuss mistakes that you are making. Such conversations may not be easy, because bad news is not pleasant. However, if you and your mentor avoid difficult conversations, the value of the relationship will be drastically diminished.

When I started work at Mobil, my approach to discussing technical work with colleagues was based on what I had experienced in the rough and tumble world of academia at MIT and Stanford. On top of that, I had grown up in Brooklyn, which did not instill in me a demure and retiring demeanor. I was accustomed to seminars being vigorous debating matches with attendees trying to pick holes in the research.

That was not Mobil's way. Eventually a kindly, older colleague took me aside and explained that, as a result of my questions in research presentations, I had acquired a reputation as a piranha (the sharp toothed South American fish that sometimes attacks human beings in a wild feeding frenzy). He made clear that Mobil's company culture was to "praise in public and punish in private." Only minor suggestions for improvement were to be voiced in open seminars. If the basic premise of the work was faulty, discussion of that was to be reserved for a closed-door session.

Many people avoid unpleasant situations and as a result are reluctant to share criticism. If someone is willing to risk a negative reaction and provides you with valuable feedback on what you are doing wrong, don't get angry; thank them profusely. I have tried to receive unpleasant criticism in an open receptive way, so as to encourage people to share it with me as soon as possible. It is not easy, but you are much better off knowing about your mistakes, so that you can try to correct them. What you don't know about how your behavior is perceived will hurt you.

Whether they are called "soft skills," "emotional intelligence quotient," "organizational citizenship behaviors," "people skills," "critical thinking," "interpersonal communication skills," or something else, your personal style can prevent you from receiving the rewards that you have earned from exceptionally good achievements on your assigned tasks. Frequently, it is not what you get done, but how you get it done that matters most.

Employers want good "team players." Organizational citizenship behaviors, which were defined by D. W. Organ as "individual behavior that is discretionary, not directly or explicitly recognized by the formal reward system, and that in the aggregate promotes the effective functioning of the organization," are what is desired.[8] These traits include enthusiasm, being aware of how your behavior impacts your fellow employees, and your willingness to assist others. Good corporate citizens are supposed to serve as role models through consistent compliance with company rules, attendance at meetings that are important but are not mandatory, and by defending the organization's business and objectives. These behaviors have been described as actions above and beyond the scope of your job duties that contribute to the welfare of the organization.

Studies have determined that organizational citizenship behaviors "account for at least as much variance in managerial evaluations of performance as task performance."[9] Podsakoff and his colleagues also found that these behaviors are "positively related to performance evaluations and managerial reward allocation decisions."[10] People with good citizenship behavior tend to be considered to be more competent, to get higher overall evaluations, and to receive better compensation.

Think of the "open microphone syndrome." We have all witnessed the expensive blunders that public figures make when they assume that a mike is turned off or that what they are saying is off the record. Everything you do at work, including your casual conversations with friends at lunch, impacts your performance evaluation. What you do on your own time can also come back to haunt you on the job. When you write an e-mail or post online, imagine yourself scrawling the words on a busy hallway wall at work. Act as if your employer is aware of everything that you do.

Employers want people who can "play well together." You may be incredibly talented, but if you a loner, who can't get along with your coworkers, your career will suffer. Not only will you acquire a reputation for being a difficult person, but also you will accomplish less, because we often rely on other people's skills and knowledge.

Teamwork is critical no matter where or how we get our work done. The burden is on you to be reliable and to clearly communicate when you are available for consultation and when you expect to complete your assignment. In some ways mutual cooperation can be even more critical if you are telecommuting or working in a different location or during different hours than your colleagues. Flexible work arrangements are a privilege and your colleagues in the office may be jealous, so make every effort to keep your coworkers and management happy. If a disagreement between you and coworkers is escalated to management, you may lose access to the flexibility that you need.

Let's look at an example. Last summer, Nick received permission to telecommute after his wife was transferred to the Los Angeles area from Chicago. He suspects that a coworker, Todd, is trying to trying to make him look bad. Since late January, Todd has been sending Nick last-minute appeals for information by e-mail, burying the request in the message and not including "urgent" or "time critical" in the subject line. Nick has learned to scan his e-mail for messages from Todd before he does anything else.

One Friday morning, Nick finds a request from Todd that was sent a couple of hours earlier. Fortunately, Nick has the required data at his fingertips. After e-mailing some charts, Nick picks up the phone and calls Todd, "Glad I caught you, Todd, do you have a few minutes to chat? I wanted to make sure that you received everything you need."

"Yeah, sure, Nick. Good thing you weren't at the beach and were able to get it to me on time."

"Anytime. I'm happy it is what you required, Todd. Please keep in mind that with the two-hour time difference, I usually don't check my email until a couple of hours after you get to the office. If fast action is imperative, please add 'urgent' to the subject line. By the way, we don't live anywhere near the beach. With traffic, getting to the ocean can take an hour. We have only been there twice since we moved."

"Well at least you are not dealing with snow. Earlier this week there were a couple of days when I was late picking my daughter up from daycare and had to pay extra."

"Sorry to hear that. Maybe you can leave early on snowy days and catch up on your work at home."

"Thanks for the suggestion, but that is impossible for me. My house is a zoo. The kids and the dog won't leave me alone. I can't find a quiet place to think."

"Yes, that is a problem. The housing prices here are much higher, so we ended up with a house half as big as what we had in Chicagoland. Making things even worse, I must have a room dedicated to work. My kids are not happy about sharing a bedroom and our kitchen is so tiny we are tripping over each other."

Nick has learned that Todd's problem is that he is jealous. To smooth the relationship, Nick makes a habit of calling Todd to confirm that he has received what he wants. When he calls, Nick takes the time to commiserate with Todd. He downplays the positive aspects of where he lives, such as being able to take his kids to Disneyland and to drive to Yosemite National Park over President's Day weekend and go snowshoeing at Badger Pass. Instead he empathizes with Todd and talks about the higher cost of living, smog, traffic, and child care issues. Their relationship improves without involving their team leader.

BUILDING RAPPORT

In everything there is risk and reward. In sharing unnecessary personal tidbits with a manager (or a subordinate), you are taking a risk. However, if you always keep everything strictly to business, you will never build relationships. The casual chitchat at the beginning and/or the end of a face-to-face or virtual meeting is an important part of the meeting. Even if you are under a lot of time pressure, budget the time for the pre and post meeting networking into your schedule.

Both remotely and in person, the sharing of little confidences can build rapport. Think of the time spent on small talk as part of your work. Pick and choose what you mention, evaluating the responses. No matter how different our cultures and our backgrounds, we all struggle with many of the same personal problems. People bond over shared challenges and experiences.

In making yourself vulnerable by discussing personal issues, you also become a "real person" and not just a box on the organizational chart. Engaging in mutual mentoring discussions is a fantastic way to build friendships. Keep it short and be sure that you give the other person more than half of the time to talk, balancing the "air time." We tend to think the other person talks longer than we do, even when that isn't the case.

If people working at home fail to establish a personal relationship with their managers, they risk being overlooked for promotions. Those who use nontraditional work arrangements can suffer from being stigmatized as less ambitious. If the manager is required to have the performance ratings of his team conform to a "bell curve," people using flexible work arrangements may be easy targets to be pushed to the lower end.

Recently, I encountered a man who demonstrated to me how quickly it is possible to create rapport with a disgruntled person without face-to-face contact. "VS" is a Microsoft employee in New Delhi, India, whose job is to provide second-level technical support. By the time I spoke with VS, I had wasted more than four hours over five days trying to get Windows 10 to function properly on my computer. My appointment with VS had been made 48 hours previously. Needless to say, I was not thinking positive thoughts about Microsoft or its staff when VS called shortly before the scheduled time.

When VS began interjecting "small talk," I wondered why he was wasting my time. VS started showing me a picture of his office building in New Delhi and its interior, when I was impatient for him to get my Windows 10 start menu functioning again. While his various tests of my computer system slowly cranked away in the background, VS prompted me to share that I had visited India multiple times on business between 1995 and 2001. Then VS shared pictures of famous locations in India, quizzing me on which ones I had seen. Meanwhile, I was hoping that he wouldn't run out of time without fixing my problem.

Although zero- and first-level Microsoft support had been completely unable to fix my problem, VS soon resolved my start menu problem and moved on to fixing all of the nasty glitches that I had encountered with Windows 10. He waited while I found the disk for my multifunction printer/scanner and then wrote a driver for the scanner, because Canon had not yet made one available. VS patiently stayed on line, while I tested that my scanner was working and that I could still print. When I was completely satisfied, VS asked, "Do I deserve a box of chocolates?"

I was confused, but in about an hour, VS had cajoled me into liking him. He explained that, in a few days, I would receive an e-mail asking me about my experience. He emphasized that the e-mail would be about the service that he had provided and not the previous calls that had not fixed anything. Then he got me to agree to positively respond to the Microsoft survey on his performance.

Over the next few days, I kept getting various surveys on my overall Windows 10 experience. Each time, I carefully checked to make sure that the survey on which I was giving low marks was not for VS's service. Finally, I received the e-mail asking about him and gave him top marks.

Would I have graded him as highly if he had not engaged me and built rapport during the call? I doubt it. At the end of the call, I carefully made a record of his name, so that I could include that when I was asked about his work. I never saw VS's face, but he certainly left me feeling very positive about him and willing to take the time to provide his virtual "box of chocolates" in the form of top marks on the survey.

TESTIMONIALS

We all have clients. When I needed assistance from Microsoft in fixing my Windows 10 problem, I was VS's client. After he did a wonderful job repairing my operating system, VS was in effect asking me to write a testimonial for him (a public tribute to him and to his achievements). VS knew that just doing a good job was not sufficient to get recognized and rewarded. Testimonials are important when decisions are being made as to who gets promoted and a good increase in compensation.

Clients can be inside or outside of our organization. If you make a valuable contribution to a major project of another subsidiary of your business, a letter from your primary contact on that work describing how you contributed to the overall success of the endeavor is more effective than your statement of what you accomplished. Sometimes your clients are colleagues who report to the same manager as you. A note from a teammate is useful in illustrating your good organizational citizenship behaviors. If anyone takes the time to thank you with a note, save it and forward it to your boss. If you have an annual appraisal, save all of the thank-you notes and attach them or include quotes from them even if you have already shared them with your supervisor. Third-party praise is much more powerful than your assessment of your performance.

If you don't get a note and you know that your client was happy, don't be shy. E-mail or call your primary contact person and ask if he or she would do you the favor of sending a note to your boss with a copy to you. You can always explain that it could make a big difference on your annual appraisal. It is important to ask for a copy, because by the time of salary action and promotions, your boss may have forgotten. If you have a copy, you can remind your supervisor by attaching it.

You may scoff at this as being contrived, but it works. Chevron had a formal mentoring program. For one of the six-month periods, I was coaching a midcareer woman, "Beth," who wanted to get promoted.

Beth was convinced that her boss didn't properly recognize the value of her contributions. When we discussed the problem Beth mentioned that she had received multiple e-mails from clients within the company. I suggested that she include quotes from the thank-you notes on her annual review form. After the next appraisal cycle, Beth thanked me for helping her get promoted.

NETWORKING

In my over 35 years in the petroleum industry, I have endured wild swings in oil price accompanied by frantic hiring when the price skyrockets and massive layoffs when the price plummets. People who have endured and been able to secure good positions during hard times are those with the best professional networks.

Every profession has affinity groups. Often there are multiple, separate, but overlapping nonprofit societies that focus on various facets of your discipline. Each of these organizations provides you with an opportunity to meet people beyond your company and to create a more robust personal network.

You may argue that as a member of a dual-career couple and also perhaps as a parent, there is no way that you have time to get involved with a professional society. But you do. It is all a matter of prioritizing your time.

Over my career, I have been an active member of multiple societies. When my daughter was only four years old, I collaborated with a friend to found the Society of Core Analysts. During the initial year of that group's existence, I organized "the first annual meeting" and brought my daughter to the evening opening reception. That society is now 30 years old and has held meetings all over the world including in Abu Dhabi, Canada, England, France, the Netherlands, Norway, and Scotland.

My professional interests evolved away from core analysis. As a result, I have not attended one of that society's meetings in more than two decades. However, I have maintained contact with people, whom I met through the Society of Core Analysts. We continue to do important favors for each other.

How did I find the time to get involved in volunteer activities? I gave up watching television. It is amazing how much time that frees up. We all have ways in which we fritter away time. Analyze how your nonwork hours are spent. Prioritize and look for ways to be more effective and efficient.

I considered the hours that I spent on professional society activities as an investment in myself. To create a financially secure retirement, we save money throughout our careers. Analogously, I have for decades invested much of my time in volunteer activities building my reputation and network. My carefully nurtured professional society "nest eggs" have paid off big dividends for years and continue to do so.

To have a robust career parachute ready to deploy, sustained effort is required to create and maintain your professional network. Your personal safety net is woven by working side by side on committees and projects with people who work for many different employers. Fellow committee members know what it is like working with you. When you want to look for a new job, you have numerous professional association friends, who are ready to help you.

Volunteer work also provides access to skill-building experiences that you may not receive through your employment. Leadership experience can be acquired by volunteering to chair committees and organize events. Engaging in volunteer projects publicly displays your leadership skills and ethics.

Depending on your career, other types of volunteer organizations such as civic, religious, charitable, and special-interest groups may serve the same function for you that professional societies have for me. You may want to attend meetings of several groups, before focusing on one. Pick something that you enjoy and get involved.

A friend, fellow active volunteer, and member of a dual-career couple, Janeen Judah, posted, "A good network depends on paying it forward to others BEFORE you ask for something in return."[11]

How robust is your career parachute? If it is flimsy, get busy volunteering.

STRENGTHEN YOUR RÉSUMÉ

If you have a boss who champions your cause or another well-placed sponsor, you may not feel that it is necessary to bolster your résumé. However over your career, you will probably work for many different bosses. Also, if you have just one or two supporters, you may find your career stagnating, when they are no longer in a position to support you. I have seen many highflyers stall out when they lose a critical sponsor.

Prepare for your "rainy day." To build career resilience, take a defensive posture with regard to providing evidence of your competency and impact. Whenever possible provide an estimate of the economic impact of your personal work. You should do this not only on your résumé, but also on company performance appraisal documents.

If you can be credentialed in your profession, whether it is engineering, law, accounting or something different, take the exam as early in your career as possible. While you gain experience with time, you usually become more specialized. Taking the exam to be certified is often easiest when you are fresh out of school and remember all of the basics that you may not recall later.

Relocating to another state to follow your partner can be a problem, if you must take a test to get a new license to practice your profession. For example, there is not reciprocity between all states for working as an attorney.[12] I knew a lawyer in her mid-fifties who relocated to another state to follow her husband. She was working as a technology protection adviser, because that position did not require a license to practice law. Despite years of legal experience, my friend had not passed the bar exam the first time in her new state.

As you get older, "senior moments" are a significant handicap in passing timed tests. Declining ability to memorize and slower recall of information may make getting relicensed tough even for a competent, skilled individual.

Depending on your profession, publications can be important. Internally within your organization, writing reports documents your involvement with major projects. Don't leave the recording to others. If you author the report, you are more likely to get the credit that you deserve.

If possible market your work externally. Leverage every chance you get to speak to groups and to author articles in trade journals. These activities will bolster your professional reputation both within your profession and within your current organization. Every time you give a talk or get an article published, add it to your list. It is much easier to capture the accomplishments as they occur than to try to generate the lists of speeches and publications later.

People may have trouble providing evidence of their professional accomplishments because their work is confidential. Some companies have teams of patent attorneys, but limit technical publications. That was the situation for me early in my career. I learned that if you can't publish, but you can patent, do so. Patents are wonderful credentials and great résumé builders.

Highly desirable employees are in a stronger position to negotiate concessions of all kinds. Throughout your career, starting in school, you should be continuously building your résumé—leadership positions, academic and professional accomplishments, awards, publications, patents, and so on. Keep a real-time record of all of them so that you can quickly assemble a résumé or biographical sketch by selecting what to cite depending on the audience.

RESILIENCE

Fairy tales end with everyone living happily ever after. Life doesn't usually work out that way. Unanticipated mergers, new technologies, market crashes, and other circumstances beyond our control can upset our meticulously constructed plans and arrangements. We always need to be prepared to hunt for a new position.

The happily ever after of having two great jobs in the same geographic area may get thrown into turmoil by one or both partners being offered a relocation or losing a job. Build and strengthen your security net by acquiring and maintaining credentials, keeping your résumé updated, and continually networking internally and externally. Nurture your network by doing favors for others, because you never know when you will need kindness in return or who will turn out to be your savior in times of need. It is much easier to maintain your readiness than to launch a crash effort in a crisis.

Resilience is the key to long-term success. When you are knocked down, don't be embarrassed. Job loss happens to many amazingly talented people. Swallow your pride, dust yourself off, and leverage your personal network. As a member of a dual career couple, you may feel constrained by the logistics involved in coordinating two careers, but when you fall on hard times, your partner's career can keep your family afloat until you find a new position.

CHAPTER 9

Why Both Partners Should Maintain Their Careers

We all have those days when we want to scream, "Take this job and shove it." That line written by David Allan Coe resonates with many people. In 1977, Johnny Paycheck's recording of Coe's song reached the top of the country music charts.

Much as you might want to, don't quit. Follow the money. When you lose your income, you have less control over your life. Your relationship with your partner will change. You will become your mate's dependent rather than his or her peer. And you will change. It does not happen instantaneously, but it does.

BALANCE OF POWER

I literally learned about the balance of power at my mother's knee. In the 1940s, my mother struggled to establish herself as a "fashion artist." By her late twenties, she had moved from Washington, DC, to Manhattan and was earning a good living illustrating advertisements for clothing and accessories in newspapers and magazines. When she married my father in 1949, she was making more money than he was as an assistant district attorney in Brooklyn.

My parents both loved their work. While my mother had dreamed of being a children's book illustrator, she was making a good income as an artist. My father lived in the world that many years later was chronicled in the television series, *Law and Order*. He would ride around with the police investigating high-profile crimes and even testified before Congress about a baby-selling adoption scandal. Life was good, but my mother wanted five children.

My mother managed to continue working from home after I was born even though there was just over two years' age difference between my older brother and myself. However, after my younger brother arrived, less than two years after me, the juggling act became unsustainable for her. When my mother stopped working, my father also had to give up the job that he loved. His salary as an assistant district attorney was insufficient to support his growing family. He resigned and went into business as a defense attorney. Within weeks, his income soared, but he hated defending criminals instead of locking them up.

My mother proceeded with her plan to have five children, but loathed having to ask my father for money. She pleaded for a weekly household allowance, but he refused, because his income stream was sporadic, depending on when his clients paid. My father also firmly believed that since it was his money, he should call the shots.

When my youngest sibling was seven years old, my parents had a fight over the purchase of a lawn chair. My mother wanted an inexpensive, lightweight chair that she could easily carry up and down the stairs to the basement. My father insisted on acquiring from a friend a chaise lounge with a robust metal frame and a heavy mattress. The lawn chair was rarely used, because of the nuisance of hauling the bulky mattress up the steep, narrow steps. That battle prompted my mother to commence the struggle to revive her career.

In the dozen years that my mother was out of the workforce, technology had largely eliminated fashion art. Photographs had displaced drawings in advertisements, so she decided to revert to her original career dream of being a children's book illustrator. Two years later a children's book that she illustrated was published, but work continued to be scarce. She turned to writing her own manuscripts so that she could illustrate them. Within a couple of years, the first of the 29 children's fantasies that she wrote and illustrated was issued under her maiden name, Ruth Chew. Her last book was released when she was 78 years old.

My mother reveled in having her own income stream that enabled her to make her own decisions. When my father disowned my hippie older brother, she subsidized his lifestyle. When I graduated from college and wanted to borrow her car to get to a summer job in Houston, she surprised me with the gift of a new car. She regained "equal earner" status, and at the end of her life, the income she had saved from the royalties on her books covered a decade of care in assisted living.

The passage of decades has not eliminated the link between money and who has the power in a domestic relationship. Wednesday Martin, a social researcher, studied the glamorous, stay-at-home moms of the upper east side of Manhattan. These women were in their thirties, possessed advanced degrees from big name universities and business schools, and had three or four children younger than 10. Their husbands were wealthy men who often managed private equity and hedge funds. Martin made it clear that she didn't envy them. "Access to your husband's money might feel good. But it can't buy you the power you get by being the one who earns, hunts or gathers it. The wives of the masters of the universe, I learned, are a lot like mistresses—dependent and comparatively disempowered. Just sensing the disequilibrium, the abyss that separates her version of power from her man's might keep a thinking woman up at night."[1]

According to Martin, an "annual wife bonus was not an uncommon practice in this tribe." The wife bonus, "might be hammered out in a pre-nup or post-nup, and distributed on the basis of not only how well her husband's fund had done but her own performance."[2] The negotiated compensation positions these women as their husband's employees with some of their work metrics related to sex.

Men married to wealthy female executives may have a more difficult time than their female counterparts. One evening at a dinner reception in Houston, I was amused to overhear the confusion of our Norwegian host, when he asked "Herb," the husband of American executive "Traci," "What do you do?" Herb replied, "I support Traci."

The Norwegian, who was fully fluent in English, repeated his question, because he thought he hadn't properly heard the response. Herb's answer was so different from what the Norwegian was anticipating; Herb almost had to spell it out.

The Norwegian's confusion is particularly noteworthy because Norway is very progressive with regard to women's role in society. Norway's paid paternity leave program is designed to encourage men to take time off to care for their children. Furthermore, in 2003 Norway became the first country in the world to impose gender quotas on the boards of directors of large corporations. About 500 companies were required to increase the proportion of women on their boards to 40 percent. Thus, it was enlightening to witness the surprised reaction of a Norwegian to an American man who had made "a career" of being the supportive executive spouse.

We seldom find a man devoting his life to supporting his wife's career. However, it is the model that many companies prefer for their female executives. Herb's full-time support and role as homemaker enabled Traci to assume the sole-breadwinner executive lifestyle and to successfully climb high into the upper ranks of a giant corporation. However, Herb lost his independence.

Male or female, when we leave the working world and are fully supported by our partner, we take on a subservient role. As with Martin's Manhattan moms, who "exercised themselves to a razor's edge" and "joked about possible sexual performance metrics," house hubbies like Herb are subordinate to their wives and live in a much narrower world than their spouses.[3]

PERSONAL IMPACT

As individuals we are constantly changing. We literally are what we eat and drink in the very real sense that an adult human body contains 55 to 65 percent water and the cells in our blood and many vital organs are replaced over time spans varying from a few days to a few months.[4] Only few parts of our body such as our nervous system and the lenses of our eyes are not replaced and regenerated during our lifetime.

Similarly, our personalities are constantly evolving depending on how we spend our time. When we cease to interact with people at work and receive relatively little intellectual stimulation at home, we regress. If your partner, who has been immersed all day in high finance, cutting-edge engineering, or major marketing issues, comes home and asks, "How was your day?" and all you do is complain about how many diapers you changed or how many junk phone calls you received or that you forgot to buy sandwich bread, you are diminished in your mate's eyes.

In the first four months of 2012, Gallup conducted telephone interviews of more than 60,000 women in the United States as part of the Gallup-Healthways Well-Being Index Survey. The report noted that, "Stay-at-home moms at all income levels are worse off than employed moms in terms of sadness, anger, and depression, though they are the same as other women in most other aspects of emotional wellbeing. Employed moms, however, are doing as well as employed women without children at home—possibly revealing that formal employment, or perhaps the income associated with it, has emotional benefits for mothers."[5]

The results of the Gallup poll suggest that if you are feeling sad and frustrated about your work–life balance, quitting to stay home with your children is not going to improve your mental health and may make it worse. Don't leap into action even if your spouse is as fabulously wealthy as the husbands of the upper east side of Manhattan moms that Martin chronicled. Pause to reflect.

You can't craft an appropriate solution until you accurately characterize the source of your misery. Take the time to understand what is causing your sadness, anger, and depression. If your career is important to you, quitting to stay home may as the Gallup poll suggests make you less well off with regard to those factors. Perhaps you need to change jobs, not lifestyles!

IDENTIFY THE REAL PAIN POINTS

As discussed in Chapter 6, if you are dissatisfied with your opportunities at work, you are more likely to consider your work–life balance to be unacceptable. Your true frustration may be with your career, not the demands that your personal life is imposing on you.

If your job is unsatisfying, can you clearly articulate what is wrong? Do you feel that you are "spinning your wheels" because you are learning nothing new and you are bored? Does your boss remind you of the pointy-haired idiot in Scott Adams's Dilbert comic strips? Are your coworkers hostile or unsupportive? Do you feel as if you must work longer hours or travel more frequently than you want? Is your job too stressful? Understanding what is wrong can help you craft a solution with your current employer or know what to look for with a new organization.

If, on reflection, you recognize that you need to change your work environment, don't quit until you have secured another position even though your partner can support you. Generally, it is easier to find new employment while you are currently employed.

If your angst is really because of the life side of the balance, be sure that you fully understand the issues and how long-lasting they will be. If you want more time with your children, is that just while they are infants or preschoolers, or for the next 20 years? In either case, if you can secure a leave of absence or work part-time, you can test to see if that change makes you happier or sadder, while making it easier to return to full-time work.

When you find your current situation unsustainable, there are usually alternatives to exiting the working world. Don't rush to stop your pain by resigning. Take the time to analyze your anxiety and consider alternatives. When we are stressed out, we may feel more cornered and think that quitting is the only way out. Careful consideration can reveal multiple doable alternatives.

DOMESTIC OVERLOAD

If you can afford to quit, you can also bear the cost of additional household help, right up to the amount of what your after-tax income would be if you continued to work. It might seem insane to continue working if most of your earnings are consumed by paying someone to handle domestic chores, but it isn't. Soldiering on maintains your career skills and preserves your earning ability.

Often a domestic meltdown is associated with caring for preschool children. However, even if you have a large number of children like my mother, they grow up. Completely cutting your ties with the working world alters your relationship with your partner, changes your experiences and perspectives, and makes it more difficult to resume your career.

When you feel overwhelmed by child care or by supporting an ailing relative, pause to consider your alternatives. If you feel that you must take a complete break, consider using the unpaid leave provided to eligible employees under the Family and Medical Leave Act of 1993. Carve out some of that time to explore your options to work in a less demanding role, part-time, or from home.

HOURS IN TRAFFIC

It is never fun to be stuck in traffic, but when daily commuting consumes large amounts of time, it is extremely frustrating to me. According to the U.S. Census Bureau, the average commute to work is now about 26 minutes.[6] That implies that many people find roughly 30 minutes each way to be tolerable. Personally, I find that wasting more time than that drives me nuts. I visualize my life draining away idling on the freeway.

When we left Stanford and started work in the Dallas area, we had a 16-month-old toddler. I didn't want to move into an apartment and then have to move a second time after we found a house. My new employer recommended a realtor, who "sold" us a house on the opposite side of Dallas from where I would be working, and claimed that it would be a counter-commute for me. Wrong, wrong, wrong! I found myself trapped in traffic for an hour or more on my way home. A little over two years later and a few weeks after our second child was born, we moved into a new home that cut my commute in half.

Even with a commute that usually was about 30 minutes each way, I tried to make the time more productive by listening to audio books. My employer had a library with a variety of recordings on business topics. My kids would make fun of me, but I learned some useful things during time that would otherwise have been wasted.

After flexible working hours became available, I found myself leaving earlier and earlier in order to shave time off my morning commute. Before I retired, I was leaving at 6:15 a.m. and even then one of the highways would regularly be slowed to a crawl, but mercifully despite bad traffic my trip took only about 20 minutes each way.

I am far from alone in my negative reaction to having a long commute, because of horrendous traffic. Hilbrecht et al. found that, "Traffic congestion can contribute to frustration, negative moods and decreased satisfaction with both one's job and home life due to the unpredictability of traffic flow, physical obstacles and lack of situational control."[7]

However, Hilbrecht et al. reported that other researchers have concluded that commuting can have some positive aspects. "Commuting provides transition time allowing a mental shift between different activity spheres. It can create a time out from other commitments and responsibilities, which could include pleasureable activities such as listening to music, enjoying the scenery or simply allowing some coveted time alone."[8]

With two job locations and one residence, it is more challenging to minimize both commutes. Spending more on housing, like paying for additional domestic assistance, might provide more quality time and improve your work–life balance. Would moving to a more expensive area shorten one or both commutes? Can you downsize and move closer? Can you use the time to listen to worthwhile recordings? Can you carpool or take public transportation so that you can work during the commute? Is working from home a few days a week a possibility? Everyone's situation differs and we have different tolerances for time lost in traffic jams, but when we get creative, there are often ways to reduce the pain.

FINANCIAL SECURITY

As a member of a dual-career couple, you may feel constrained by the logistics involved with coordinating careers, but when you encounter hard times, one partner's income can keep your family afloat until the unemployed partner secures a new position. Even if you and your partner are in similar roles in the same industry, couples with two incomes can find it easier to weather recessions than sole breadwinners.

President Truman liked to say, "A recession is when your neighbor loses his job; a depression is when you lose your job."[9] For dual-career couples, the saying could be modified to "A recession is when one partner is fired; a depression is when both partners lose their jobs."

Business cycles are inevitable. The frequency and the magnitude of the changes in unemployment rate are not predictable. Since I received my bachelor's degree a little over 40 years ago, there have been six recessions in the United States, varying in length from 6 to 18 months. Twice the unemployment rate has spiked to 10 percent or more, but the other recessions were milder. No matter what your profession, you will face recessions and periods of downsizing during the course of your career.

The industry in which you work may have a different business cycle pattern than the economy as a whole. I worked in the petroleum industry, which had a more than 20-year recession, while the overall economy experienced shorter contractions. When I was hired by Mobil Oil in 1978, the number of people employed in the oil industry was soaring. However, between 1982 and 2003, I endured a seemingly endless series of layoffs.

Depending on how diversified your community is, you may find yourself tied to the business cycle of another industry. For example, in communities in which the petroleum industry dominates, the financial well-being of attorneys, accountants, realtors, and those in service industries can be linked to the price of oil or natural gas.

Living in the greater San Francisco/Silicon Valley area, I have seen the impact of the booms and busts of the "tech" or "dot-com" sector. In the early part of this century after the dot-com collapse, congestion on the local highways was noticeably decreased and housing prices collapsed. In the 2008 bust, our next door neighbor lost his job and his home was foreclosed. However, during that period, employment in the petroleum industry was relatively stable. Now, although oil industry is rapidly retrenching, the tech sector is booming. Thus, where I live, housing prices have soared and freeway traffic is horrific. My oil company stocks may be down, but the value of my house is up.

The job security of having two working people in a household is a key reason that many people gave as a good reason to be part of a dual-career couple. As many of them commented, "You don't want to have all of your eggs in one basket."

CHAPTER 10

Why You Shouldn't Wait for the System to Change

The shift from a predominantly sole breadwinner to a dual-career couple workforce is well documented. In 2013, the Pew Research Center reported that women comprised 47 percent of the U.S. workforce with 68 percent of women and 79 percent of men of working age active in the labor force. Between 1960 and 1990 as more women continued working after marriage, the percentage of families with two earners soared from only about 25 percent to approximately 60 percent, and the percentage of married couples with children under the age of 18 in which only the father was employed plummeted from about 70 percent to 30 percent. Since 1990 approximately 60 percent of families with children under 18 have been dual income.[1]

With sole breadwinners a shrinking fraction of the workforce, you might assume that most organizations would aspire to be a preferred employer for members of dual-career couples. Unfortunately not! Although as a member of a dual-career couple you may see the writing on the wall that changes are needed, far too many executives do not. Outdated hiring preferences, career development programs, work styles, and parental leave policies linger in numerous establishments. The modifications that you want may not be implemented within a time frame that benefits you.

WHO MOVED MY CHEESE?

In the allegorical story, "Who Moved My Cheese?" that was written by Spencer Johnson, two indecisive miniature humans, "Hem" and "Haw" and two mice, "Sniff" and "Scurry" live in a maze, eating cheese which represents happiness and success. When the cheese vanishes from its customary location, the tiny people fear the unknown and blame each other for their hunger. Eventually, Haw realizes that he will starve waiting for the cheese to reappear in its customary location, and reconciles himself to scouting for alternative supplies. Before embarking on his search, Haw writes on the wall of the empty cheese station, "If You Do Not Change, You Can Become Extinct." As the story progresses, Haw continues scrawling messages about embracing change on the walls of the maze.[2]

In the late 1990s numerous organizations distributed copies of "Who Moved My Cheese?" to employees and held group discussions about embracing change. My company, Mobil, distributed the story during a time of draconian downsizings and reorganizations. Management's goal was to convince my coworkers and me to accept the need for unpleasant changes. They wanted those of us who survived the cuts to stay productive and to maintain a positive attitude in the face of uncertainty about our continued employment.

Although management embraced Johnson's allegory as a way to persuade its employees to change, many organizations are resistant to transformations when faced with their own equivalent of the cheese disappearing. In this case, lifestyles are evolving and single earners no longer constitute the bulk of the workforce. Instead of "Who Moved My Cheese?" for traditional supervisors, it is "What Happened to My Workforce?" Traditional sole breadwinners not cheese are disappearing.

Like the miniature humans, Hem and Haw, in "Who Moved My Cheese?," the management of many organizations is still stuck in the mind-set that the old ways of working are tried and true. The traditional workers are becoming scarcer, but many old-fashioned managers are determined to staff their organization with dominant breadwinners like themselves as long as any are available. These managers see no need to change the old system to better accommodate members of dual-career couples.

There is a natural tendency for people to hire and promote "in their own image." In many large, long-established organizations, the majority of leaders are sole breadwinner males with a wife responsible for all of the household logistics. Even though the percentage of the workforce without a working mate is dwindling, many "old guard" executives continue to insist that their young protégés mimic their lifestyle.

In those organizations there is often an emphasis on a career path that tends to exclude members of dual-career couples. Members of the "old guard" are convinced that the appropriate way to develop leadership skills is the same way that they did. These bosses seek as their successors those who share their lifestyle and values. As long as traditional managers can fill their ranks with younger clones, they see no reason to change. Along the lines of "Who Moved My Cheese?" sole breadwinners are getting scarcer, but some are still available, so why change until the supply completely vanishes?

Sole breadwinner managers may be less inclined to accept flexible work practices that ease work–life integration for people in dual-career couples. Even if the organization's policies allow flexible work alternatives, old-fashioned managers may frown on the practice and discriminate against their subordinates who use them. When skilled workers have better alternatives, eventually inability to attract critical talent will provide the impetus for change. There is some evidence of that trend emerging. Individuals in dual-career couples are more likely than dominant earners to report changing employers, because of a conflict with their managers.[3]

Just as Hem waited until he was famished to embrace change, employers will wait to take action until they have trouble attracting and retaining people with critical skills. Many valuable staff members will have to exit before employers react.

The more valuable your skills, the harder you are to replace, and the greater attrition there is of others with your expertise, the more likely it is that management will make concessions. Companies in technology, finance, and professional services are offering generous parental leave packages not because they are enlightened, but because they are having difficulty attracting and retaining the highly skilled staff that they require.

If you try and fail to get the flexible work arrangements that you need or find yourself blocked from advancing, waiting for your boss or your organization to change is analogous to starving, because your cheese has vanished. You need to make the existing system work for you or find a new organization where you have the opportunities that you want and the flexibility that you crave.

IMMEDIATE SUPERVISOR

While large organizations have policies and procedures to enforce uniformity, the attitude of your immediate supervisor can make a huge difference. Your boss controls your performance evaluation and has a huge influence on your ability to get promoted. Even if your organization offers flexible work arrangements, they are often at the discretion of your immediate supervisor, who determines whether or not using them adversely impacts the enterprise. Your manager is a gatekeeper who can choose to focus on the quality and quantity of your work or on your work style—when and how you work.

There are many variations of the saying "People don't leave companies, they leave bosses." Your relationship with your direct supervisor has a huge impact on your satisfaction with your job. If you and your manager clash, you have a major problem and need to escape to another group in the same organization, to a new employer, or to self-employment.

FORGIVENESS IS EASIER THAN PERMISSION

Rear Admiral Grace Murray Hopper, who was a U.S. naval officer and an early computer programmer, was quoted in the U.S. Navy's *Chips Ahoy* magazine in July 1986, when she was 79 years old as saying, "It is often easier to ask for forgiveness than to ask for permission."[4]

Grace married in 1930 at the age of 25, before she obtained her doctorate in mathematics from Yale. She had no children, and her husband died about 15 years later during World War II. As one of the female pioneers in computer programming and in the navy, she must have encountered many barriers. Without a doubt, she spoke from personal experience about the benefits of pushing the limits and asking for permission afterward.

When you ask your manager for permission to do something unusual, you place her or him in a potentially risky position. Many people are risk averse. To protect themselves, they are predisposed to decline your request. After you have been explicitly told no, it is not a good idea to defy the verdict. However, if you stretch the rules and are successful, as Admiral Hopper recommended, the objections may vanish. By not asking permission until you have evidence of success, you have minimized the risk for your boss.

As an individual, you should be careful about deciding when to push boundaries. Do not abuse the situation. If you decide to leave early, arrive late, or occasionally work from home for personal reasons, make sure that you get your work done and meet your deadlines. If you follow the rules, you can complain that there was too much work for the time available, albeit at the risk of being condemned as less productive.

In contrast, if you choose to bend the rules, flexing your time or occasionally working from home without explicit permission, you need to meet or exceed performance expectations.

If you are in a professional role and there isn't a known need for face time in the office on a given day at a specific time, you can slip away and work from home or catch up at another time. However, if you are planning to take the day off and don't have clear permission to be out of the office, you might get caught, if a last-minute business crisis pops up and you are unavailable.

My daughter asked me to fly halfway across the country for her baby shower. When we made our plans, she said that she would take the day off, so that we could prepare and have some mother-daughter time. While I was in the air, her boss called to ask her to assist with a project that needed results by noon the following day. My daughter was able to remind her boss that she was already on the record as not being available that Friday.

TIME MARCHES ON

Through much of this volume, I have emphasized the importance of money in understanding what motivates people and the impact of each partner's income on the balance of power in a couple. In looking at the trade-offs between quitting and spending more money for domestic support, the relationship between time and money was the focus. In many ways time is a form of currency or as we often say, "time is money." That saying goes back to Benjamin Franklin, who in 1748 in "Advice to a Young Tradesman, Written by an Old One" explained that if you can work for wages, choosing to be idle is the same as spending money.[5]

In some instances, time is more valuable than money. If you lose money, you may be able to recoup it, but you can never recapture lost time. I find myself constantly weighing whether I am using my time wisely. Is the time spent worthy of the potential rewards? How would I invest my time if I did something else? Even time doing nothing—relaxing, sleeping, commuting, and so on—as Ben Franklin explained has a cost and a value.

If your employer doesn't provide the flexibility and/or opportunities you desire, taking no action and waiting for change is equivalent to making a decision. That is different from carefully considering all of your alternatives and deciding to stay the course, because you don't think you have a better alternative. In the first case, you just let time slip away, and in the second, you make a conscious decision and can take steps to position yourself for a future move.

There may be compelling reasons for choosing to remain in a job that is unsatisfying. I did so, because there were no better employment options for me that didn't involve splitting the family and/or pulling my kids out of schools in which they were thriving, but I still wonder if it was the correct decision. I didn't let the time slip away, but rather made a conscious decision to live with the situation and increased my activity in professional societies to enhance my marketability and to build my personal network. When the time was ripe, my ongoing personal initiatives paid off and I had alternatives.

You must decide for yourself whether it is better to stay the course with a less than satisfying job, "the devil you know," or to assume greater risk and take on "the devil you don't." Continuing will impact your career, your personal life, and your health. A period of career stagnation can make it difficult, if not impossible, to achieve certain goals. Missed experiences with your family because of an inflexible work schedule cannot be recaptured. Persistent stress may have a major adverse impact on your health and your relationships.

Timing can be critical in access to career opportunities. You may have more ability to switch employers or career tracks before your compensation exceeds a threshold. Age can also be a factor. Despite rules against age discrimination, certain types of opportunities are generally reserved for younger people. Wait too long to try to jump-start your career and you will find yourself handicapped by being viewed as having "a short runway." If that happens, your best alternative may be starting your own business, which may be more feasible when your children are grown and out of college, and you have a nest egg to live on.

Your children are only infants for a brief period of time. All too often we are so overwhelmed by caring for a newborn that we don't give ourselves the luxury of savoring precious moments snuggling with them. Indulge yourself. Time spent helping with homework is a long-term investment in your children's future well-being and success. The quiet time reading bedtime stories and cuddling is perfect for bonding. Don't let work pressures rob you of the chance to enjoy your children, but prioritize what you do. Focus on quality time rather than the quantity of time.

Family has always been important to me, even though my husband and my children may not have always agreed with me on my assessment of which activities were time-worthy. In high school my daughter ran cross-country and wanted me to attend her events. I went to a race once during business hours only to see her vanish into the trees and return later. Besides the cross-country run, I took time off to watch one of her track meets. She doesn't remember that I ever was present for a single one of her high school athletic events. While it gave her something to complain about, it didn't stop her from becoming a marathoner or seriously damage our relationship. And importantly, I don't feel guilty or have regrets.

If you are miserable at work, because of lack of flexibility and/or opportunity, don't underestimate the impact of the stress. Years ago, I was friends with a woman who headed employee relations at Mobil's Field Research Laboratory. (That was back before "employee relations" was renamed "human resources" in recognition of the reality that the focus was on serving management not employees.) She mentioned to me that she wasn't concerned about complaints from my research colleagues about work stress, because they didn't drop dead as frequently as their counterparts in operations.

MANAGING STRESS

Don't underestimate the devastating impact stress can have on your health. According to the National Institute of Mental Health, "People under chronic stress are prone to more frequent and severe viral infec tions . . . routine stress may lead to serious health problems, such as heart disease, high blood pressure, diabetes, depression, anxiety disorder, and other illnesses."[6]

The American Institute of Stress notes, "Numerous studies show that job stress is far and away the major source of stress for American adults and that it has escalated progressively over the past few decades. Increased levels of job stress as assessed by the perception of having little control but lots of demands have been demonstrated to be associated with increased rates of heart attack, hypertension and other disorders. In New York, Los Angeles and other municipalities, the relationship between job stress and heart attacks is so well acknowledged, that any police officer who suffers a coronary event on or off the job is assumed to have a work related injury and is compensated accordingly (including heart attack sustained while fishing on vacation or gambling in Las Vegas)."[7]

Stress related to the pressures of work, family, and other daily responsibilities is insidious with the potentially devastating impacts creeping up on you. According to the National Institute of Mental Health, "changes in health from routine stress may be hardest to notice at first. Because the source of stress tends to be more constant than in cases of acute or traumatic stress, the body gets no clear signal to return to normal functioning."[8]

Most of us can implement one of the National Institute of Mental Health's recommendations for reducing stress: to exercise regularly—30 minutes a day of gentle walking. Over the years when I have felt frustrated I have often gone out for a brisk walk either alone or with a friend. While walking I often remember things that I should do or think of solutions to nagging problems. One of my cures for writer's block is to go outside and walk. All sorts of solutions and ideas come to me when I do.

If you have small children and think you can't get away, take them with you. When I am helping with my grandchildren, I take them out for a walk. Babies sleep better with the motion and I get exercise. Invest in a good running or walking stroller and take off.

Admittedly, I live in California, which offers great weather, but with the right clothes and equipment, even if the climate is miserable, you can get out. In Scandinavian countries, I have seen people out walking with plastic rain covers for the baby carriages and strollers. I went on a half-day walking tour in Europe in a cold deluge, and stayed dry with waterproof boots, rain pants, and a Gore-Tex jacket.

With my fixation on maximizing my use of time, I love walking. I can get exercise while I think and solve problems or socialize. For multitaskers like me, it is a great option.

Everyone is faced with stress and the solutions vary. The basics that we all need are good nutrition, sleep, exercise, and social engagement. Having someone to talk with is beneficial, but depending on their familiarity with the problem that you are discussing, they may or may not provide helpful advice. Still, just having someone to whom you can "vent" can be helpful, but pick your confidant carefully and critically evaluate any advice you receive.

A good hug is also a great stress reliever and can make you feel much better. Give and receive hugs generously.

CHAPTER 11

Surviving and Thriving as a Dual-Career Couple

Planning is valuable, but no one can predict life's twists and turns. Those who thrive know their priorities, understand the trade-offs involved in risk–reward and pain–gain decisions, and are prepared to negotiate both with their employer and with their partner.

LIFE'S JOURNEY

In life, transitions are full of both risk and opportunity. The shift from the overwhelmingly male, sole breadwinner workforce to one filled with dual-career couples is a major revolution. The old rules and patterns no longer apply. Gender roles and work patterns are evolving. We have the opportunity to shape our destiny and determine whether the saying "May you live in interesting times" is a blessing or a curse.

Planning is important, but we should recognize that many of the best opportunities present themselves without advance warning. Life is a journey. As with a great vacation, some of the best experiences can't be planned. No matter how carefully we prepare, we may never get where we intended to go, so we should learn to enjoy the trip.

A recent adventure highlighted for me how much fun and memorable "a journey" can be. As my husband and I strolled past the Palazzo Reale (Royal Palace) in Naples, Italy, I noticed a sign to the Biblioteca Nazionale (National Library). I remembered reading that tourists could view some of the collection of over 1,800 Roman era papyri (papyrus scrolls) that were unearthed from beneath the 50-foot-thick flow of volcanic mud that buried Herculaneum in 63 CE. Pompeii vanished under volcanic ash in the same series of eruptions. We set off following small signs through extensive construction zones to the Biblioteca Nazionale. We zigzagged through courtyard after courtyard. Finally we arrived at a small cluttered office.

Since neither of us speak Italian, I said just one word to the man at the desk at the entrance, "Papyri?" Without asking for any identification, he handed us two slips of paper and pointed us toward the rear of the office. Another man silently led us to an elevator and pushed the button for the top floor. When we got there, we found ourselves alone in a large book-filled room. Taped to one wall was a small, color-coded list. After I found papyri with a pink bar next to it, I inferred that we should follow the pink bits.

We wandered through numerous deserted rooms that were stuffed from floor to ceiling with ancient dusty volumes. After climbing a small staircase, the pink patches led through a wildly twisting corridor that was too constricted to have any bookshelves. I suspected that we were in a passage tucked under the eaves of the palace.

After the narrow maze, we entered a series of long, dark, book-lined corridors. I felt like a character in one of the Dan Brown novels, such as *The Da Vinci Code* and was glad that I was not alone. It was before lunch, so I reassured myself that the odds of getting locked in overnight were low.

Finally, we turned a corner into a better lit hall with a brightly illuminated room at the end. The center of the room was filled with a large rectangular table with people seated around it studying documents. A lady approached us and I asked, "Papyri?" She indicated that we should sign a guest book, and rattled off a list of languages. I responded, "Inglese." Handing us a sheet of paper in English, she led us into an adjacent, darkened room with a number of dusty displays in small glass cases and departed.

We were trying to match the numbers on our printed sheet with the nondescript, charcoal-colored chunks in the cabinets, when the lady reappeared with a young English woman, who was spending six months in Naples studying the papyrus scrolls. The young woman graciously took the time to explain the machines built in the early 19th century to unroll the scrolls. The process was somewhat successful, but many of the scrolls were destroyed in the process, breaking into small fragments. Now, lasers are used to map the writing on the scrolls by detecting the presence of ink without unraveling them. The young woman remained with us until all of our questions were answered.

The next day on our tour, we visited the Museo Archeologico Nazionale. In a clean, brightly lit room, there were some of the charred bits that were scrolls from Herculaneum and machines that had been used in attempts to unroll them. The exhibit had detailed explanations in Italian and English. Our group paused briefly before passing on to see some of the other treasures in the museum. I was glad that we had trekked through the Biblioteca Nazionale, which was more memorable than the museum with its fantastic treasures.

Life is an adventure. Even with the best-laid plans, we take detours, hit dead-ends, and retrace our steps. We may never get to where we plan to go. However, as with my visit to the papyri in the Biblioteca Nazionale, the journey can turn out to be far more fun and memorable than the destination. Even when there is light at the end of a dark passage, the prize you have been seeking may not be there. The true value may be in the aggregate of the small seemingly inconsequential experiences along the way. Many things that we covet and sacrifice to obtain turn out not to be as wonderful as we imagined.

In my 35-year career in the petroleum industry, I didn't climb the corporate ladder as high as I hoped that I would, but I have fulfilled many other goals. Along the way, I have frequently considered alternatives, pondering the potential impact on my life in terms of Maslow's hierarchy of needs. I would ask myself if seizing the opportunity would improve my position in Maslow's hierarchy. About the time I left Mobil after 21 years, I ran into a former boss and spoke with him briefly. For some unknown reason, he blurted out, "You don't know how successful you have been."

His comment puzzled me. I didn't feel that my career with Mobil was particularly successful. I've often wondered if he was congratulating me on my approach to work–life balance.

Having children was always a major part of my plan and I am convinced that my working full time has not harmed them. At one point when they were in their teens and they were complaining about having been sent to daycare, I asked them, "What was so bad about daycare?"

All they could come up with was, "They made us eat spinach," and "They made us take naps and the cots were hard." Not exactly a deprived existence. Perhaps the greatest vindication of my decision to work full time throughout their childhood is that they have chosen to embrace a similar lifestyle; both are part of dual-career couples.

Whenever I was furious with my husband about something, I knew that I could walk away and still maintain my lifestyle. I envisioned myself a little bird sitting on an open palm. If the hand started to close, I would have flown away. Because I had freedom, I was willing to accept that no one is perfect and ignore behaviors that otherwise might have driven me away.

TRANSITIONS

Dual-career couples in which men and women are true equals are distinctly different than traditional families. Patriarchal societies have persisted in most areas for countless generations creating cultural traditions that are deeply ingrained in societies and that linger in many subtle ways. The unconscious prejudice that endures continues to make life challenging for people in dual-career couples, especially the women.

We are making progress toward true gender equality. However, for individual women, the improvements can be frustratingly slow. Each generation is advancing a little further, but women tend to be more disappointed with their career success than their male counterparts. When the Harvard Business School (HBS) asked alumni about their experiences versus their expectations at the time that they graduated, HBS "identified a pattern of frequent unmet expectations among women, while men's experiences more often aligned with their expectations."[1]

Over the course of my career, I have witnessed women progress from begging to be allowed in the room, to now when they are being urged by Sheryl Sandberg to take a seat at the table. However, since people generally are employed for over 30 years, there are still plenty of individuals in the workforce, and often in top management, who have attitudes more representative of the past than the present. Far too often, the highest level executives are among the most antiquated in their beliefs, because they have spouses who have assumed a subservient role. For people caught in the transition, the gap between corporate rhetoric and reality can be extremely frustrating.

Traditions evolve slowly. Many men and even some women resist the changes. Don't expect the dinosaurs to change or rapidly become extinct. However, in transitions there are local "sweet spots" with more enlightened attitudes. Improve your chances of career success and happiness by discovering and migrating to a more progressive and egalitarian environment. Vote with your feet.

I learned to look for greener pastures as an undergraduate at MIT in the early 1970s. At that time, only some of the faculty considered women to be worth educating. I wanted to be an earthquake seismologist. The professor of seismology, whom I approached about a research project, assigned me to work for course credit with a Turkish research associate who barely spoke English. I spent a year collecting and analyzing data only to have the faculty member and the research associate coauthor a paper based on my work. I was not even credited in the acknowledgments. Simultaneously a male contemporary, who occasionally would copy my homework, was paid to do research for that faculty member and allowed to coauthor the resulting paper. When an enlightened faculty member in a different aspect of geophysics, Professor William F. Brace, invited me to work with him on a research project, I jumped at the opportunity. I learned an important lesson. Don't try to teach an old dog new tricks. Find one who already behaves properly.

If for some reason you deliberately choose to stick with an unsatisfying work situation, seek other outlets for your talents. Volunteer activities can display your skills and expertise. Noncompensated endeavors may pave the path to a new and more rewarding career.

GATHER STATISTICS

Besides finding the sweet spots, collect statistics to demonstrate bias and drive change. My role model for using statistics to demonstrate bias was Professor Nancy Hopkins at MIT. After gathering data that illustrated the unequal treatment of female faculty, she went to see the president of MIT, who at that time was Charles Vest. When Professor Hopkins shared her facts, President Vest told her, "I see it. I get it. And we're going to take it on."[2]

President Vest followed up on his pledge by initiating a study that transformed MIT's policies and practices on gender. The changes President Vest made at MIT cascaded through universities across the United States, positively transforming the experiences of female faculty.

What were these powerful statistics? Was it a lengthy and expensive study? No, Professor Hopkins used a standard carpenter's metal tape measure to compare the amount of lab space assigned to faculty.

For academics, access to space to conduct research is essential. In 1994, after having been denied 200 additional square feet of lab space, Professor Hopkins took measurements and calculated the square footage allocated to male and female faculty members. She found that junior professors averaged 2,000 square feet and full professors received between 3,000 and 6,000 square feet. Although she was a full professor, Hopkins had only 1,500 square feet of lab space.

With her tape measure, Hopkins demonstrated that powerful, statistical evidence of bias can be collected not only by management, but also by those who are suffering from discrimination. The cost and effort involved in collecting the data can be miniscule in comparison to the impact. The trick is to amass information that clearly proves your case, and then to use that evidence to convince a major decision maker to take appropriate action.

Collection of statistics can be a powerful way of documenting inequities and the success of mitigation programs. If top management is behind the effort to change as in the MIT example, tremendous progress can be made. Without a strong champion, organizations may only grudgingly collect data and, even worse, try to disguise problems. When metrics are distorted and contrived, they lose their power to stimulate appropriate corrective action.

Currently, many employers are under pressure to address discrimination against women. To be competitive in recruiting, these groups may feel compelled to monitor and report the percentage of women at different levels. Without a strong champion within the organization, those responsible for the information may attempt to manipulate the reporting of the results rather than tackle the underlying problems.

One giant corporation reported and shared with employees the percentages of women, up to the executive level. At the executive level, the metric abruptly switched from being "percentage of women" to being "percentage of women and minorities." The combined percentage of women and minorities was still much lower than the percentage of women alone in the immediately subordinate group in the corporate hierarchy. A careful reader of the report was left wondering, "Why did the analysts have to hide the data? Whom did they think they were fooling? Was the real percentage of women in executive ranks so low that the company was ashamed?"

It is far better to admit to a deficiency and to take action than to try hide it. As in the MIT example, acknowledging that a problem exists is a crucial first step in fixing it. Hiding the information under a rug of obfuscation strongly signals that top management doesn't intend to fix the problem.

Greater transparency is required to eliminate persistent gender pay inequities. One way to push corporations to release relevant data is through shareholder proposals. As an experiment, I submitted a shareholder proposal to ExxonMobil requesting an annual report on the percentages of women at different percentiles of compensation. Statistics on the percentages of women in each salary grade would expose whether or not women are underrepresented in the upper tiers of organizations. Annual updates would reveal whether there was any progress in eliminating glass ceilings.

ExxonMobil tried to avoid including my proposal in its proxy statement, but the Securities and Exchange Commission sided with me. My initiative didn't pass, but I learned that if you already own at least $2,000 worth of a company's stock, you can submit a shareholder proposal and have it included in the proxy statement at essentially zero out-of-pocket cost.[3]

Data can be useful in highlighting discrimination against underrepresented groups. Members of disadvantaged demographic groups should be included in the design of surveys, because they often have the best insight into the underlying problems. This kind of approach can be used to determine if members of dual-career couples are scarce in the upper ranks of corporations and to identify corrective actions.

Organizations benefit if they understand their customers. Dual-career couples are an important part of the population and a major market for goods and services. Businesses that lack insight into the priorities and needs of dual-career couples may be less successful than their competitors.

DEFINITION OF SUCCESS

The HBS conducted a survey in 2012 to develop a better understanding of the current professional and personal lives of alumni.[4] The study found that for alumni of all ages and both genders, quality of personal and family relationships was most important.

The average MBA student at Harvard is 28 when he or she graduates. At the time of the survey, members of Generation Y (Gen Y) were under the age of 30. Those in Generation X (Gen X) were in the ages 31–47. Baby boomers were between the age of 48 and 66.

In the HBS survey, there were large variations by gender and generation in the ranking of the importance of "compatibility of work and personal life." With many women delaying childbirth into their thirties, relatively few of the Gen Y group would have been parents at the time of the study. Childless, hard-charging Gen Y of both genders ranked "compatibility of work and personal life" last in fifth place, and agreed on the relative ranking of all of the other factors. In contrast, members of Gen X were of prime child-rearing age. There were major gender differences in the ranking of priorities including "compatibility of work and personal life." The female Gen X put "compatibility of work and personal life" in second place, while the male Gen X, who were apparently not carrying their fair share of family duties or had spouses in a domestic support role, ranked that fourth. The largely empty nest baby boomers were back in agreement on all of the factors and rated that factor third. The HBS study indicates that the toughest period of life for ambitious professionals is midlife when they are balancing work and family and that women are still disadvantaged.

The survey asked not only about priorities, but also about satisfaction. "Work that is meaningful and satisfying and compatibility of work with personal life are of top importance to both men and women, but on both measures, men report greater satisfaction."[5]

We tend to be unhappy when our priorities and our self-audit of our relative success are out of sync. What is your relative ranking of the importance of the following factors?

- Quality of personal and family relationships
- Compatibility of work with your personal life
- Opportunities for career growth
- Meaningful and satisfying work
- Ability to make a contribution to society
- Professional accomplishments
- Time for leisure and personal development
- Spirituality
- Wealth

How satisfied are you with the factors that are of greatest importance to you? What do you think you should do differently to feel more successful? How would changes that you might make to feel more successful impact your relationship with your partner? How would changes affect your relationships with other people you love? At the end of your life what do you think will be most important to you? What might you regret doing or not doing?

How does your partner rank these factors? Are there major differences between you and your partner in prioritization and satisfaction? How does that impact your relationship? What should you do to reduce any friction within your household?

Trade-offs are inevitable. Make sure that when you sacrifice something important to you that you are receiving value for that loss in another way. For example, a work trade-off could have its reward in the form of maintaining your personal and family relationships. Do not succumb to peer pressure to make accommodations that you do not think are necessary. Match your work–life balance to your priorities not to other people's expectations.

Even from an early age your kids can be skilled at making you feel guilty. Don't let them. Rationally evaluate what you think your offspring really need. Don't compromise your career any more than you think is necessary.

Besides your children there are many other people, who may voice judgments about your lifestyle. Traditional women and men may condemn your choices. Mothers, who stayed home with their children or assumed the role of assistant to their spouse, often think that it is nature's order and may be very critical of your goals and priorities. Ignore peer pressure that you think is unjustified. Be true to yourself.

COMMUNICATION

Good communication is more than just sharing everything that you are thinking. Having been married well over 40 years, I often find myself keeping silent rather than saying something that I think will create conflict with no upside. I once heard the expression that "long marriages are built on more what isn't said than what is."

Forgiveness can be easier than permission at home as well as at work. You don't need to discuss and come to agreement on everything. You are a coequal, so make decisions and deal with the dispute if and when it occurs. In the absence of a fight, your partner may not remember that he or she had any objections to what you wanted to do.

In partnerships, money can be a source of conflict. You need to discuss with your mate whether or not you will maintain separate financial accounts and the mechanics of sharing household expenses. You can also agree to pay different percentages of specific shared expenses that you value differently. If you don't have to concur that an expenditure makes sense, the person who wants to spend the money can decide if he or she is willing to pay the entire amount. If you keep your earnings separate, you can vote your priorities with your money.

My husband and I have very different investment philosophies, so I am glad that we have kept our funds separate. When my retirement takes a hit from a market crash, I have no one to blame, but myself. In effect we have diversification that tends to balance out the cycles.

Remember the theme about following the money? Keeping control of your finances also protects you if your relationship turns sour. We have a friend, who was completely blindsided after many years of marriage and two children. Her husband methodically schemed to steal the family assets and marry someone else. He depleted shared accounts and hid the assets, leaving her with huge debts. If she had maintained separate accounts in her name alone, he could not have left her so completely economically destitute.

"Love is blind." When you are infatuated it is tempting to completely trust the other person. Unlike the traditional housewives, who may have had no business or financial experience, as a member of a dual-career couple, you do. Put your business hat on and look at your domestic arrangement a business deal. "Trust but verify" and maintain your independence and economic well-being.

REWRITING THE RULES

The large number of female professionals and the associated increase in members of dual-career couples in the workforce combined with new communications technologies introduced new ways of working and new lifestyles. Traditional work patterns are under attack, because they don't work for a large fraction of the population. The old rules are being broken and discarded and new ones are being formulated. Depending on your perspective, it can be a blessing or a curse. We are living in interesting times.

The rules that I live with are as follows:

- Don't let others impose their value system on you. Be true to yourself.
- Set your own priorities.
- Relationships with family and friends are a major component of happiness and success.
- Focus on the quality of time that you spend with the people that you love, not the quantity of time.
- Time is money. Use money to replace time in low-value activities.
- Money is not everything. It can be useful in predicting people's actions, but not always.

- Follow the money to better understand power relationships.
- Money of your own combined with the ability to support yourself is emancipating.
- Forgiveness is easier than permission.
- Network. Do favors for others, because you never know when you will need one.
- You should enjoy life's journey, because you may never get to where you hoped to go.
- Plan your life to minimize regrets at the end. Write your own obituary and undertake the appropriate actions now to accomplish what you hope to achieve both in your personal life and professionally.

Notes

PREFACE

1. Nevada National Security Site History, Sedan Crater, http://www.nv
.energy.gov/library/factsheets/DOENV_712.pdf.

INTRODUCTION

1. Laura Pecenco and Mary Blair-Loy, "Legal Professions: The Status of
Women and Men," Center for Research on Gender in the Professions, UC
San Diego (2013), http://crgp.ucsd.edu/documents/GenderinLegalProfess
ionsCaseStudy.pdf.

2. Catalyst, "Catalyst Quick Take: Women in Law in Canada and the U.S."
(2015), http://www.catalyst.org/knowledge/women-law-canada-and-us.

3. For example, Corinne A. Moss-Racusin, John F. Dovidio, Victoria L. Brescoll,
Mark J. Graham, and Jo Handelsman, "Science Faculty's Subtle Gender
Biases Favor Male Students," Proceedings of the National Academy of Sciences of the United States of America, 109, no. 41 (August 21, 2012): 16474–
16479, doi: 10.1073/pnas.1211286109, http://www.pnas.org/content/109/41/
16474.full.

4. Moss-Racusin et al., "Science Faculty's Subtle Gender Biases Favor
Male Students."

5. Eve Sprunt and Susan Howes, "Results of Dual-career Couple Survey,"
Journal of Petroleum Technology 63, no. 10 (October 2011): 60–62; and Eve
Sprunt and Susan Howes, "Dual-Career Couple Survey Results," 151971-MS,
Society of Petroleum Engineers (2011), OnePetro, http://www.onepetro.org/
mslib/app/Preview.do?paperNumber=SPE-151971-MS&societyCode=SPE.

6. L. Schiebinger, A.D. Henderson, and S.K. Gilmartin, "Dual-Career Academic Couples, What Universities Need to Know," Michelle R. Clayman Institute for Gender Research, Stanford University (2008), 98, ISBN 978–0–9817746–0–2, http://www.carriere2.ch/site/wp-content/uploads/2010/09/Etude-Stanford-2008.pdf.

7. L. Schiebinger, A.D. Henderson, and S.K. Gilmartin, "Dual-Career Academic Couples, What Universities Need to Know," Michelle R. Clayman Institute for Gender Research, Stanford University (2008), 98, ISBN 978–0–9817746–0–2, http://www.carriere2.ch/site/wp-content/uploads/2010/09/Etude-Stanford-2008.pdf.

8. Eve Sprunt and Susan Howes, "Factors Impacting Dual-Career Couples, Results of December 2011 Talent Council Survey," SPE paper number 160928 (2012), http://www.onepetro.org/mslib/app/Preview.do?paper Number=SPE-160928-MS&societyCode=SPE; and Eve Sprunt and Susan Howes, "Factors Impacting Dual-Career Couples, Results of the December 2011 Talent Council Survey," *The Way Ahead* 8, no. 2 (2012): 6–9, https://www.spe.org/twa/print/archives/2012/2012v8n2/06_v8n2HRDiscussion.pdf.

9. Harvard Business School, "Life and Leadership after HBS" (2015), http://www.hbs.edu/women50/docs/L_and_L_Survey_2Findings_12final.pdf.

10. Eve Sprunt, Susan Howes, and Michael Pyrcz, "Impact of the Big Crew Change on Employee Retention," *Journal of Petroleum Technology* 66, no. 3 (2014): 80–86, http://www.spe.org/jpt/article/5908-talent-technology-impact-of-the-big-crew-change-on-employee-retention/; Eve Sprunt, Susan Howes, and Michael Pyrcz, "Attraction and Retention of Employees," Results of 2013 SPE Talent Council Survey, SPE paper number 168112 (2013), http://dx.doi.org/10.2118/168112-MS.

11. Eve Sprunt, Nancy House, and Maria Angela Capello, "SEG Survey on Dual-Career Couples and Women: The Hidden Diversity of Dual-Career Couples," *The Leading Edge* 33, no. 7 (2014): 812–816, doi: 10.1190/tle33070812.1; and Eve Sprunt, Nancy House, and Maria Angela Capello, "SEG Survey on Dual-Career-Couples and Women: Implications for the Future of Our Society," *The Leading Edge* 33, no. 4 (2014): 460–462, doi: 10.1190/tle33040460.1.

CHAPTER 1

1. Wendy Wang and Kim Parker, "Record Share of Americans Have Never Married: As Values, Economics and Gender Patterns Change," Washington, DC: Pew Research Center's Social & Demographic Trends project (September 24, 2014), http://www.pewsocialtrends.org/2014/09/24/record-share-of-americans-have-never-married/.

2. See data from the National Committee on Pay Equity, http://www.pay-equity.org/info-time.html.

3. Anonymous response to a survey the author conducted in May 2011.

4. Eve Sprunt, Susan Howes, and Michael Pyrcz, "Impact of the Big Crew Change on Employee Retention," *Journal of Petroleum Technology* 66, no. 3 (2014), http://www.spe.org/jpt/article/5908-talent-technology-impact-of-the-big-crew-change-on-employee-retention/; Eve Sprunt, Susan Howes, and Michael Pyrcz, "Attraction and Retention of Employees, Results of 2013 SPE Talent Council Survey," SPE paper number 168112 (2013), http://dx.doi.org/10.2118/168112-MS.

5. Anonymous discussion comment in response to survey the author conducted in 2013.

6. Dame Stephanie Shirley, "Why Do Ambitious Women Have Flat Heads," filmed in March 2015, https://www.ted.com/talks/dame_stephanie_shirley_why_do_ambitious_women_have_flat_heads?language=en.

CHAPTER 2

1. U.S. Equal Employment Opportunity Commission, the Pregnancy Discrimination Act of 1978, http://www.eeoc.gov/laws/statutes/pregnancy.cfm.

2. U.S. Census Bureau, "Statistical Abstract of the United States, 2012," Table 599 "Employment Status of Women by Marital Status and Presence and Age of Children: 1970 to 2009," http://www.census.gov/compendia/statab/2012/tables/12s0599.pdf.

3. U.S. Department of Labor, "Employee Rights and Responsibilities under the Family and Medical Leave Act," http://www.dol.gov/whd/regs/compliance/posters/fmlaen.pdf.

4. Pew Research Center, "Childlessness Falls, Family Size Grows among Highly Educated Women" (May 2015), http://www.pewsocialtrends.org/files/2015/05/2015-05-07_children-ever-born_FINAL.pdf.

5. Audrey Brixner, "Mother—My Memories of Her," unpublished memoir dated August 25, 1884, which she distributed to family members. Audrey Chew Brixner died on July 19, 1996, at the age of 81.

6. The White House, Washington, National Equal Pay Task Force, "Fifty Years after the Equal Pay Act, Assessing the Past, Taking Stock of the Future" (June 2013), https://www.whitehouse.gov/sites/default/files/image/image_file/equal_pay-task_force_progress_report_june_10_2013.pdf.

7. U.S. Bureau of Labor and Statistics, Report 1045, "Highlights of Women's Earnings in 2012" (October 2013), http://www.bls.gov/cps/cpswom2012.pdf.

8. Rakesh Kochhar, "How Pew Research Measured the Gender Pay Gap" (December 11, 2013), http://www.pewresearch.org/fact-tank/2013/12/11/how-pew-research-measured-the-gender-pay-gap/.

9. The White House, Washington, National Equal Pay Task Force, "Fifty Years after the Equal Pay Act, Assessing the Past, Taking Stock of the Future."

10. Institute for Women's Policy Research, "New Study: Men Earn More Than Women within Nearly All the Most Common Occupations" (April 17, 2012), http://www.iwpr.org/press-room/press-releases/new-study-men-earn-more-than-women-within-nearly-all-the-most-common-occupations.

11. Institute for Women's Policy Research, Press Release, "New Study: Men Earn More Than Women within Nearly All the Most Common Occupations."

12. Anthony T. LoSasso, Michael R. Richards, Chiu-Fang Chou, and Susan E. Gerber, "The $16,819 Pay Gap for Newly Trained Physicians: The Unexplained Trend of Men Earning More Than Women," *Health Affairs* 30, no. 2 (February 2011): 193–201, doi: 10.1377/hlthaff.2010.0597.

13. U.S. Bureau of Labor and Statistics, "Median Weekly Earnings of Full-Time Wage and Salary Workers by Detailed Occupation and Sex" (February 12, 2015), http://www.bls.gov/cps/cpsaat39.htm.

14. Pew Research Center, "The Narrowing of the Gender Wage Gap, 1980–2012" (December 10, 2013), http://www.pewsocialtrends.org/2013/12/11/on-pay-gap-millennial-women-near-parity-for-now/sdt-gender-and-work-12-2013-0-02/.

15. Data from Tables 23, 24, and 25 of the U.S. Bureau of Labor and Statistics, "Women in the Labor Force: A Databook," Report 1049 (May 2014), http://www.bls.gov/opub/reports/cps/womenlaborforce_2013.pdf.

16. Eve Sprunt and Susan Howes, "Results of Dual-career Couple Survey," *Journal of Petroleum Technology* 63, no. 10 (October 2011): 60–62; and Eve Sprunt and Susan Howes, "Dual-Career Couple Survey Results," 151971-MS, SPE, OnePetro (2011), http://www.onepetro.org/mslib/app/Preview.do?paperNumber=SPE-151971-MS&societyCode=SPE.

17. Eve Sprunt, Nancy House, and Maria Angela Capello, "SEG Survey on Dual-Career Couples and Women: The Hidden Diversity of Dual-Career Couples," *The Leading Edge* 33, no. 7 (2014): 812–816, doi: 10.1190/tle33070812.1.

18. Sreedhari D. Desai, Dolly Chugh, and Arthur Brief, "Marriage Structure and Resistance to the Gender Revolution in the Workplace" (2012), http://c.ymcdn.com/sites/www.newonline.org/resource/resmgr/research/marriageandgenderdiversity.pdf.

19. U.S. Bureau of Labor and Statistics, Economic News Release, "Employment Characteristics of Families Summary" (April 23, 2015), http://www.bls.gov/news.release/famee.nr0.htm.

CHAPTER 3

1. Interaction Associates, "The Challenge of Advancing Women in Leadership Roles: New Workplace Survey Points to Where Organizations Can Make Progress" (June 10, 2015), http://www.businesswire.com/news/home/20150610005372/en/Challenge-Advancing-Women-Leadership-Roles-Workplace-Survey#.VZQGF_lVhBc.

2. Catalyst, "Pyramid: Women in S&P 500 Companies," New York: Catalyst (April 3, 2015), http://www.catalyst.org/knowledge/women-sp-500-companies.

3. Sandrine Devillard, Sandra Sancier-Sultan, and Charlotte Werner, "Moving Mind-Sets on Gender Diversity: McKinsey Global Survey results," McKinsey & Company (January 2014), http://www.mckinsey.com/insights/organization/moving_mind-sets_on_gender_diversity_mckinsey_global_survey_results;and Sandrine Devillard, Sandra Sancier-Sultan, Charlotte Werner, Ina Maller, and Cecille Kossoff, "Women Matter 2013—Gender Diversity in Top Management: Moving Culture, Moving Boundaries," McKinsey & Company (2013), http://www.mckinsey.com/insights/organization/moving_mind-sets_on_gender_diversity_mckinsey_global_survey_results.

4. U.S. Bureau of Labor and Statistics, "TED: The Economics Daily, Daily Time Use among Married Mothers" (May 8, 2015), http://www.bls.gov/opub/ted/2015/daily-time-use-among-married-mothers.htm.

5. EY, Press release, "Study: Work-Life Challenges across Generations, Millennials and Parents Hit Hardest" (May 5, 2015), http://www.ey.com/US/en/About-us/Our-people-and-culture/EY-work-life-challenges-across-generations-global-study.

6. EY, "Global Generations: A Global Study on Work-Life Challenges across Generations, Detailed findings" (2015), http://www.ey.com/Publication/vwLUAssets/EY-global-generations-a-global-study-on-work-life-challenges-across-generations/$FILE/EY-global-generations-a-global-study-on-work-life-challenges-across-generations.pdf.

7. *Los Angeles Times*, "Millennials Want Flexibility in Work Schedules" (June 4, 2015), http://www.sfgate.com/business/article/Millennials-want-flexibility-in-work-schedules-6307541.php.

8. Eve Sprunt and Susan Howes, "Factors Impacting Dual-Career Couples, Results of December 2011 Talent Council Survey," SPE paper number 160928 (2012), http://www.onepetro.org/mslib/app/Preview.do?paperNumber=SPE-160928-MS&societyCode=SPE; and Eve Sprunt and Susan Howes, "Factors Impacting Dual-Career Couples, Results of the December 2011 Talent Council Survey," *The Way Ahead* 8, no. 2 (2012): 6–9, https://www.spe.org/twa/print/archives/2012/2012v8n2/06_v8n2HRDiscussion.pdf.

9. Anonymous comment received in response to the SPE survey that was distributed in December 2011. Selected results and comments from that survey were reported in Sprunt and Howes, "Factors Impacting Dual-Career Couples, Results of December 2011 Talent Council Survey."

10. Ibid.

11. EY, "Global Generations: A Global Study on Work-Life Challenges across Generations, Detailed findings."

12. Teresa A. Taylor, *The Balance Myth: Rethinking Your Work-Life Success* (Austin, TX: Greenleaf Book Group Press, 2013), ISBN: 978-1-60832-564-1.

13. Taylor, *The Balance Myth: Rethinking Your Work-Life Success*, 24–31.

14. Eve Sprunt, Nancy House, and Maria Angela Capello, "SEG Survey on Dual-Career Couples and Women: The Hidden Diversity of Dual-Career

Couples," *The Leading Edge* 33, no. 7 (2014): 812–816, doi: 10.1190/tle33070812.1; and Eve Sprunt, Nancy House, and Maria Angela Capello, "SEG Survey on Dual-Career Couples and Women: Implications for the Future of Our Society," *The Leading Edge*, 33, no. 4, (2014): 460–462, doi: 10.1190/tle33040460.1.

15. Comment made anonymously in response to a survey that I led.

16. Sprunt et al., "SEG Survey on Dual-Career Couples and Women: The Hidden Diversity of Dual-Career Couples"; and Sprunt et al., "SEG Survey on Dual-Career Couples and Women: Implications for the Future of Our Society."

CHAPTER 4

1. Eve Sprunt, Susan Howes, and Maria Angela Capello, "Bridging the Generation Gap," *Journal of Petroleum Technology* 64, 5 (May 2012): 80–81.

2. Anonymous quotes from the results of a SPE survey. The overall results of the survey were not published, just a few of the anonymous quotes in Sprunt et al., "Bridging the Generation Gap."

3. Sprunt et al., "Bridging the Generation Gap."

4. Meg Whitman and Joan O'C. Hamilton, *The Power of Many: Values for Success in Business and Life* (New York: Random House, 2010), 25.

5. Whitman and Hamilton, *The Power of Many: Values for Success in Business and Life*, 55.

6. Whitman and Hamilton, *The Power of Many: Values for Success in Business and Life*, 15.

7. Whitman and Hamilton, *The Power of Many: Values for Success in Business and Life*, 83.

8. Whitman and Hamilton, *The Power of Many: Values for Success in Business and Life*, 257.

9. Sheryl Sandberg, *Lean In: Women, Work and the Will to Lead* (New York, Alfred A. Knopf: 2013), 111.

10. U.S. Department of Health and Human Services, National Institute of General Medical Services, "Sepsis Fact Sheet," http://www.nigms.nih.gov/Education/Pages/factsheet_sepsis.aspx.

CHAPTER 5

1. Career Builder, "Thirty-Eight Percent of Workers Have Dated a Co-Worker, Finds CareerBuilder Survey: Twenty Percent of Office Romances Involve Someone Who Is Already Married" (February 12, 2014), http://www.careerbuilder.com/share/aboutus/pressreleasesdetail.aspx?sd=2%2F13%2F2014&id=pr803&ed=12%2F31%2F2014.

2. Eve Sprunt, Susan Howes, and Michael Pyrcz, "Talent & Technology—Impact of the Big Crew Change on Employee Retention," *Journal of Petroleum*

Technology 66, no. 3 (2014), http://www.spe.org/jpt/article/5908-talent-techno logy-impact-of-the-big-crew-change-on-employee-retention/; and Eve Sprunt, Susan Howes, and Michael Pyrcz, "Attraction and Retention of Employees, Results of 2013 SPE Talent Council Survey," SPE paper number 168112 (2013), http://dx.doi.org/10.2118/168112-MS.

3. Vault, "Love Is in the Air: Vault's 2014 Office Romance Survey, Vault Careers" (February 12, 2014), http://www.vault.com/blog/workplace-issues/ love-is-in-the-air-vaults-2014-office-romance-survey/.

4. Sprunt et al., "Talent & Technology—Impact of the Big Crew Change on Employee Retention"; and Sprunt et al., "Attraction and Retention of Employees."

5. Sprunt et al.,, "Talent & Technology—Impact of the Big Crew Change on Employee Retention"; and Sprunt et al., "Attraction and Retention of Employees."

6. Eve Sprunt and Susan Howes, "Factors Impacting Dual-Career Couples, Results of December 2011 Talent Council Survey," SPE paper number 160928 (2012), http://www.onepetro.org/mslib/app/Preview.do?paperNum ber=SPE-160928-MS&societyCode=SPE; and Eve Sprunt and Susan Howes, "Factors Impacting Dual-Career Couples, Results of the December 2011 Talent Council Survey," *The Way Ahead* 8, no. 2 (2012): 6–9, https://www.spe .org/twa/print/archives/2012/2012v8n2/06_v8n2HRDiscussion.pdf.

7. Sprunt et al., "Talent & Technology—Impact of the Big Crew Change on Employee Retention"; and Sprunt et al., "Attraction and Retention of Employees."

8. The external group to which the woman's husband was referred, www .jobseekers.org, still has a website, but there is a note that as of September 1, 2014, it is ceasing operations.

9. In the SPE surveys, gender was captured, but not the identities of those responding. Thus, we don't know who made individual comments, but we know their gender and selected other characteristics. Some of the results of those surveys were reported in Sprunt et al., "Talent & Technology—Impact of the Big Crew Change on Employee Retention"; and Sprunt et al., "Attrac-tion and Retention of Employees."

10. Anonymous comments collected in the 2013 SPE survey, the results of which were reported in Sprunt et al., "Talent & Technology—Impact of the Big Crew Change on Employee Retention"; and Sprunt et al.,, "Attraction and Retention of Employees."

11. Anonymous comments collected in the 2013 SPE survey, the results of which were reported in Sprunt et al., "Talent & Technology—Impact of the Big Crew Change on Employee Retention"; and Sprunt et al., "Attraction and Retention of Employees."

12. Anonymous comments collected in the 2013 SPE survey, the results of which were reported in Sprunt et al., "Talent & Technology—Impact of the Big Crew Change on Employee Retention"; and Sprunt et al., "Attraction and Retention of Employees."

13. Anonymous comments collected in the 2013 SPE survey, the results of which were reported in Sprunt et al., "Talent & Technology—Impact of the Big Crew Change on Employee Retention"; and Sprunt et al., "Attraction and Retention of Employees."

14. Anonymous comment collected in the 2013 SPE survey, the results of which were reported in Sprunt et al., "Talent & Technology—Impact of the Big Crew Change on Employee Retention"; and Sprunt et al., "Attraction and Retention of Employees."

15. U.S. Government Publishing Office, "Part 825—The Family and Medical Leave Act of 1993, Section 825.201(b)," http://www.ecfr.gov/cgi-bin/text-idx?c4b2de7c5b2ac0d5ca0b64a0dd&rgn=div5&view=text&node=29:3.1.1.3.54&idno=29#se29.3.825_1201.

16. U.S. Department of Labor, "Family and Medical Leave Act Final Rule to Revise the Definition of 'Spouse' under the FMLA," http://www.dol.gov/whd/fmla/spouse/.

17. National Conference of State Legislatures, "Common Law Marriage by State," http://www.ncsl.org/research/human-services/common-law-marriage.aspx.

18. Find Law, "Common Law Marriage by State: The Basics," http://family.findlaw.com/marriage/common-law-marriage.html.

19. Anonymous comment collected in the 2013 SPE survey, the results of which were reported in Sprunt et al., "Talent & Technology—Impact of the Big Crew Change on Employee Retention"; and Sprunt et al., "Attraction and Retention of Employees."

20. Sprunt et al., "Talent & Technology—Impact of the Big Crew Change on Employee Retention"; and Sprunt et al., "Attraction and Retention of Employees."

CHAPTER 6

1. Eve Sprunt, Susan Howes, and Michael Pyrcz, "Talent & Technology—Impact of the Big Crew Change on Employee Retention," *Journal of Petroleum Technology* 66, no. 3 (2014): 80–86, http://www.spe.org/jpt/article/5908-talent-technology-impact-of-the-big-crew-change-on-employee-retention/; and Eve Sprunt, Susan Howes, and Michael Pyrcz, "Attraction and Retention of Employees, Results of 2013 SPE Talent Council Survey," SPE paper number 168112 (2013), http://dx.doi.org/10.2118/168112-MS.

2. Sprunt et al., "Talent & Technology—Impact of the Big Crew Change on Employee Retention"; and Sprunt et al., "Attraction and Retention of Employees."

3. Sprunt et al., "Attraction and Retention of Employees."

4. Sprunt et al., "Attraction and Retention of Employees."

5. Sylvia Ann Hewlett, Carolyn Buck Luce, Lisa J. Servon, Laura Sherbin, Peggy Shiller, Eytan Sosnovich, and Karen Sumberg, "The Athena Factor: Reversing the Brain Drain in Science, Engineering and Technology," Harvard

Business Review Research Report (2008), 100, http://documents.library.nsf
.gov/edocs/HD6060-.A84–2008-PDF-Athena-factor-Reversing-the-brain-
drain-in-science,-engineering,-and-technology.pdf.

6. Sprunt et al., "Attraction and Retention of Employees."

7. A.H. Maslow, "A Theory of Human Motivation," *Psychological Review*
50, no. 4 (1943): 370–396, http://psychclassics.yorku.ca/Maslow/motivation
.htm.

8. The Workplace Bullying Institute, http://www.workplacebullying.org/
individuals/problem/being-bullied/, offers useful resources that can help you
combat bullying.

9. Laura Sydell, "Silicon Valley Companies Add New Benefit for Women:
Egg-Freezing," National Public Radio, All Tech Considered (October 17, 2014),
http://www.npr.org/sections/alltechconsidered/2014/10/17/356765423/
silicon-valley-companies-add-new-benefit-for-women-egg-freezing.

10. Sydell, "Silicon Valley Companies Add New Benefit for Women:
Egg-Freezing."

11. USC Fertility, "Frequently Asked Questions about Egg Freezing,"
accessed October 7, 2015, http://uscfertility.org/egg-freezing-faqs/.

12. USC Fertility, "Frequently Asked Questions about Egg Freezing."

13. Eve Sprunt, Nancy House and Maria Angela Capello, "SEG Survey
on Dual-Career Couples and Women: The Hidden Diversity of Dual-Career
Couples," *The Leading Edge* 33, no. 7 (2014): 460–463.

14. Eve Sprunt and Susan Howes, "Factors Impacting Dual-Career Couples,
Results of the December 2011 Talent Council Survey," *The Way Ahead* 8, no. 2
(2012): 6–9, https://www.spe.org/twa/print/archives/2012/2012v8n2/06_v8n2
HRDiscussion.pdf.

15. Permits Foundation, International Mobility and Dual Career Survey
of International Employers, http://www.permitsfoundation.com/wp-content/
uploads/2013/06/Permits+Global+Survey+2012nw.pdf.

16. Sprunt et al., "SEG Survey on Dual-Career Couples and Women: The
Hidden Diversity of Dual-Career Couples."

17. Cathleen Benko and Anne Weisberg, *Mass Career Customization* (Boston:
Harvard Business School Press, 2007).

18. Not his real name.

CHAPTER 7

1. Changing Minds, "The Need for a Sense of Control," http://changing
minds.org/explanations/needs/control.htm.

2. Kenneth Matos and Ellen Galinsky, "Workplace Flexibility in the United
States: A Status Report," Families and Work Institute, 2011, 27, http://families
andwork.org/site/research/reports/www_us_workflex.pdf.

3. Matos and Galinsky, "Workplace Flexibility in the United States: A Status
Report."

4. Kim Parker and Wendy Wang, "Modern Parenthood, Roles of Moms and Dads Converge as They Balance Work and Family," Pew Research Center, March 14, 2013, 65, http://www.pewsocialtrends.org/2013/03/14/modern-parenthood-roles-of-moms-and-dads-converge-as-they-balance-work-and-family/.

5. K. Matos and E. Galinsky, "Workplace Flexibility among Professional Employees," Families and Work Institute, 2011, 17 pp. http://familiesand work.org/site/research/reports/WorkFlexAndProfessionals.pdf.

6. Parker and Wang, "Modern Parenthood, Roles of Moms and Dads Converge as They Balance Work and Family."

7. Working Mother Report, "What Moms Think, Career vs. Paycheck" (2010), 26, http://www.wmmsurveys.com/25thanniversary.pdf.

8. Sheryl Sandberg, *Lean In: Women, Work, and the Will to Lead* (New York, Alfred A. Knopf, 2013), 113.

9. Sandberg, *Lean In: Women, Work, and the Will to Lead*, 108.

10. Sandberg, *Lean In: Women, Work, and the Will to Lead*, 109.

11. E. M. Rehel, "When Dad Stays Home Too: Paternity Leave, Gender and Parenting," *Gender & Society* 28, no. 1 (2014): 110–132, http://gas.sage pub.com/content/28/1/110.full.pdf+html.

12. Rehel, "When Dad Stays Home Too: Paternity Leave, Gender and Parenting."

13. M. Huerta, W. Adema, J. Baxter, W. Han, M. Lausten, R. H. Lee, and J. Waldfogel, "Fathers' Leave, Fathers' Involvement and Child Development: Are They Related? Evidence from Four OECD Countries," OECD Social, Employment and Migration Working Papers, No. 140, OECD Publishing (2013), doi: 10.1787/1815199x.

14. International Labour Organization, "Maternity and Paternity at Work, Law and Practice across the World" (2014), p. 118, http://www.ilo.org/wcm sp5/groups/public/---dgreports/---dcomm/---publ/documents/publication/ wcms_242615.pdf.

15. International Labour Organization, "Maternity and Paternity at Work, Law and Practice across the World."

16. Mike Ramsey, "Men Need Work/Life Balance, Too: Paternity Leave Proves To Be a Potent Benefit for Today's Working Fathers," Society for Human Resource Management, *HR Magazine* 59, no. 11 (November 1, 2014), http://www.shrm.org/publications/hrmagazine/editorialcontent/2014/1114/ pages/1114-paternity-leave.aspx#sthash.fk6Gu3dZ.dpuf.

17. Ron Lieber, "Paid Leave for Fathers. Any Takers?" *New York Times*, August 8, 2015, page B1 of the New York edition, http://www.nytimes.com/ 2015/08/08/your-money/bringing-paternity-leave-into-the-mainstream.html.

18. Ray Hennessy, "Did Mark Zuckerberg Really Take 'Paternity Leave?'" Entrepreneur, http://www.entrepreneur.com/article/270088.

19. Eve Sprunt and Susan Howes, "Factors Impacting Dual-Career Couples, Results of December 2011 Talent Council Survey," SPE paper number 160928 (2012), One Petro, http://www.onepetro.org/mslib/app/Preview.do? paperNumber=SPE-160928-MS&societyCode=SPE.

20. Rehel, "When Dad Stays Home Too: Paternity Leave, Gender and Parenting."

21. Employment Development Department, State of California, "Paid Family Leave: Ten Years of Assisting Californians in Need, July 1, 2004–July 1, 2014" (2014), 9, http://www.edd.ca.gov/disability/pdf/Paid_Family_Leave_10_Year_Anniversary_Report.pdf.

22. Employment Development Department, "Paid Family Leave: Ten Years of Assisting Californians in Need, July 1, 2004–July 1, 2014."

23. International Labour Organization, "Maternity and Paternity at Work, Law and Practice across the World."

24. U.S. Department of Labor, "DOL Factsheet: Paid Family and Medical Leave," accessed October 3, 2015, http://www.dol.gov/wb/PaidLeave/Paid Leave.htm.

25. National Conference of State Legislatures, "Paid Family Leave," accessed October 3, 2015, http://www.ncsl.org/research/labor-and-employ ment/paid-family-leave-resources.aspx.

26. Employment Development Department, "Paid Family Leave: Ten Years of Assisting Californians in Need, July 1, 2004–July 1, 2014."

27. Sprunt and Howes, "Factors Impacting Dual-Career Couples, Results of December 2011 Talent Council Survey."

28. Susan Wojcicki, "Paid Maternity Leave Is Good for Business: When We Increased Paid Leave at Google to 18 Weeks, the Rate at Which New Mothers Left Fell by 50%," *Wall Street Journal* (December 16, 2014), http://www.wsj.com/articles/susan-wojcicki-paid-maternity-leave-is-good-for-business-1418773756.

29. Claire Zillman, "Wall Street's Latest Perk for New Moms: Flying Nannies," *Fortune* (August 13, 2015), http://fortune.com/2015/08/13/perk-maternity-leave-flying-nannies/.

30. Michal Lev-Ram, "No More Pump and Dump: IBM Plans to Ship Employees' Breast Milk Home," *Fortune* (July 13, 2015), http://fortune.com/2015/07/13/ibm-ship-employee-breast-milk/.

31. Mari Rege and Nina Drange, "Trapped at Home: The Effect of Mothers' Temporary Labor Market Exits on Their Subsequent Work Career," CESIFO Working Paper No. 3833, Category 4: Labour Markets (May 2012), http://ideas.repec.org/p/ces/ceswps/_3833.html.

32. Sprunt and Howes, "Factors Impacting Dual-Career Couples, Results of December 2011 Talent Council Survey."

33. Richard Holguin, "Commerce to Try New Work Hours for City Employees," *Los Angeles Times* (May 5, 1988), http://articles.latimes.com/1988–05–05/news/hd-3745_1_city-employees.

34. Kate Lister and Tom Harnish, The State of Telework in the U.S., How Individuals, Business, and Government Benefit, Telework Research Network (June 2011), http://www.workshifting.com/downloads/downloads/Telework-Trends-US.pdf.

35. Global Workplace Analytics, "Latest Telecommuting Statistics" (updated September 29, 2015), accessed October 3, 2015, http://globalworkplaceana lytics.com/telecommuting-statistics.

36. Scott Sayare, "In France, a Move to Limit Off-the-Clock Work Emails," *New York Times* (April 11, 2014), http://www.nytimes.com/2014/04/12/world/europe/in-france-a-move-to-limit-off-the-clock-work-emails.html?ref=todayspaper. A version of this article appeared in print on April 12, 2014, on page A4 of the New York edition with the headline, "Deal Seeks a Respite from Email."

37. The origin of the TED talks was a conference in 1984 in which technology, entertainment, and design converged.

38. Dame Stephanie Shirley, "Why Do Ambitious Women Have Flat Heads?" https://www.ted.com/talks/dame_stephanie_shirley_why_do_ambitious_women_have_flat_heads?language=en.

39. Nicholas Bloom, James Liang, John Roberts, Zhichum Jenny Ying, "Does Working from Home Work? Evidence from a Chinese Experiment," National Bureau of Economic Research Working Paper 18871 (2013), www.nber.org/papers/w18871. Revised Nov 2014 version https://web.stanford.edu/~nbloom/WFH.pdf.

40. Nicholas Bloom, James Liang, John Roberts, Zhichum Jenny Ying, "Does Working from Home Work? Evidence from a Chinese Experiment."

41. Society for Human Resource Management, "Telecommuting Policy and Procedure #1" (May 30, 2014), http://www.shrm.org/templatestools/samples/policies/pages/cms_000573.aspx.

42. Society for Human Resource Management, "Telework Policy Template," http://www.shrm.org/templatestools/samples/policies/pages/cms_000573.aspx.

43. Lister and Harnish, "The State of Telework in the U.S., How Individuals, Business, and Government Benefit."

44. Judith Warner, "The Opt-Out Generation Wants Back In," *New York Times*, Magazine Section (August 7, 2013), http://www.nytimes.com/2013/08/11/magazine/the-opt-out-generation-wants-back-in.html?pagewanted=all&_r=0. A version of this article appeared in print on August 11, 2013, on page MM25 of the *New York Times* Sunday Magazine with the headline "Ready to Rejoin the Rat Race."

45. Eve Sprunt, Nancy House, and Maria Angela Capello, "SEG Survey on Dual-Career Couples and Women: The Hidden Diversity of Dual-Career Couples," *The Leading Edge* 33, no. 7 (2014): 460–463.

46. Eve Sprunt and Susan Howes, "Results of Dual-Career Couple Survey," *Journal of Petroleum Technology* 63, no. 10 (October 2011): 60–62.

CHAPTER 8

1. Clancy Susan, "The Hidden Reason Women Aren't Making It to the Top," *Forbes* (March 31, 2014), http://www.forbes.com/sites/85broads/2014/03/31/the-hidden-reason-women-arent-making-it-to-the-top/.

2. Curt Rice, "How Blind Auditions Help Orchestras to Eliminate Gender Bias," *Guardian* (October 14, 2013), http://www.theguardian.com/women-in-leadership/2013/oct/14/blind-auditions-orchestras-gender-bias.

3. Corinne A.Moss-Racusin, John F. Dovidio, Victoria L. Brescoll, Mark J. Graham, and Jo Handelsman, "Science Faculty's Subtle Gender Biases Favor Male Students, Proceedings National Academy of Sciences" (approved August 21, 2012), http://www.pnas.org/content/109/41/16474.full.pdf.

4. Mana Nakagawa, "Male 'Identity Threat' Can Disadvantage Women in High-Status Professions," Gender News, Clayman Institute for Gender Research, Stanford University (April 10, 2014), http://gender.stanford.edu/news/2014/male-identity-threat-can-disadvantage-women-high-status-professions?utm_source=April+15&utm_campaign=4%2F15%2F2014+Gender+News+email&utm_medium=email.

5. Eve Sprunt, Nancy House, and Maria Angela Capello, "SEG Survey on Dual-Career-Couples and Women: The Hidden Diversity of Dual-Career Couples," *The Leading Edge* 33, no. 7 (2014): 812–816, doi: 10.1190/tle33070812.1; and Eve Sprunt, Nancy House, and Maria Angela Capello, "SEG Survey on Dual-Career-Couples and Women: Implications for the Future of Our Society," *The Leading Edge* 33, no. 4 (2014): 460–462, doi: 10.1190/tle33040460.1 as well as unpublished findings from the survey.

6. Sara Murray, "How One Company Put Women in Charge," *Wall Street Journal* (April 1, 2014), http://blogs.wsj.com/atwork/2014/04/01/how-one-company-put-women-in-charge/tab/print/.

7. Dan Ariely, "You Are What You Measure," *Harvard Business Review* (June 2010), http://hbr.org/2010/06/column-you-are-what-you-measure/ar/1.

8. D. W. Organ, *Organizational Citizenship Behavior: The Good Soldier Syndrome* (Lexington, MA: Lexington Books, 1988).

9. Nathan P. Podsakoff, Brian D. Blume, Steven W. Whiting, and Philip M. Podsakoff, "Individual- and Organizational-Level Consequences of Organizational Citizenship Behaviors: A Meta-Analysis," *Journal of Applied Psychology* 94, no. 1 (2009): 122–141, http://www.uni-kiel.de/psychologie/AOM/tl_files/Dokumente/Gesichert/Studium/SeminarAO_UK/OI_4.pdf.

10. Podsakoff et al., "Individual- and Organizational-Level Consequences of Organizational Citizenship Behaviors: A Meta-Analysis."

11. Janeen Judah, "Your Network: Build It Before You Need It," LinkedIn Post (August 26, 2015), https://www.linkedin.com/pulse/your-network-build-before-you-need-janeen-judah?trk=hb_ntf_MEGAPHONE_ARTICLE_POST.

12. American Bar Association, Center for Professional Responsibility Policy Implementation Committee, "Admission by Motion Rules" (October 2, 2015), accessed October 4, 2014, http://www.americanbar.org/content/dam/aba/administrative/professional_responsibility/admission_motion_rules.authcheckdam.pdf.

CHAPTER 9

1. Wednesday Martin, "Poor Little Rich Women," *New York Times*, May 16, 2015, http://www.nytimes.com/2015/05/17/opinion/sunday/poor-little-rich-women.html. A version of this op-ed appeared in print under the same title on May 17, 2015, on page SR1 of the New York edition.

2. Martin, "Poor Little Rich Women."

3. Martin, "Poor Little Rich Women."

4. Anne Marie Helmenstine, "How Much of Your Body Is Water?" About Education, http://chemistry.about.com/od/waterchemistry/f/How-Much-Of-Your-Body-Is-Water.htm; "How Quickly Do Different Cells in the Body Replace Themselves?" Cell Biology by the Numbers, http://book.bionum bers.org/how-quickly-do-different-cells-in-the-body-replace-themselves/.

5. Elizabeth Mendes, Lydia Saad, and Kyley McGeeney, "Stay-at-Home Moms Report More Depression, Sadness, Anger," Gallup Well-Being (May 18, 2012), http://www.gallup.com/poll/154685/stay-home-moms-report-depress ion-sadness-anger.aspx.

6. Beth Jarosz and Rachel T. Cortes, "In U.S., New Data Show Longer, More Sedentary Commutes," Population Reference Bureau, accessed October 4, 2015, http://www.prb.org/Publications/Articles/2014/us-commuting.aspx.

7. Margo Hilbrecht, Bryan Smale, and Steven E. Mock, "Highway to Health? Commute Time and Well-Being among Canadian Adults," *World Leisure Journal* 56, no. 2 (2014): 151–163, doi: 10.1080/16078055.2014.903723.

8. Hilbrecht et al., "Highway to Health? Commute Time and Well-Being among Canadian Adults."

9. Although President Truman often used the phrase, according to *The Yale Book of Quotations*, edited by Fred R. Shapiro (New Haven, CT: Yale University Press, 2006), 49, the quote is originally attributed to the labor leader, David Beck.

CHAPTER 10

1. Wendy Wang, Kim Parker, and Paul Taylor, "Breadwinner Moms," Pew Research Center (May 29, 2013), http://www.pewsocialtrends.org/files/2013/05/Breadwinner_moms_final.pdf.

2. Spencer Johnson, "Who Moved My Cheese? An Amazing Way to Deal with Change in Your Work and in Your Life," 1998, http://classes.sdc.wsu.edu/classes/cstm301/readings/who%20moved%20my%20cheese.pdf.

3. Eve Sprunt, Susan Howes, and Michael Pyrcz, "Talent & Technology—Impact of the Big Crew Change on Employee Retention," *Journal of Petroleum Technology* 66, no. 3 (2014), http://www.spe.org/jpt/article/5908-talent-technology-impact-of-the-big-crew-change-on-employee-retention/.

4. Brainy Quote, "Grace Hopper Quotes," http://www.brainyquote.com/quotes/quotes/g/gracehoppe170166.html.

5. Quote Investigator: Exploring the Origins of Quotations, "Time Is Money. Benjamin Franklin?" accessed October 4, 2015, http://quoteinvestigator.com/2010/05/14/time-is-money/.

6. National Institute of Mental Health, "Fact Sheet on Stress," accessed October 4, 2015, http://www.nimh.nih.gov/health/publications/stress/index.shtml.

7. The American Institute of Stress, "Workplace Stress," accessed October 4, 2015, http://www.stress.org/workplace-stress/.

8. National Institute of Mental Health, "Fact Sheet on Stress."

CHAPTER 11

1. Harvard Business School, "Life and Leadership after HBS: Findings" (May 2015), http://www.hbs.edu/women50/docs/L_and_L_Survey_2Findings_12final.pdf.

2. Ashley Southall, "Charles M. Vest, 72, President of M.I.T. and a Leader in Online Education, Dies," *New York Times*, December 15, 2013, http://www.nytimes.com/2013/12/16/us/charles-m-vest-72-president-of-mit-and-a-leader-in-online-education-dies.html.

3. Eve Sprunt, "Shareholder Activism as a Means to Advance Pay Equity for Women, A Step-by-Step Guide to Submitting a Shareholder Proposal," *AWIS Magazine* 47, no. 2 (Summer 2015): 12–16, http://magazine.awis.org/t/71103-assoc-for-women-in-science.

4. Harvard Business School, "Life and Leadership after HBS: Findings."

5. Harvard Business School, "Life and Leadership after HBS: Findings."

Index

About the Author

Eve Sprunt earned her BS and MS degrees from the Massachusetts Institute of Technology (MIT) and was the first woman to earn a PhD in geophysics from Stanford University. She was among the first women to be hired as an oil industry research scientist. In her early years of employment, she was busy proving that women deserved a place in the petroleum industry. Decades later, after having served as the 2006 president of the Society of Petroleum Engineers and as manager of Chevron's university philanthropy and worldwide college recruiting, she recognized that although women were still struggling for equality, they were an essential part of the workforce. Laws requiring equal pay for equal work have had a huge impact. In decades past no matter how well educated a woman was, her husband's career took precedence. Now, that has changed. Eve was moved to action when she heard about women being brought to tears, because their managers demanded that they decide whether their career or their spouse's took precedence. To better understand dual-career couples, Eve persuaded professional societies to survey their members and performed detailed analysis of more than 10,000 responses, the results of which have been published in articles in periodicals.